Stephen Castles
with Heather Booth and Tina Wallace

Here for good
Western Europe's new ethnic minorities

Pluto Press
London and Sydney

First published in 1984 by Pluto Press Limited,
The Works, 105a Torriano Avenue, London NW5 2RX
and Pluto Press Australia Limited, PO Box 199, Leichhardt,
New South Wales 2040, Australia

Cover designed by Michael Mayhew

Photoset by Photobooks (Bristol) Ltd
Printed in Great Britain by St Edmundsbury Press,
Bury St Edmunds, Suffolk

British Library Cataloguing in Publication Data
Castles, Stephen
   Here for good.
   1. Minorities——Europe
   I. Title   II. Booth, Heather   III. Wallace,
   Tina
   305.8′0094   D1056

ISBN 0–86104–752–4

This book is dedicated to the memory of Cemal Kemal Altun, who jumped to his death from the sixth floor of the West Berlin administrative court on 30 August 1983.

Altun was a 23-year-old Turkish refugee. He had been active in student politics before the military coup of September 1980. Altun came to West Germany in search of political asylum. The West German authorities informed the Turkish police, who applied for his extradition. Altun was kept in a West Berlin gaol for 13 months, awaiting return to Turkey where he had every reason to fear torture and death in the prisons of the junta. A West Berlin court agreed to his extradition. The federal minister of justice, Engelhard (FDP), gave his consent. After a visit to Ankara in July 1983, the federal minister of the interior, Zimmermann (CSU), called for speedy extradition of Altun and other Turkish refugees wanted by the junta. Despite a campaign by civil rights organisations to save Altun, he lived in daily fear of deportation. He took the only way out that seemed open to him.

The death of Cemal Kemal Altun was caused by the close links between the ruling classes of West Germany and Turkey. The transfer of labour power from Turkey to West Germany, which has led to the creation of a new ethnic minority, was another expression of this co-operation.

Contents

Acknowledgements

The first part of chapter 3 of this book was written by Tina Wallace. The second part of chapter 4 was written by Heather Booth. Heather Booth and Tina Wallace also contributed substantially to the reworking of the first draft and helped with discussion, criticism, provision of data and preparation of statistics. However, responsibility for the information and views in the various sections lies with the respective authors. We are not in complete agreement about everything said in the book. All translations of foreign quotations are by Stephen Castles.

Many people have helped in one way or another (often indirectly and without being aware of it) with the preparation of this book. Special thanks to: Uli Baier, Freyja Castles, Paul Crane, Armagan Konrat, Richard Kuper, Detlef Lüderwald, Annie Phizacklea, Vicky Straw, Eva Weber, Jenny Wüstenberg and Wiebke Wüstenberg.

Stephen Castles
Frankfurt, September 1983

Abbreviations

BfA	Bundesanstalt für Arbeit (German Federal Labour Office)
CDU	Christlich Democratische Union (Christian Democratic Party)
CSU	Christlich Soziale Union (Christian Social Union)
DGB	Deutsche Gewerkschaftsbund (German Trade Union Federation)
EEC	European Economic Community
ESN	Educationally sub-normal
EVWs	European Voluntary Workers
FDP	Freidemokratische Partei (Free Democratic Party)
GEW	Gewerkschaft Erziehung und Wissenschaft (German Teachers' Union)
ILO	International Labour Office, Geneva
NCWP	New Commonwealth with Pakistan
NICs	Newly Industrialising Countries
NPD	National Demokratische Partei (National Democratic Party)
OECD	Organisation for Economic Co-operation and Development
OECD SOPEMI	OECD Continuous Reporting System on Migration
ONI	Office National d'Immigration, Paris
OPCS	Office of Population Censuses and Surveys
OPEC	Organisation of Petroleum Exporting Countries
SDP	Sozialdemokratische Partei Deutschlands (German Social Democratic Party)
TUC	Trades Union Congress
UNECE	United Nations Economic Commission for Europe

1. Introduction

Writing in 1729, the Irish clergyman and satirist Jonathan Swift put forward a novel solution to the economic problems of a society being ravaged by British colonialism: the poor should turn to 'baby farming', and earn a living by selling their children as fresh meat to the British landlords.[1] Two centuries later, in the decades following the second world war, baby farming became a widespread activity not only in Ireland, but also in many other countries on the periphery of the areas of rapid economic growth. The difference was that the human exports sent to the booming industrial countries of Western Europe were consumed not as meat on the tables of the bourgeoisie, but as labour power in their factories.

From 1945 until the mid seventies, and most particularly during rapid expansion in the last 15 years of that period, the import of labour power was a marked feature of all advanced capitalist countries. Employers were looking for flexible labour units. Temporary foreign workers matched this requirement; they provided labour as and where required, without inflationary effects on wages or social expenditure. They were expected to remain only a few years, and to be easy to get rid of if no longer needed.

Something like 30 million people entered the Western European countries as workers or workers' dependants in the post-war period, making this one of the greatest migratory movements in human history. Many did indeed return to their countries of origin after a while, but others stayed: altogether, the population of Western Europe increased by about 10 million between 1950 and 1975 as a result of net migration[2] (the difference between migration in and out). Immigration of workers was not of course the only migratory current of Western Europe in this period. In the late forties and the fifties there was considerable overseas migration, leading to a net loss for the whole of Europe of 3 million people. Europe gained population as colonists returned from countries like India, Algeria, Angola and Mozambique. The aftermath of the second world war and the beginning of the cold war caused large-scale refugee movements. But labour migration was the largest factor in the development of immigrant populations, now amounting to over 16 million.

Because migration and settlement have been spontaneous and unplanned, the resulting social costs and tensions have been imposed on those social groups least able to absorb them: the migrants themselves, the indigenous working class and groups marginalised by the market mechanisms of capitalist society (the unemployed, the elderly, the handicapped, welfare recipients). Members of such groups have tended to see immigration as a cause of their increasing problems. And politicians and the media have encouraged this belief. So as migrant workers have become settlers, racism and unrest have grown. Immigration and settlement have become explosive political issues throughout Western Europe, and the right has used racism as a lever to make fascism a real threat once more.

The character of the migrations has been complex and varied. They have included political refugees, black workers from colonies or former colonies, and 'guest workers' brought in from under-developed areas of Europe (Southern Europe, Finland, Ireland) often through organised labour recruitment. Each Western European country is a special case, where specific historical, demographic, economic and social conditions have shaped particular patterns of migration. Yet it is no coincidence that all Western European countries resorted to the use of migrant labour at the same time. The general use of imported labour reflects a particular stage in the development of the capitalist mode of production, in which a long period of expansion made it essential to transcend the boundaries of national labour markets. (This also applies to the USA[3] and Japan.) The need for migrant labour in this period was not merely a result of quantitative expansion but also of its form: increasing use of such methods of mass production as increasing division of labour, conveyor-line production, shift-work and piece-work. This form of growth meant not only an increase in the number of workers needed, but also deskilling of large sections of the labour force. The new jobs were often dirty, monotonous, unhealthy and unpleasant. In a situation of expanding employment opportunities, some sections of the indigenous workforce were able to refuse such jobs and move into skilled, supervisory and white-collar positions. Expansion could only be sustained by the large-scale import of workers compelled by their social, economic and legal position to take unpleasant jobs.

The stage of development of the labour process which required mass labour migration ended in the early seventies – at least so far as Western Europe is concerned. The new slogans were increased automation and moving capital to labour – that is, the export of capital and places of work for low-productivity, low-technology, labour-intensive production processes to the European and American periphery and to Third World countries. This new stage also involves mass labour migration, but mainly within these areas, rather than between them and the advanced industrial countries. All Western European governments (except the British one) stopped the entry of workers at almost exactly the same time: 1973/4. This was the beginning of the long-drawn-out period of economic stagnation and social crisis, which still persists at the time of writing.

The British government took steps to restrict the entry of workers from the Commonwealth much earlier, in 1962. The reasons were mainly political, although early signs of impending economic stagnation may have played a part. It is commonly argued, both in Britain and the rest of Western Europe, that compared to other European countries Britain's migrant population lives in completely different circumstances. This view mainly prevails because of differences in the law. Immigrants to Britain have been seen as having a legal right to remain permanently. Apart from some migrants from former colonies in France and the Netherlands, those in the rest of Western Europe have a legal right only to temporary residence.

This distinction is less clear cut than often claimed. In Britain there has been a gradual move away from legal permanence and security. In other countries, there has been a gradual if reluctant move towards more long-term security of residence, with right of entry for dependants and longer-term work and residence permits (see chapter 3).

The similarities between Britain and other Western European countries are clearest in the actual patterns of migration and settlement. The process began with the migration of workers and progressed to family migration. The dominant motivation was economic. Migration took place on a trial basis, although almost unconsciously it was often extended indefinitely.

The main difference between Britain and other countries in Western Europe lies in the stage of development. British migrants are more advanced in the process of settlement than those elsewhere, partly from an earlier start, partly from the fact that young single women migrated (from the West Indies), and partly from the early absence of legal obstacles to family migration. In addition the expectation of permanency, even if not universal, caused the migrant community to become settled relatively quickly and more demographically balanced. There is now a second generation, and cultural and political conflicts have emerged. In view of the maturity of migration, the British experience offers useful lessons for other countries.[4]

The 'guest worker' system is dead. But the expectation that the superfluous labour units would quietly pack up and go away has proved fallacious. Many of the migrants have become settlers. More and more are sending for their dependants and opting to stay for the foreseeable future. Now second and third generations are growing up. While links with their parents' countries of origin are increasingly tenuous, their future lies in countries where they may be treated and experience themselves as outsiders.

It is now clear that *new ethnic minorities* have been formed. Immigrants and their descendants form groups characterised by nationality, certain physical traits, language, culture and lifestyle, distinct from the indigenous populations. These minorities are to a certain extent isolated from the rest of the population, and they are discriminated against. They form communities with their own institutions and identity.

A process of class formation is also taking place. This is, above all, a restructuring of the working class. Immigrants and their descendants make up a large proportion of the urban industrial labour force and are concentrated in unskilled and semi-skilled employment in mass-production sectors and in certain service industries. Many have jobs where working-class organisation and militancy have traditionally been strongest. Problems of class organisation and consciousness arise because the interests of immigrant and indigenous workers may diverge. While immigrants may form majorities in some unions, the control of the labour movement has remained largely in the hands of indigenous workers or officials.

Sociologists have tended to emphasise exclusively either the class position or ethnic minority status of immigrants. In reality, these two aspects interact with each other at a time when class structure, the labour market and the very nature of work are undergoing rapid transformation. Whether ethnic and class consciousness are in contradiction to each other, or correspond with and reinforce each other, depends on factors like segregation of the workplace, segregation of housing, institutional discrimination, racism in the arts and the media. The way the labour and housing markets functioned during the sixties and seventies meant that immigrant communities developed in the poorest inner-city areas of the industrial conurbations. Today, many immigrants prefer to stay there, rather than move out to better private or council accommodation, because of fear of racist attacks and discrimination.

Racism is on the upsurge in all the countries of immigration. It can force immigrant workers to depend more on ethnic solidarity than on class solidarity to defend their interests. But effective ethnic organisation can strengthen class solidarity if it leads to acceptance of immigrant workers as a group with legitimate special interests which can be integrated into a broader movement.

Racism has taken various forms: media campaigns against immigrants, articulation of fears of 'foreign swamping' of the national culture, racist attacks, growth of neo-Nazi organisations, emphasis on racial problems in the policies of major political parties. The phenomenon is growing because the consolidation of the new ethnic minorities is taking place at a time of economic crisis and restructuring of the labour process. The objective increase in insecurity for all workers is intensified by a subjective threat in the form of foreign groups who are portrayed as competing for increasingly scarce jobs and social resources. Employers, politicians and the media promote the image of immigrants as the cause of the crisis, rather than as fellow victims, and this idea falls on fertile ground. Immigrants no longer appear to be useful 'guest workers' who do the dirty work, but as an alien and growing threat to culture and society. This shift matches a transformation in ruling-class strategy. In the boom period, immigrant workers were seen mainly in their economic role as providers of extra labour power; now the ideological role of a useful scapegoat for the crisis is becoming predominant.

The basic determinant of migration was employers' demand for labour. Unemployment and underemployment in countries of the European periphery and the Third World were the necessary pre-conditions for mass labour migration rather than the dynamic factors shaping its course. Once labour migration took on a significant volume, the states of the receiving countries set up agencies and designed policies to cope with it. In general they reacted to events in an ad hoc way, rather than planning migrations according to social and economic needs. Even West Germany's highly organised recruitment system (with offices in Verona, Belgrade, Athens and Istanbul) merely responded to employers' short-term labour requirements, without any form of long-term labour-market planning.

France was the only country that made some plans for permanent settlement of the people recruited as workers and set up an Office National d'Immigration in 1945. Heavy war losses and low birth rates made this seem demographically desirable. But the number of settlers expected was far lower than the actual number who stayed.

Mass international migrations almost always lead to settlement and to the development of ethnic minorities. As a migratory current matures, workers – predominantly young men – tend to bring in their dependants. Once children start going to school in the new country, settlement of a kind becomes inevitable. So the new ethnic minorities may be seen as the natural result of the policies of mass recruitment of migrant workers. What is surprising is not the fact of settlement, but that the states concerned did not seem to expect it, and did little or nothing to plan accordingly. The extreme case of this head-in-the-sand attitude is West Germany. Even today, with an immigrant population of 4.7 million, the government and major parties continue to intone, 'The German Federal Republic is not a country of immigration,' as if the ritual chant could make the problems go away.

The explanation for the lack of planning is quite simply that the priority was to meet capital's labour requirements as quickly and cheaply as possible. Since all major industrial countries were using migrant labour, any country that failed to do so was likely to lose out in international competition. Similarly, heavy expenditure in social capital (housing, schools, social facilities), needed to ease the process of settlement, would have generated inflationary pressures, harmful to economic growth. So governments took the easy way out, letting migration and settlement take place spontaneously, pushing its social costs on to the migrants and other inhabitants of the inner city.

A decade ago, one of the authors of the present book, Stephen Castles, and Godula Kosack described and analysed what may in retrospect be seen as the first phase of the migratory process, the phase of mass labour migration. Our book *Immigrant Workers and Class Structure in Western Europe*[5] was written largely as a contribution to the debate taking place at that time on Commonwealth immigration to Britain. Most people tended to see the presence of black workers in Britain as an historically unique phenomenon connected with the decline of the Empire. Most sociological studies were based on an 'immigrant–host' framework, and conflicts were often examined in social-psychological terms, as problems of 'race relations'. British sociologists made comparative studies with race problems in the USA and South Africa, colour–class systems in Brazil or patterns of ethnic interaction in Malaysia. But most British academics seemed to be ignorant of the presence of millions of migrant workers in other Western European countries, or at least to see no parallels in the situation.

We therefore examined the situation of immigrant workers in France, Switzerland and West Germany in comparison with Britain, with the aim of showing that labour migration was a general feature of post-war Western European capitalism. Despite the differences in the patterns of migration to the various countries, we argued that the basic causes were similar, and that they could only be understood in the historical context of the uneven development of the capitalist system. We tried to show that immigrant labour had become a structural necessity for Western European economies, and that this was likely to have long-term effects, even where the migration appeared initially to be temporary. We saw the major impact of immigration in a trend towards the restructuring of the working class. For many reasons immigrant workers entered the labour market at the bottom and tended to stay there. This situation was duplicated in the housing market and access to social facilities. In their relationship to the means of production, immigrants were members of the working class, but were apparently becoming a specific stratum within it. We advanced the hypothesis that this allowed social advancement to sections of the indigenous working class; this took the form both of objective upward mobility through occupational promotion and improved income, and of subjective mobility in higher status relative to a new low-status group. It was helping to change class consciousness, and was conducive to ideas of individual advancement, rather than collective advancement through class struggle.

Immigrant Workers and Class Structure in Western Europe was published in the very year that was to prove to be the turning point from mass labour migration to family migration and settlement. A lot has changed in the decade since, not only in the situation of immigrants, but also with regard to the economic and social framework in which the process of migration and settlement is taking place. The present work is an attempt to describe and analyse the new phase. It deals with events up to 1973 only to the extent necessary for understanding subsequent developments. Again the aim is to go beyond the specific characteristics of the various Western European countries, and to show general features, which arise from basic structures (and structural changes) of contemporary Western European capitalism. The approach is necessarily interdisciplinary. The basic framework of analysis cuts across the fields of political economy, sociology and demography – fields in which the authors are relatively at home. But it is also necessary to trespass into the preserves of law, political science, history and culture. We do not attempt a comprehensive survey of the relevant theory in these various fields.

The early chapters of this book are concerned with Western Europe as a whole. Chapter 2 puts labour migration and settlement in the broad historical perspective of the changing political economy of the capitalist world market. Chapter 3 presents statistics and a description of patterns of migration and settlement for the seven main countries of immigration: Britain, Belgium, France, the Netherlands, Sweden, Switzerland and West Germany. While the emphasis is on the peculiarities of each case, general patterns do start to emerge.

The second part of the book presents far more detailed information on West Germany, and draws attention to parallels and differences with Britain. The interest of this comparison lies in the fact that the two countries appear at first sight to be so different: Britain with relatively early migrations of black workers from former colonies who had rights of permanent settlement; West Germany with a highly organised system of temporary 'guest workers' from Southern Europe who had no right of settlement. The two countries are at opposite ends of the spectrum. If it can be shown that there are parallel patterns of development of the new ethnic minorities, then there is every reason to believe that this applies to the other countries as well. Nonetheless, where possible, differences and similarities in other countries will be pointed out.

Chapter 5 examines some demographic and sociological aspects of the transition from labour migration to settlement. Chapter 6 deals with the changing position of migrant or minority workers in the labour process. Chapter 7 discusses the situation of minority youth, and the extent to which their class position and consciousness corresponds with that of their parents. Chapter 8 is concerned with the growth of racism, its causes, and its political impact. Chapter 9 tries to assess varying perceptions of class position. This leads to a discussion of the anti-racist movement and the role of the left within it.

The sources of information for this study are listed in the notes and references and the bibliography. They fall into the following categories:

Statistics, reports and studies provided by international organisations such as the ILO, OECD, United Nations and EEC. The most useful single source in this category is the OECD's Continuous Reporting System on Migration (known as SOPEMI).

Material issued by the appropriate government agencies of the countries concerned. This includes statistics provided by census offices and statistical agencies, reports from home affairs ministries, education authorities and social affairs departments, and the findings of state commissioned research.

Academic publications and research findings on all aspects of migration and settlement.

Documents and statements of organisations concerned with immigrants, such as trade unions, employers' associations, welfare bodies, churches, immigrants' associations.

Materials issued by political parties.

Press reports.

Migrants' accounts of their experience in literary or verbal form.

Background information obtained from the main author's work in the field of social-work training and youth work in Britain and West Germany.

2. The rise and fall of the guest worker system

The migratory process

There have been three phases in the process of international migration which have led to the development of the new ethnic minorities. The phases have merged into each other, though during each phase a particular aspect of the migratory process has been predominant.

The first may be designated as *the phase of mass labour migration*. In most of the seven countries dealt with in this book, entry of migrant workers started about 1945, gained momentum in the fifties, expanded dramatically in the late sixties and early seventies, and then stopped fairly suddenly in 1973/4.

There are two exceptions: West Germany did not start recruiting foreign workers until 1956, because the labour market had to absorb large numbers of German refugees (from East Germany and the former eastern territories lost to Poland and the Soviet Union) in the early post-war years. From the early sixties, recruitment of foreign workers was so rapid that West Germany had caught up with the other countries in the use of migrant labour by the end of the decade. Britain stopped entries of migrant workers in 1962, except for certain categories of highly skilled people. (The detailed patterns of labour migration to the various countries will be examined in chapter 3.)

In the early years, labour migration was, on the whole, seen as a temporary necessity, caused by the need to compensate for war losses and to provide labour for post-war reconstruction. Labour migration was not expected to go on for long, nor were many of the workers expected to settle. The still-vivid memories of the world economic crisis of the thirties led most people to expect an early end to the post-war boom. So various states took measures to keep the migrants mobile, and were often supported in this by unions and employers. A system of residence and labour permits of restricted duration were evolved for this purpose. Often workers were bound to specific occupations and employers. The migrants were denied political and civil rights, and often not permitted to bring in family members. Typically, there were clauses calling for the revoking of labour permits in the event of deterioration of the employment situation. Sometimes, such networks of institutional discrimination were linked to official, state, migrant labour recruitment frameworks: the European Voluntary Worker scheme in Britain, the Belgian *contingentensysteem*, the French Office National d'Immigration, the West German Federal Labour Office recruiting scheme. In other countries like Switzerland, Sweden, the Netherlands, state regulations controlled workers recruited directly by employers or coming of their own accord. This system of institutionalised discrimination, designed to recruit and control temporary migrant workers, is referred to as the *guest worker system*.

Of course, not all migrant workers were part of the guest worker system. Britain, France and the Netherlands also received large numbers of migrant workers from their colonies or former colonies. These migrants generally had better legal rights than the guest workers; often they held citizenship of the country of immigration. Many of the workers from the colonies saw themselves as temporary labour migrants, but they did have the right to stay. Some planned to settle, and were expected to by people in the receiving countries. This 'colonial immigration' was the main form of labour migration to Britain; it was as important as the guest worker system for the Netherlands; and was a major factor for France, although smaller in numbers than entries from Southern Europe.

The overwhelming majority of migrant workers recruited through the guest worker system, and a fair proportion of workers coming from the colonies, intended to stay for a few years only. Their aim was to save enough money to buy land and livestock, to build a house, or to set up a business in the country of origin. This intention of temporary migration is common to the initial phase of most migratory movements – even to those seen in retrospect as permanent, such as migration to the USA, Latin America and Australia. The aims of the migrants in the first phase of the process of migration to Western Europe matched the intentions of the employers and states of the immigration countries.

But as time went on, many migrant workers found that it was impossible to earn and save enough to achieve their economic aims. Moreover, the deterioration of the political and economic situations in some of the countries of origin made an early return seem less and less feasible. As the prospect of going home receded, a life of nothing but hard work, frugality and social isolation seemed less acceptable. Workers began bringing in their wives or husbands and children. Others started new families in the country of immigration. The second phase of the migratory process, *the phase of family reunification*, got under way. Family reunification usually did not imply a decision to settle permanently or even to stay on for a long period. Indeed, many migrants actually thought that it would speed return, for their family members came as workers rather than mere dependants. But family immigration developed a logic of its own. Family housing and other needs raised migrants' cost of living, so that saving was harder than for single workers. Once children were born in Western Europe and started going to school, the prospect of return receded even further. Family reunification therefore generally meant a much longer duration of stay.

Family reunification contradicted the original aims of the guest worker system. It made migrant labour less mobile and harder to get rid of in the event of a recession. It increased the need for investment in housing and other social amenities, or – more realistically since the necessary social investments were rarely made – it increased the social tensions in the inner-city areas where migrants were forced to live. So it is necessary to ask why the states of Western Europe permitted family reunification, despite the existence of discriminatory regulations designed to prevent it.

One explanation was the growing competition for labour during the boom of the sixties and early seventies. Labour market authorities were under pressure from employers to meet their labour needs quickly. Demand was especially high for workers with skills and industrial experience, and there was considerable competition to attract such workers. This led to improvements in legal status and social conditions for migrants – a trend reinforced by policies of governments of the countries of origin, which demanded guarantees concerning pay and conditions before permitting their workers to emigrate. The resulting bilateral agreements between sending and receiving countries generally permitted family reunification after a certain period. Trends towards European integration also led to international agreements that improved migrants' rights.

A further factor was the desire of many employers to maintain a stable labour force. The policy of 'rotation' of migrant workers, called for by labour market authorities in Switzerland and West Germany, was all very well for firms that specialised in exploiting the cheap labour power of unskilled, temporary and rightless foreign workers. But the big industrial enterprises were becoming increasingly dependent on migrant labour, and they often needed trained workers, with appropriate skills and experience. Such employers wanted a reliable and stable work force, even if this could only be obtained by allowing workers to bring in dependants and settle for longer periods.

But the main cause of family reunification was simply that migrants were not willing to accept the denial of the basic human right of living with their wives, husbands and children. Dependants were brought in legally where possible, illegally where this right was refused. Once large-scale labour migration became established, family immigration was inevitable. State measures to restrict it caused misery and hardship for millions of families, but they could not enforce permanent separation for all.

By the time large-scale labour migration was halted, the trend to family reunification was well established. The phase of family reunification was the dominant aspect of the migratory process in the subsequent decade. The state labour-market authorities of the Western European countries had hoped that stopping labour migration would cause large-scale return migration of both workers and dependants. As will be shown in more detail below, large numbers of migrant workers did leave, but those workers who remained continued to bring in dependants, so that immigrant populations became stabilised or even increased.

In the meantime, the majority of migrants have brought in dependants. The average length of residence is increasing, and ties with the countries of origin are becoming more tenuous, especially for the increasing proportion of migrants' children actually born in Western Europe. Many migrant families have of course re-migrated. Those who stay on are becoming more firmly established, and are likely to stay permanently, often without making a conscious decision to do so. The migratory process has entered its third and final stage: *the phase of permanent settlement and development of new ethnic minorities*. The description and analysis of various aspects of this third phase is the main theme of the second part of this book.

World market and labour migration

Labour migration, along with commodity exchanges and capital flows, plays an important part in the development of the capitalist mode of production throughout its history, although its forms have varied considerably. A brief look at the forms taken by these relationships in the past makes it easier to understand current trends. But first it is necessary to define what is meant by 'centre' and 'periphery' of the capitalist system.

According to Samir Amin, the pre-condition for a theory of capital accumulation on a world scale is the comprehension that exchange relations exist between two differing types of socio-economic formation, 'capitalism of the centre' and 'capitalism of the periphery':

> The concrete socio-economic formations of the centre bear this distinctive feature, that in them the capitalist mode of production is not merely *dominant* but, because its growth is based on expansion of the internal market, tends to become *exclusive*. These formations therefore draw closer and closer to the capitalist mode of production, the disintegration of precapitalist modes tending to become complete and to lead to their replacement by the capitalist mode, reconstituted on the basis of the scattered elements issuing from this break-up process . . . The socio-economic formations of the periphery, however, bear this distinctive feature, that though the capitalist mode of production does indeed predominate, this domination does not lead to a tendency for it to become exclusive, because the spread of capitalism here is based on the external market. It follows that pre-capitalist modes of production are not destroyed but are transformed and subjected to that mode of production which predominates on a world scale as well as locally – the capitalist mode of production.[1]

The geographical location of centre and periphery has varied in the different epochs of capitalist development, but the essential distinction has been maintained. Advanced forms of production as well as control of world trade have tended to be concentrated at the centre, while peripheral areas have been pushed into a subordinate role as suppliers of labour power and certain types of commodities, and as markets for the industrial products of the centre. 'Underdevelopment' of the countries of the periphery is the result. In other words, as Amin puts it, their 'process of transition has been blocked'.[2]

The survival of pre-capitalist modes of production in peripheral areas is essential to the development of the capitalist system. It permits continuing processes of 'primitive accumulation',[3] through which value is transferred from the peripheral areas to the centre. This encourages capital accumulation and economic growth in the advanced central areas of capitalism. Migrant labour is one form of this 'hidden transfer of value from the periphery to the centre, since the periphery has borne the cost of education and training this labour power'.[4] Or, 'Labour migration is a form of development aid given by the poor countries to the rich countries.'[5]

During the centuries preceding the industrial revolution – the *mercantile period* – relations between Western Europe ('the centre in process of formation')[6] and the countries then being colonised ('the new periphery') were vital for the genesis of capitalism. World trade was mainly between Western Europe on the one hand, and the New World, Asia and Africa on the other. The commercial metropoles of Western Europe (first the cities of Northern Italy, later the Hanse towns of Germany, then Spain and Portugal, and from the seventeenth century the ports of Holland and Britain) redistributed gold, spices and agricultural and craft products obtained overseas. The centre got hold of such products through a variety of methods, including exchange, plunder and the organisation of production in the colonies. The consequence was the transformation of the relations of production and the imposition of new forms of subjugation of labour both at the periphery and the centre.

The slave economies of the New World were based on enforced migration of labour from one area of the periphery (Africa) to another (America). At the same time, the development of agrarian capitalism at the centre (especially in Britain) was causing displacement, through the enclosures, of masses of formerly independent small farmers. As the landlords turned arable land into sheep pastures and pulled down the cottages of their tenants, these had no choice but to migrate to the towns. Hordes of beggars, disciplined and intimidated by draconian poor laws, provided labour power for the workhouses and manufactures, foreshadowing the industrial revolution.[7]

During the *period of industrialisation at the centre* – starting in the mid eighteenth century in Britain, and continuing until the late nineteenth century in continential Europe, the USA and finally in Japan – trade between the centre and the periphery changed in character. The centre exported manufactured goods such as textiles to the periphery, and obtained in return agricultural products, either from the traditional agriculture of the East (tea, for example) or from the highly productive capitalist agriculture of the New World (for example, wheat, meat, cotton). The international specialisation between industrial and agricultural countries became established. In addition, as new countries like France, Germany and the USA began industrialising, the exchange of manufactured and mineral products between the countries of the centre gained in importance. World trade began to split into two groups of exchange relationships: exchange between centre and periphery, and internal exchange within the centre.[8]

In this period, primitive accumulation continued at both centre and periphery, giving rise to a variety of forms of labour migration, both internal and international. In Britain, for instance, displaced small farmers and agricultural labourers moved from rural counties to become wage workers in the new factories of the Midlands, Lancashire, Yorkshire and elsewhere. They were joined by former hand-weavers and other artisans who had lost their livelihood through the competition of the machines. At an early stage in the industrial revolution, British capital began employing workers from one of its colonies for some of the hardest and worst paid jobs. Many of the 'navigators' who dug the canals as well as factory labourers came from Ireland. Irish labour was plentiful because of the depredation of Ireland by British landlords and the flooding of the Irish market with cheap manufactured products, which had ruined many peasants and artisans and caused widespread poverty.

Similarly, in France industrialisation led to migrations from

Brittany, Normandy and the south-west to Paris and the north-east. Soon, French industrialists started recruiting labour in Italy and Poland. In Germany, a large proportion of the workers recruited for the coal mines and iron-works of the Ruhr were Poles.[9]

But many of the small farmers and artisans displaced by agrarian capitalism and by industrialisation sought to better their lot through emigration from Western Europe to the colonies or the USA: labour migration from the centre to the periphery. The migrants became soldiers, farmers, traders, craftspeople, overseers, managers and clerks, often settling permanently and playing a vital part in the development of the colonial economies and societies. This type of overseas migration grew throughout the nineteenth century, although its peak was during the later period of imperialism.

In the countries of the periphery, colonial expansion was beginning to incorporate some sections of peasant agriculture and artisan production into the capitalist mode of production. The pulling of these pre-capitalist forms into the world market, and the expropriation of their surplus products was causing increasing poverty, landlessness and debt. Displaced and underemployed farmers and artisans were thus 'freed' from their traditional relations of production, and were forced to seek a means of survival elsewhere. Initially they migrated as wage labour for colonial plantations, mines, docks and so on, or became domestic servants of the colonists.

From about 1870 new structural trends in the capitalist economy led to a speeding-up of the integration of peripheral areas into the world market. The *imperialist period* was characterised by the merging of industrial and financial capital resulting in the control of production by the banks, and increasing monopolisation of key areas of industry and commerce. The states of the capitalist countries took on a new and vital role in providing and safeguarding the conditions for profitability, through both domestic and foreign policies. Increasing competition between the growing number of capitalist powers, and the trend towards falling rates of profits at the centre, caused the scramble for colonies between 1870 and 1914. By the latter date, the capitalist countries of Western Europe and North America had transformed most of the rest of the world into colonies or semi-colonies (economically dependent areas like Turkey, Iran and China).

Imperialism involved an enormous expansion of capital export from centre to periphery. This did not replace the export of commodities; indeed it further stimulated it. The plantations, mines, oil wells and (later) factories, set up in the countries of the periphery as a result of imperialist investment, increased dependence of the periphery on the centre. Now most of the products of the periphery were produced in enterprises directly controlled by the capital of the centre. Trends towards incorporation of peasant agriculture and artisan production in the world market continued, with increasing control of finance and distribution by transnational agribusiness. However, the relative importance of traditional products in the exports of the periphery declined. Amin estimates that 'three-quarters of the exports of the periphery come from highly productive modern sectors which are the expression of capitalist development in the periphery, to a large extent the direct result of investment of capital by the centre'.[10]

The tendency of the imperialist form of capitalism – which is still the prevailing form of the world market today – is to progressively integrate all areas of production into a single system, in which centre and periphery are interdependent sectors. Integration is based not only on markets for commodities and capital, but also for labour and for production sites. But the imperialist form of integration of the world economy is very far from being a smooth, continuous and planned process. It is marked by constant struggles of various kinds: between capital and labour, between various sectors of capital on the national and international level, and between imperialist states struggling for bigger shares in the pickings. Domination of production in peripheral countries by the monopolies of the centre has often given rise to resistance from nascent national bourgeoisies, sometimes consisting of white settlers (as in the case of Rhodesia).

It is impossible to go into the complexities of these struggles here, though there can be no doubt that the long-term trend is towards greater integration of the world economy, with increasing control of finance, production and distribution by transnational corporations. Imperialism has developed in a succession of phases, in which periods of expansion and integration have been followed by periods of economic and political crisis. In each of these phases, labour migration has taken a different form.

The period of imperialist expansion from the 1890s to 1914 led to large-scale intra-European labour migration. The proportion of foreign workers in the Ruhr and north-east France was comparable to that reached again half a century later. At the same time, overseas emigration from Europe reached new peaks, due to the growing opportunities in the USA and the colonies. In the countries of the periphery, imperialism led to accelerated primitive accumulation, 'freeing' increasing numbers of people to become contract workers in the rapidly expanding mines and plantations.

The crisis of imperialism, which expressed itself in the first world war and in the period of stagnation that followed it, put a virtual stop to intra-European labour migration. Growth in the countries of the periphery also declined. France did recruit Polish workers to compensate for war losses, but many were sent home as the crisis deepened in the early thirties. The Nazi war economy led to a new upsurge in labour migration, recruiting foreign workers from 1936 onwards. By 1944, 7.5 million foreign workers – many of them prisoners of war or people conscripted by force in occupied countries – were employed in munitions and other industries, replacing Germans called up for military service.

In most capitalist countries, labour migration resumed after 1945. This new current had several novel features, one of which was the high volume of migration from Third World countries to Western Europe and North America.

In the current period of restructuring of capitalism, which is marked by stagnation of production and world trade, and decline in employment at the centre, labour migration to Western Europe has again virtually ceased. New currents of labour migration include movements into oil-producing countries, of both highly skilled personnel from developed countries and manual workers from poorer surrounding areas. Labour migration into new industrial areas within the Third World from other countries of the periphery is also taking place. (These two most recent periods will be examined in the final sections of this chapter.)

Mass labour migration during the post-war boom

The long wave[11] of expansion from 1945 to the early seventies saw the most rapid and sustained development of production in recorded history, with world capitalist output doubling in the period from 1952 to 1968 alone.[12] The boom was marked by high rates of capital accumulation: on average the stock of the means of production grew by nearly 6 per cent annually from 1950 to 1970.[13] More and better machinery was continually brought into service, leading to production of more commodities, and raising labour productivity. Capitalists were able and willing to invest because the conditions for both production of surplus value and realisation of that surplus values were favourable. In other words, on the supply side, the factors of production (labour, raw materials, machinery) were readily available, so that expansion of production did not immediately lead to cost inflation. On the demand side, it was possible to sell the commodities produced at prices which permitted adequate rates of profit.

The causes of the long boom were complex and closely inter-dependent. The hegemony of US capital which emerged from the second world war allowed a restructuring of world financial and commodity markets. US capital reorganised large sectors of industrial production in Western Europe, while its growing domination of newly independent, Third World countries secured cheap raw materials and agricultural products. The advanced sectors of capital became transnational, as they strove to integrate production and trade on a world scale. The weakening of the working class through fascism and war (especially in the later 'economic miracle' countries of West Germany, Italy and Japan) kept wages relatively low in relation to productivity growth in the early post-war years, allowing high rates of surplus value. Labour was readily available due to the dislocation caused by the war and its aftermath. Post-war reconstruction led to initial high demand for goods of all kinds. Re-armament, the cold war and the 'Korea boom' revived demand when it began to show signs of flagging. The opportunities for the renewal of fixed capital due to the expansion of new high-technology-based industries further stimulated demand. It is not feasible to adequately analyse the causes of the long boom here.[14] But for the theme of the present book, it is necessary to look a little more closely at the question of availability of labour and its relationship to wage and profit levels.

On average, employment in the advanced capitalist countries grew by about one per cent per year during the period of expansion. This seems little compared to the rate of capital accumulation (nearly 6 per cent per year) yet growth of labour supply was an essential pre-condition for capital accumulation.[15] If no new workers had been available, capitalists wishing to expand production, to set up new factories, or to introduce new methods of working would have had to offer higher wages to attract labour away from competitors. These in turn would have had to pay more to retain labour. The resulting increased rate of inflation would have led to a stop–go economy, reducing economic growth and causing an early end to the boom. On this basis, the US economist C.P. Kindleberger has argued that the ready availability of labour was vital to post-war economic growth in Western Europe:

> The major factor shaping the remarkable economic growth which most of Europe has experienced since 1950 has been the availability of a large supply of labour. The labour has come from a high rate of natural increase (the Netherlands), from transfers from agriculture to services and industry (Germany, France, Italy), from the immigration of refugees (Germany), and from the immigration of unemployed and underemployed workers from the Mediterranean countries (France, Germany and Switzerland). Those countries with no substantial increase in the labour supply – Britain, Belgium and the Scandinavian nations – on the whole have grown more slowly than the others.[16]
>
> An OECD study has summed up the function of labour migration: To permit the industrialised countries to fill job vacancies with reduced upward pressure on wages and profits. This added to national output in those countries and protected their competitive position in world trade.[17]

Now of course these two statements oversimplify the issue, because they imply that labour power is an homogeneous commodity, which can be treated in purely quantitative terms. In reality, migrant workers, along with the other additional sources of labour power mentioned by Kindleberger, provided particular types of labour power needed for economic growth and structural change. This point will be returned to below.

Capital's requirement of additional and flexible sources of labour is in no way a new feature of post-war Western Europe, but rather a general condition of the mode of production; only the specific form is new. Marx showed that 'a surplus population of workers' is not only a necessary product of capital accumulation, but is also conversely 'the lever of capitalist accumulation' and 'a condition for the existence of the capitalist mode of production'.[18] Only by bringing ever more workers into the production process can the capitalist accumulate capital, which is the pre-condition for extending production and applying new techniques. These new techniques often make redundant the very men and women whose labour allowed their introduction. They are set free to provide an 'industrial reserve army' which is available to be thrown into other sectors, as the interests of capital require.

> Modern industry's whole form of notion therefore depends
> on the constant transformation of a part of the working
> population into unemployed or semi-employed 'hands'.[19]

The pressure of the industrial reserve army forces those workers who do have jobs to accept long hours, poor conditions and deskilling. Above all:

> Taking them as a whole, the general movements of wages
> are exclusively regulated by the expansion and contraction
> of the industrial reserve army, and this in turn corresponds
> to the periodic alternations of the industrial cycle.[20]

If employment grows and the number of people out of work contracts, workers are in a better position to demand higher wages. When this happens, profits and capital accumulation diminish, investment falls and employment begins to contract again. Then the reserve army grows and wages begin to fall. This is one cause of the capitalist 'business cycle' with its regularly alternating phases of expansion and recession.

Marx identified three forms taken by the 'relative surplus population' or 'industrial reserve army': 'the floating, the latent and the stagnant'.[21] The 'floating surplus population' refers to workers who have been employed in industry and then dismissed in recession. Such workers can quickly be brought back to work in event of expansion. The 'latent surplus population' is the result of capitalist transformation of agrarian production, which reduces the amount of labour needed on the land, and impoverishes small farmers and artisans. Some of these become available for industry, and are compelled to seek employment as wage workers in the towns.

> Part of the agricultural population is therefore constantly on the point of passing over into an urban or manufacturing proletariat, and on the lookout for opportunities to complete this transformation . . . But the constant movement towards the towns presupposes, in the countryside itself, a constant latent surplus population, the extent of which only becomes evident at those exceptional times when its distribution channels are wide open.[22]

The 'stagnant surplus population' refers to people impoverished and marginalised by capitalist exploitation: domestic workers, orphans, the handicapped and chronically sick, prostitutes, vagabonds and criminals. Marx speaks of 'the lowest sediment of the relative surplus poplation' which 'dwells in the sphere of pauperism'. Today, one speaks of the 'impoverished' or the lowest stratum of the working class.

Marx's concept of 'relative surplus population' has been dealt with at some length because it helps us to understand the form of development taken by Western European capitalism and the resulting labour migrations. The three types of 'relative surplus population' have all been present throughout the history of industrialisation, but their relative importance has varied. For instance, during the period of the industrial revolution, the presence of a 'latent surplus population' of unemployed and underemployed rural workers was vital to growth. The movement of these workers into the new factories took the form of internal rural–urban migration (for example, from the Highlands to Glasgow, from Brittany to the Lorraine) or of international labour migration (Ireland to Manchester, Poland to the Ruhr). In the inter-war period, the major forms of the industrial reserve army in Western Europe were the 'floating' and the 'stagnant' ones. Mass unemployment and increasing impoverishment kept wages low and forced workers to accept rationalisation and poor conditions. But the resulting political tensions were so severe that they threatened the existence of the capitalist system. The response of the ruling class was the establishment of fascist regimes in the areas where it was most threatened, in order to suppress the labour movement through violence. The failure of this strategy, culminating in the defeat of fascism in 1945, was accompanied by the reinforcement of an alternative system in Eastern Europe and Asia, and by a new upsurge of the labour movement in some Western European countries.

Policies leading to mass unemployment and impoverishment were politically untenable in this period. The states of Western Europe had to aim for full employment and improved social welfare. Their new policies were embodied in the strategies of Keynsian economics and of the welfare state. These strategies were a potential threat to the profitability of capitalist production. Capital's response was to aim at constant growth through increased productivity and mobilisation of new sources of labour.

These sources varied. In West Germany, for instance, the collapse of the war economy and the demobilisation of millions of soldiers provided a large reserve army of the 'floating' type. These workers were eager to get any jobs they could, and generally had training and industrial experience. They were joined by millions of refugees and expellees from East Germany and the former eastern territories of the Reich. West Germany, hence, had a huge industrial reserve army. This, together with the weakness of the labour movement in the aftermath of fascism, provided ideal conditions for capitalist expansion, and was the essential cause of the 'economic miracle'.

As the boom got under way, mobilisation of other internal labour reserves also became important. Agricultural reform led to increased rural–urban migration, and increasing numbers of women were drawn into wage employment. West German industry had absorbed all these reserves by the end of the fifties, and it was at that point that capital began to call for mobilisation of the 'latent surplus population' of Southern Europe to meet its labour needs. The result was the establishment of a system of highly organised labour recruitment by the state.

No other country had such large and flexible labour reserves. Italy, the Netherlands, France and Switzerland were able to benefit from a certain amount of rural–urban migration. The two former countries also had fairly high rates of natural growth. Increase in women's participation in the labour force also played a part, although the limiting factor was always the social expenditure necessary to provide child-care. So all these countries started recruiting foreign workers, or encouraging them to enter, more or less immediately after the second world war. (Italy is a special case in which the migration was internal – from the underdeveloped Mezzogiorno to the industrial north.)

Britain was in a particularly unfavourable position with regard to labour supply. Because the agrarian revolution had been so early, there was little reserve labour in rural areas. The number of women in the labour force was already high at the end of the war. It was essential to obtain additional workers through migration from abroad. British capital turned to its old labour reserve, Ireland, and also started recruitment of 'European Voluntary Workers' in the refugee camps. Information on the good prospects of finding work in Britain gave rise to a new stream of labour migrants from the Commonwealth countries from the fifties. But, taking account of emigration from Britain, the supply of labour had been more or less stagnant since 1945. This, together with the strength of the labour movement, which has resisted attacks on the incomes and conditions of workers, is at the root of the chronic crisis of profitability of British capital.

The significance of immigrant labour grew in the sixties, as the internal labour potential of the countries concerned stagnated or even declined. Birth rates were so low in some countries (West Germany, for instance) that the indigenous population was actually declining. At the same time, the proportion of the population in the labour force was falling due to increased length of education and earlier retirement. Cuts in working hours also reduced the amount of labour available. These trends could only be partially countered by increasing women's labour force participation. So the recruitment of migrant workers was the main additional source of labour for West Germany, France, Luxembourg, Sweden and Switzerland. It was an important additional source of labour in Britain, Belgium and the Netherlands, where the largest sources of new labour were either natural increase or increased employment of women.[23]

The employment of migrant workers has been important in processes of restructuring of the labour process and segmentation of the labour market throughout the post-war period. Migrants have entered the labour market for specific types of work and have often tended to remain there, for reasons of lack of education and industrial training, language difficulties, racial prejudice, systems of institutional discrimination which hinder job-changing and promotion.

Migrant workers have generally had to take the least qualified jobs with the lowest pay and the worst working conditions, with important consequences. First, as the labour market has expanded, migrants have replaced a proportion of indigenous workers in the least desirable jobs. The latter (or their children) have been able to gain education and training, and hence to obtain promotion into skilled or white-collar employment. Second, a substantial part of the indigenous working class has not obtained such promotion, and has worked side by side with migrant workers. Problems of communication along with the development of racism often endanger the unity of the work force and weaken union organisation. Third, the weak socio-economic position of migrant labour often makes it particularly flexible and easily controllable for employers. In many cases, employers have recruited migrants into new jobs as part of restructuring measures which deskill the labour force. The newcomers were far less able to resist such processes than well-established, local labour forces, which was important from the early sixties, when declining profit rates began endangering the post-war boom.

The response of capital was the accelerated introduction of forms of organisation of the labour process designed to intensify work and raise productivity. These methods included splitting work processes into simple operations to reduce the need for skilled workers; increased use of assembly lines, piece-work and bonus payments; and the introduction of continuous shift working. The increased employment of migrant workers was crucial to this trend, as is shown for West Germany in chapter 5.

All in all, countries with the most flexible supplies of labour, and which made most effective use of migrant workers, had the highest growth rates in the post-war boom. As the quotation from the OECD study on page 22 above indicates, migrant labour has helped to hold back wage inflation and to keep profit rates high. This fact is often mistakenly taken to imply that the long-term impact of labour migration is to keep wages lower in countries of high immigration than in countries of low immigration. The opposite is the case. By sustaining a boom which would otherwise have collapsed due to inflation, the use of migrant labour permitted wage rates to improve more in absolute terms in the long run, compared with countries having restricted labour supplies where growth was slow.

In the boom period there was a strong correlation between economic growth, increase of labour supply and improvement in productivity.[24] In West Germany and Switzerland, for instance, the labour force grew very fast and there was also large investment in modern plant with high productivity. In the long run, the economy grew steadily and fast, and wages increased too. In Britain, on the other hand, the labour force grew little, the profit rate remained too low to encourage large investment in new and more productive plant, economic growth was slow and sporadic, and wages in the long run increased less than in West Germany. The effect of abundant labour supply in the long run was not to keep wages down absolutely, but to keep down their relative share in national income, allowing profits and investment to remain high.

During the sixties, some economists argued that the possibility of importing relatively cheap labour was harmful to growth, because it reduced the incentive for rationalisation, leading to investment in the form of 'capital widening', that is, the extension of production using relatively backward, labour-intensive techniques.[25] On that basis, rationalisation should have been more rapid in Britain than in Germany, France or Switzerland. That was of course not the case.

In fact high profit rates permitted by relatively abundant labour generally led to both capital widening and capital deepening. In other words, the new jobs created to employ migrant workers also used new techniques that raised productivity. The real lesson of the British economy is that lack of labour and low profit rates did not lead to rationalisation, but rather to unwillingness to invest in the country at all. British capital has been exported to countries with higher profit rates, while transnational companies have been very reluctant to invest in Britain.

Halting labour migration to Western Europe

Migrant labour played an important part in economic growth and in the restructuring and rationalisation of the production process. This role was especially marked in the late sixties and early seventies, when recruitment of migrant workers reached peak levels in several countries, including West Germany and France. In retrospect, it seems curious that these two countries should so suddenly have halted further entries of new workers (from outside the EEC) in 1973 and 1974 just after the peaks of migration. At the time it was stated that the so-called oil crisis of 1973–5 was reducing labour demand. But a decade later, recruitment of migrant labour has still not resumed, and it is obvious that the 'oil crisis' was merely the harbinger of a long period of recession and stagnation in the capitalist economy.

It had been expected that migrants would pack up and go if recession made their labour superfluous, so that some of the social costs and political strains of unemployment could be exported. These expectations were based on a failure to understand the migratory process, and to see that the phase of mass labour migration was necessarily merging into a second phase of family reunification. By the late sixties in most countries, and earlier in Britain and Switzerland, the consequences of the shift were being felt at economic and political levels. This led to disputes between sectors of capital, the unions and the state about the wisdom of maintaining policies of mass labour migration.

The mobility and flexibility of migrant labour was declining as non-working dependants were brought in. As migrants became settlers, demands for expenditure on housing, schools, medical and social facilities increased. Such costs were rarely met by employers, but where the state did make social capital available, the effect was inevitably to divert investment from industrial to social purposes. This in turn was expected to stimulate inflationary pressures and harm international competitiveness. Apart from a few restricted schemes in France and West Germany,[26] very little in the way of housing or social amenities was provided especially for migrants.

The strategy was rather to leave them to market forces, which pushed them into the most disadvantaged inner-city areas. As living conditions there deteriorated, indigenous workers often came to blame the immigrants, and far-right groups took the opportunity to fan the flames. The result was outbreaks of racial violence, and rapid decay of the social fabric in the areas concerned. Sections of the ruling class ceased to see migrants as a welcome source of additional labour power, but rather as a threat to public order and safety.

Such trends received further impetus from the growing trade union and political militancy of migrant workers. In the first phase of the migratory process, aspirations had been geared to return, and migrants' associations were primarily concerned with the political questions in their countries of origin. But even at this early stage, there were strikes and protests against particularly oppressive forms of exploitation in Western Europe. As migrants stayed on longer, and brought in dependants, their focus shifted to working and living conditions in the new country. Migrants' associations demanded better schooling and social facilities, and fought racism and discrimination. They demanded civil and political rights. Large numbers of them joined trade unions, and demanded that the labour movement should take account of their special interests. Foreign workers in Switzerland went on unofficial strike, breaking through decades of union passivity. In France they played a leading role in the strikes of May 1968. Employers throughout Europe began to express the fear that they were importing new forms of militant class struggle through the recruitment of migrant labour. The wave of unofficial strikes in West Germany in the summer of 1973 involved mainly foreign workers, and was on a level of militancy almost without precedent for that country.[27] The banning of labour migration just a few months later was more than a coincidence.

Social and political tensions were especially marked in Britain, where post-colonial racism and advanced urban decay expressed themselves in outbreaks of racial violence in the late fifties. The severe curtailment of immigration of workers from the Commonwealth by legislation in 1962 was motivated by racism and by fears within the Conservative Party of public disorder. It does not seem to have been motivated by economic considerations, and it is arguable that the resulting constraints on labour supply may have been one cause of Britain's poor economic performance at a time when other West European economies were still growing fast.

In other countries, economic considerations remained predominant in the sixties. The main debate was on the issue of what the 'economic interests' of the country were, with each group trying to show that its interests coincided with those of the nation.

In Switzerland, where migrant workers were around one-third of the labour force, this debate started early in the decade. The unions opposed immigration, fearing pressure on wages. Small-scale capital was in favour of labour entries, but wanted rigid controls on job-changing, to prevent workers moving to higher-productivity industries, which could afford better wages. Large-scale capital (largely transnational in Switzerland) was mainly concerned with having predictable and easily controllable flows of migrant labour. To obtain a more stable labour force, large firms with relatively high productivity were often willing to pay higher wages and to support family reunification and secure residence for status for migrants.

From 1964, the Swiss state began taking measures to restrict entries of labour, and to prevent job-changing. A study commission appointed by the government emphasised the vital role of migrant labour, but at the same time expressed fears that the long-term effect would be to hold back rationalisation of production, and to cause inflation.[28] There was growing emphasis on the political effects of immigration, with the *Schwarzenbach Initiative* mobil-ising almost half the Swiss voters in a referendum against '*Überfremdung*' ('foreign swamping'). The system of migration control introduced in the early seventies was a compromise between the interests of large capital and state considerations of public order and political stability. Entry of new workers was severely limited, with emphasis on seasonal and frontier workers (the latter cross the frontier every day from neighbouring countries). But those workers already in the country with annual permits were granted improved rights on long-term stay and family reunification.

Similar conflicts were in progress in the other countries. In general, unions were worried about the impact of immigration on wages and working-class living conditions, and were often in favour of restrictive entry policies, although they demanded equal wages and conditions for migrants, once they were admitted. Small, marginal businesses were in favour of continued entry of workers, but wanted their rights to be kept as limited as possible, in order to prevent job-changing or demands for better pay. The best possible worker for many marginal businesses was the illegal immigrant without a work permit, completely lacking in rights, and hence an easy target for exploitation. Such 'tourists' or 'clandestines' were (and still are) used extensively in building, catering and domestic service. The system is particularly developed in France (and, incidentally, in the USA). Large capital wanted predictable, controllable, well-disciplined labour. Big firms were therefore in favour of discriminatory regulations, which kept wage demands down and hindered the development of militancy, but at the same time they were willing to accept family reunification and better residence rights, as this helped stabilise the labour force.

The states of Western Europe, on the other hand, were becoming more and more concerned with the economic, social and political strains of the shift from migration to settlement. The costs and tensions were the responsibility of the state, rather than of capital itself, and they were becoming increasingly difficult to manage, in view of trends towards inflation and fiscal crisis. The focus of the debate on labour-market policy was shifting away from the question of how to mobilise new sources of migrant labour. The new issue being raised by labour-market authorities, employers' associations and international economic organisations (like the OECD and ILO) can be summed up in the question: 'Is it not more rational to move the machines to the workers, rather than the workers to the machines?'

In the post-war boom period, the dynamism of Western European capitalism had led to very high rates of capital accumulation, caused in part by the inflow of US investments, especially to West Germany. The result, by the end of the sixties, was an over-accumulation of capital leading to very high demand for other factors of production. Labour was becoming scarce and increasingly dear, while the costs of necessary labour-saving expenditure investment were also soaring.[29] A further consequence of over-accumulation and over-industrialisation in a geographically restricted area was pollution and destruction of the environment. States were forced to impose emission controls, which in turn increased production costs.

Similar strains were emerging in the USA and Japan, the other main centres of capitalist production. In the current phase of restructuring which stems from these problems, the direction and character of capital flows has changed. USA and transnational capital are now being invested more in areas of the Third World – the so-called newly industrialising countries (or NICs) – and in less industrialised parts of Europe, rather than in the traditional industrial centres. Only part of the huge investment resources accumulated by OPEC countries after 1973 have flowed back to the old industrial countries, while large amounts of capital have been used for their own industrialisation, or invested in NICs.

Western European countries that were major labour importers in the boom period have now become major capital exporters. Within multinational enterprises (themselves often a result of previous US investment, or of fusion between US and other national capital), a more intense technical division of labour is permitting the transfer of labour-intensive functions to other countries. The production processes remaining in Western Europe are characterised by increased automation and intensification of work.

This trend in the imperialist integration of the world labour market has been described as 'the new international division of labour' by the marxist economists Fröbel, Heinrichs and Kreye,[30] while the West German academic establishment prefers the term 'trade in place of migration'.[31] Countries like West Germany, Switzerland and Sweden, which made the most efficient use of migrant workers before 1973, are in the forefront of the movement.

Production processes that were becoming unprofitable in Western Europe are being exported to countries where labour is plentiful, wages are low and environmental controls are minimal. The trend applies not only to traditionally labour-intensive industries like clothing, textiles, leather goods, toys, but also to engineering, optics, electrical goods and electronics. In many cases the relocation of production does not apply to the whole process of manufacture of a commodity, but only to the labour-intensive and environmentally unacceptable parts of the process. Capital-intensive stages of production, along with control of finance, design, technology and marketing generally remain in the traditional industrial countries, where the transnational companies and banks are based. So the new international division of labour does little to modify the relations of domination between centre and periphery of the capitalist system, at least in the short run, although it is arguable that some of the NICs may in future reach a stage of industrialisation in which their dependence becomes less marked.

The new flows of capital are not simply from Europe, North America and Japan to the Third World. Often they involve industrialisation within more backward areas of the centre. For instance, West German capital has been heavily invested in Southern and Eastern Europe, as well as in South East Asia and

Latin America. The new international division of labour is based on technological pre-conditions such as the availability of cheap and rapid transport and telecommunications, and the technical feasibility of splitting production processes on an international level. It also requires certain political conditions: stable (generally authoritarian) governments, able to keep labour in line, and willing to grant tax concessions and permit repatriation of profits. An efficient system of international trade and finance is also essential. These pre-conditions were being created in the sixties, as Third World countries set up 'offshore production sites', offering infrastructure and fiscal concessions to international capital. Bodies like the International Monetary Fund and the World Bank did much to encourage this, often stipulating the opening of the economy to foreign investment and trade as a condition for making loans to underdeveloped countries. Political and military intervention by the USA and various West European states have helped to make the world safe for transnational capital.

What effects have these new trends had on the conditions of workers and on labour migrations? In the areas to which labour-intensive production processes have been transferred, workers have been encouraged to move from underemployment in traditional sectors to wage work in industry – a process often marked by accelerated rural–urban migration and the development of unplanned squatter slums. Workers, mostly women, in countries like Taiwan, South Korea, Haiti and Brazil can be utilised by capital at minimal wages. Employers need not take account of the reproduction costs of labour, as reserves are large, and the governments of the countries concerned prevent trade union organisation of the workforce. Social costs – upbringing, welfare in sickness and old age – can be imposed on the traditional sectors of the economy. Long hours and poor working conditions can use a worker's lifetime labour power in just a few years, after which she or he is dismissed to a future of illness and destitution. A well-known example of this exploitation is the women who work at the microscopes of electronic and optical assembly plants: they generally become too short-sighted to continue this work after just a few years. It is appropriate to see this form of exploitation of labour as a process of primitive accumulation, in which value is being transferred from pre-capitalist to capitalist sectors of the economy.

The new international division of labour, together with the

current long wave of stagnation in world production and trade, has also had a major impact on the conditions of workers in the traditional industrial countries. Employment in manufacturing is declining as labour-intensive production processes are relocated. The character of work in those sectors of production not relocated is changing dramatically as a result of new production technologies and new forms of division of labour. Micro-electronics plays a major part in this process, often changing the character of the product itself, as well as the methods of production. The result is not only further unemployment, but also deskilling of sections of the labour force, as traditional jobs requiring long training and experience are eliminated. This permits the speeding-up of work, the worsening of working conditions, and the further reduction of workers' control over their occupational environment. Inability to effectively resist the growth of unemployment and the deterioration of working conditions weakens the labour movement.

Restructuring of the capitalist economy is an attempt to impose the costs of the crisis of over-accumulation of capital on the working class. In this way, the economic crisis is transformed into a social and political crisis. The profitability of West European capitalism cannot be adequately restored through mass unemployment and deskilling, so long as the welfare state is able partially to cushion workers from the material consequences. Restructuring, therefore, inevitably means not only the abandonment of social-democratic, full-employment policies, but also an all-out attack on the welfare state. Reaganomics in the USA, Thatcherism in Britain and, most recently, the CDU–CSU–FDP coalition in West Germany are the political expression of economic restructuring. The result is not only a decline in working-class living standards, but also a crisis in political legitimacy. Economic growth, full employment and steadily improving standards of living are no longer available as instruments to secure mass support for the capitalist system, so how is loyalty to be guaranteed?

West European capital has shifted from the strategy of mobilising an external 'latent surplus population' of unemployed and underemployed workers in underdeveloped areas of Europe and the Third World to that of creating a 'floating surplus population' of unemployed and deskilled workers at home. In those circumstances, the stopping of labour migration was seen by a panel of OECD experts as:

simply an obvious form of protection. The policy is
intended to protect domestic jobs, wages, and the 'integrity'
of social transfer systems, in the face of cutbacks in demand
for labour, public budgets, and medium-term growth
prospects.[32]

The efforts made by most West European governments to induce
migrant workers to leave after 1973 were, as the OECD experts put
it, an attempt 'to redistribute the burden of unemployment from
more advanced to less advanced countries'.[33] Part of the economic
costs and the social and political strains of recession and restructuring were to be imposed on the countries which had provided
additional labour during the boom period.

National governments and international organisations made an
effort to provide an ideological justification for the new policy.
Prior to 1973, they had claimed, generally, that labour migration
was beneficial to the countries of origin, helping to stimulate their
economic development.[34] Now officials and experts suddenly
discovered that this was not the case. The Second European
Regional Conference of the ILO, held in January 1974, stated:

It was widely felt that there should be a new concept of
cooperative development, giving more consideration to
increasing employment in developing countries. For that
reason, improving arrangements for the transfer of capital
as a way of obviating emigration for reasons of economic
need and demographic pressure was felt to be necessary.[35]

Transnational capital was shifting investment and employment to
the periphery, so now the ILO was given the task of setting up a
World Employment Programme to undertake 'case studies of
various possibilities of the transfer of industry and employment
opportunities to the countries from which migrant workers come'.[36]
The result was a series of working papers, recommending just
what was happening anyway: the stopping of labour migration
and the export of capital.

In fact, capital was not automatically going to the countries that
had previously supplied labour. This only happened when economic
and political conditions made investment particularly attractive.
West German firms were eager to invest in Spain under Franco or

Greece under the junta. But countries with democratic governments and strong unions were not regarded as suitable for investment. A well-documented study by a leading West German economic research institute, published as part of the ILO World Employment Programme, put the blame squarely on the governments that were not doing enough to keep down wages and social costs and to make themselves attractive to foreign investors.[37] The governments of countries like Turkey were urged to devalue their currencies, abandon policies of import-substitution, keep down production costs, and concentrate on labour-intensive production for the world market. Such ideas were influential. They foreshadowed the economic and social policies adopted by the Turkish military regime, which seized power in 1980. But the effect has not been to create employment and make emigration unnecessary. On the contrary, the effect has been increased unemployment, a sharp decline in working-class living standards, and the ruin of small businesses that are not able to compete with transnational capital. The 'latent surplus population' has grown, and millions of Turks are looking for a chance to emigrate in search of work.

In the Western European countries themselves, the attempt to export unemployment was only a partial success. Hundreds of thousands of migrant workers did leave, but the majority did not. At a time of world recession, the chances of finding work or setting up a successful business in the country of origin were small. Moreover, the stopping of labour entries meant that it was now impossible to return home on a trial basis, and then come back to work if things proved too difficult. The ban on migration therefore pushed many migrants into the decision to stay on longer, and to bring in dependants. So the policies adopted from 1973 onwards involuntarily accelerated family reunification and settlement. The number of migrant workers declined, but the minority populations continued to increase.

After two or three decades, migrants had become an integral part of the Western European labour force. The segmentation of the labour market – itself a result of the discriminatory guest worker system – made it impossible to dispense with them quickly. They could not be replaced readily by indigenous workers, even when unemployment reached record levels at the beginning of the eighties. Employers have, therefore, usually not been in favour of policies of mass repatriation, fearing that it would lead to acute labour shortages in certain sectors, and hence to economic bottlenecks and upward pressure on wages.

The former migrants are becoming settlers; they are not only a vital part of the labour force, but also a permanent part of the population. Settlement is taking place during a period of crisis, and under conditions of institutional discrimination and racism.

States have developed two main strategies to manage the ethnic minorities in the crisis. First, workers belonging to ethnic minorities are being used as a buffer partially to cushion other workers from the economic effects of the crisis. This is particularly easy in countries where the minority workers have inferior legal status as foreigners. National preference in hiring policies, and refusal or withdrawal of work permits ensure that foreign workers are the first to go. But even in countries like Britain, where most members of the minorities have equal legal rights, informal discrimination often causes blacks to be dismissed first. In both cases, the very structure of the labour process ensures higher unemployment for minority workers. They are generally employed in the occupations and sectors hardest hit by the processes of economic restructuring. As will be shown in chapter 5, members of the minorities are extremely vulnerable to dismissal during recessions, and their rates of unemployment are everywhere very high.

Secondly, Western European states are developing an ideological and legal offensive against the minorities, as part of their strategies of political crisis management. As working-class living standards decline, as housing in the cities deteriorates, as the destruction of the environment becomes ever more evident, as the threat of nuclear destruction looms ever greater, as youth shows less and less interest in increasingly irrelevant political institutions, the capitalist system is confronted with a crisis of political and ideological legitimacy. State efforts to reassert social control are leading to a concentration of power in the executive, an erosion of democratic institutions, a decline in the role of the political parties and a curtailment of civil liberties. One method of engendering popular support for such strategies is the construction and projection of alleged threats to society presented by the ethnic minorities. A recent British study refers to 'a racialisation of state policies in all areas of social life'.[38] Mass media and politicians present an image of blacks or foreigners who take away other workers' jobs, sponge off social security, cause the housing problem, overwhelm schools with hordes of children, and generally swamp our society and culture. Minority youths are allegedly a particular threat to public order, with high rates of criminality and drug addiction. Alien extremists are said to create social unrest through violent demonstrations, as well as through bombings and shoot-outs. The worst threat is posed by Islamic minorities, who are supposedly out to avenge the defeat of the Turks before the gates of Vienna in 1683, by destroying Europe's Christian civilisation.

The dissemination of such destructive stereotypes is designed to increase public support for measures of added discrimination against the minorities. The effectiveness of these campaigns is all the greater in that reactionary politicians like Powell in Britain or Dregger in West Germany actually appear to believe what they say. But the discriminatory measures boomerang on people willing to support racist politics. The strengthening of state powers, the reinforcement of the police and the erosion of civil liberties are not aimed exclusively at the new ethnic minorities. Their target is the working class as a whole. The intention of the campaign for 'law and order' is to secure the ideological and political conditions needed to break all opposition to the attack on working-class living conditions, which is crucial to the restructuring of the capitalist labour process.

3. International patterns of migration and settlement

The aim of this chapter is to bring out some of the specific characteristics of migration and settlement for each of the seven Western European countries that experienced large-scale immigration. Certain general features do begin to emerge. These are summarised in the final section, which returns to the notion of labour migration and the transition to settlement as structural features of post-war Western European society. We will not present data on three smaller countries of immigration: Austria, Norway and Luxemburg.[1] Of the other Western European countries, Denmark has had little immigration, while Finland and Ireland are part of the periphery with high rates of emigration. Some Southern European countries (Italy, Greece, Spain) are both countries of emigration (to Western Europe) and of immigration (from North Africa, for instance). We shall be considering only the former role in these cases.

For each of the seven countries, general information is presented on roughly similar topics: patterns of migration, the origins of migrants, the development and structure of ethnic minority population, legal and political circumstances. More detailed analysis is reserved for later chapters, which deal mainly with West Germany and Britain. The legislation in all the countries is complex and has changed frequently, so that an adequate treatment is not possible here.

This chapter involves the use of statistical material, the pitfalls and problems of which should be borne in mind. Statistical data are rarely readily comparable between countries, and even within a country different data sources may not tally. For example, West German migration data include all movements of people regardless of their intended length of stay. On the other hand, UK migration data include only migrants intending to stay for a year or more. For data on the resident foreign population, a variety of sources exist including the census, and labour and residence permit administrations, with often widely differing figures. The statistics presented should be taken as indicative of broad trends rather than precise numbers. In fact, the most accurate statistics are found in countries such as Switzerland and West Germany, where migrants suffer more severe restrictions accompanied by close statistical monitoring.

Britain

Since 1945 there have been several different groups of migrants to the UK. Irish immigration for work in Britain continued after the war, as it had done for over a hundred years, since the 1830s. Irish citizens have always been free to enter Britain, to move from job to job and to vote without restrictions. The net inflow from the Irish Republic from 1946 to 1959 was estimated at 350,000,[2] but it declined during the sixties.

A second source of migration to Britain was other European countries. About 460,000 foreigners, mainly Europeans, are estimated to have entered Britain between 1946 and 1951, although not all of them settled permanently. They came from different backgrounds and many were refugees or displaced persons. The British government recruited 90,000 'European Voluntary Workers' (EVWs) from refugee camps, and later from Italy. These workers were needed to fill temporary needs created by the post-war boom and the loss of British labour in the war. Only single people were eligible. They were not regarded as permanent settlers and their civil rights were severely restricted. Tied for three years to a specific job chosen by the Ministry of Labour, they were liable to deportation for misconduct or ill health, and single men and women recruited were rarely allowed to bring other family members with them.[3] Another group of Europeans, about 100,000 in all, came on work permits during this period, under the Aliens Restriction Act 1914, securing work permits from the Ministry of Labour which were renewable every year. Work permits were granted initially if there were no British nationals available to do the job, but once a migrant had stayed in Britain for four years, restrictions on employment were dropped and they were free to settle. Most of these migrants were from Italy and, during the 1950s, the bulk of European migrants continued to come from

Italy. In the 1960s most European work-permit holders came from Spain and Portugal.

The third and best known source of immigration was the New Commonwealth.[4] Starting after the war and building up during the 1950s, migrants came from the West Indies, India and Pakistan; countries newly independent or fighting for independence from Britain's now-crumbling colonial empire. Some came as a result of direct recruitment by London Transport or the British Hotels and Restaurants Association, but the majority came in response to the labour demands of British industry. By the mid fifties about 30,000 black workers were entering Britain every year without restriction. They had no need to seek permission to enter because they were British or Commonwealth citizens. This flow continued until it was interrupted by declining economic demand[5] and the introduction of immigration control in the early 1960s.

The final waves of primary immigration started in the 1970s when workers from countries such as the Philippines, Morocco and Latin American countries came to Britain on work permits to fill spaces in the service sector – the National Health Service, hotels and catering, domestic work. EEC workers also came after Britain joined the Common Market.

While the popular image of work-permit holders from countries like Spain or Portugal, and of New Commonwealth migrants is of simple, uneducated peasants, the reality is different. These migrants do not form a homogeneous mass; they come from different historical and political backgrounds, and from different classes within their own societies. For example, government language tests, financial guarantees and employment criteria effectively screened would-be Pakistani migrants and so ensured that only those with wealth and skills were allowed to migrate. In addition, recent research shows that some of the Indians who came to work in the foundries in the West Midlands were from the old colonial administrative class in the Punjab.[6] Many who came from the ex-colonies had experience of the struggle for independence both within the labour movement and in the wider political arena.

People migrated to Britain to work, encouraged both by the demand for labour in Britain and by unfavourable conditions at home. At a government level there was pressure on Britain to take migrants from newly independent countries where political unrest was causing concern.[7] While some may have come to earn money to save, and to return home to set up a business or a farm, others came in order to send money home to keep a family, and often members of the family came and left, rotating the responsibility of being the breadwinner abroad.[8] Yet others came to escape family pressures, poverty, or political oppression.

In 1951 there were 1.6 million people living in Great Britain who were born outside the UK. By 1981 this figure had risen to 3.4 million. Table 3.1 shows their distribution by birthplace over time.[9] For one section of the immigrant population – people of New Commonwealth and Pakistani origin – estimates of their UK-born descendants are available: less than 0.1 million in 1961, 0.1 million in 1966 and 0.5 million in 1971. In 1981, almost half of the 2.1 million people of New Commonwealth and Pakistani ethnic origin were born in the UK.[10]

Table 3.1. Residents in Great Britain born outside UK, 1951–81 (thousands)

Birthplace	1951	1961	1966	1971	1981
New Commonwealth[1]	218	541	853	1,151	1,513
Old Commonwealth[2]	99	110	125	143	153
Irish Republic[3]	532	709	739	709	607
EEC[4]	724	845	886	980	374
Other					712
Total	1,573	2,205	2,603	2,983	3,360
% of total population	3.2	4.3	5.0	5.5	6.2

Sources: OPCS, Demographic Review 1977, DR no. 1, London : HMSO 1978; 1981 Census.

Notes: 1. Including Pakistan; 2. Australia, Canada and New Zealand; 3. Including Ireland, part not stated; 4. Excluding Irish Republic.

While the early common belief was that black migrants were only in Britain on a temporary basis, there was growing concern about the presence of this population. The post-war government had already privately expressed their apprehension about allowing black labour freely into the UK and by the early 1960s this was being openly voiced. A combination of factors including a declining demand for labour, growing discontent and some racial violence

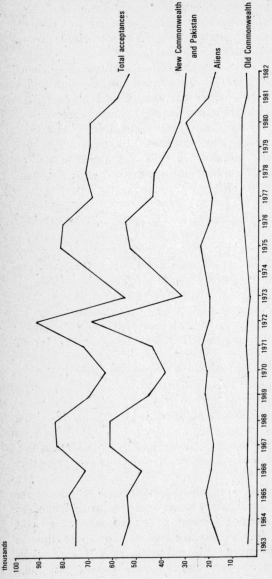

Figure 3.1. Acceptances for settlement in the United Kingdom, 1963–82

Source: Home Office, *Control of Immigration Statistics*, HMSO, Annual.

Notes: Figures for the Old Commonwealth underestimate the actual level of immigration because many Old Commonwealth citizens are patrial and hence free from immigration control. Total acceptances are underestimates of immigration for this reason and because the Irish are also excluded from immigration control.

in inner-city areas, and the visibility of this expanding black population led to the introduction of immigration controls.

The Commonwealth Immigrants Act 1962 required that all Commonwealth citizens must obtain an employment voucher before coming to Britain. No restrictions were imposed on the entry of dependants at this stage. In 1968, a second Act was passed which imposed restrictions on British passport holders from the Commonwealth; for the first time some UK passport holders could not freely travel to Britain. The 1968 Act was a response to the threatened expulsion of Kenyan Asians who still held UK passports. The 1971 Immigration Act and its accompanying administrative rules further restricted Commonwealth immigration by placing limitations on the entry of dependants. Figure 3.1 shows the general effect of these Acts in reducing immigration from the New Commonwealth while the immigration of aliens increased, at least until very recently.

Whatever the original intentions of the individual migrants about staying or returning, the imposition of severe restrictions on entry to the UK undoubtedly had the effect of preventing them leaving unless they were totally sure they never wanted to return, or could afford to return for substantial periods every two years thereby retaining their right of residence. Under the 1971 Act, Commonwealth citizens and British citizens from the Commonwealth were effectively excluded from Britain unless they obtained a quota voucher or a work permit on the same footing as all other 'aliens'. In fact, very few people now enter the UK on work permits or with special vouchers, and in 1982 about 90 per cent of those accepted for settlement were dependants.

While originally Commonwealth citizens and aliens who came to Britain on work permits were governed by different laws, over time successive immigration Acts brought their situations closer together. Only Commonwealth citizens settled in Britain prior to 1973 have been exempt from increasing restrictions. Those who came on work permits have to renew them annually and have to obtain permission from the Department of Employment if they wish to change their job. However, after four years in approved employment and continuous residence all restrictions may be removed. Once a person is settled in the UK they have very similar rights to those who came in on Commonwealth passports. They do not have to register with the police, they may take any job, they are free to move anywhere in the UK, they are entitled to social security benefits and after five years' residence they may apply for citizenship. Commonwealth citizens could, until the 1981 Nationality Act came into force in 1983, obtain British citizenship automatically through registration while aliens had to apply to become naturalised. Within five years of the new Nationality Act, registration will have ceased and citizenship will only be obtainable through naturalisation, a process which is discretionary, expensive and subject to tests of language and good conduct.

Until 1983, all children born in the UK, regardless of their parents' status and nationality, automatically had the right to British citizenship. The Nationality Act has removed this right, which is now dependent on the parents being legally settled in Britain at the time of the child's birth.

One major difference between aliens who are settled legally and Commonwealth citizens is that aliens may not vote unless they take British citizenship. Commonwealth citizens have the right to vote, though this right may be lost after the Nationality Act has been in force for five years.

While people settled in the UK do have these rights, and they are substantial when compared to other European countries, settlers are subject to a great deal of discrimination in respect to migration and settlement. Immigration legislation specifically discriminates against black people through the notion of 'patriality'.[11] Unlike patrials, non-patrials may be subject to deportation for a criminal offence at the discretion of the courts, even after years of lawful residence. Increasing numbers of people are subject to 'removal' from Britain because they are being defined as illegal entrants, based on any irregularity in their papers or interviews conducted on arrival. Deportations and removals have created a mounting sense of insecurity among the black population. The restrictions on bringing in dependants have tightened severely until the family is defined only as a spouse and children under 18. The EEC definition of a family includes children up to the age of 21, dependent parents and grandparents and other relatives living under the same roof. Only rarely now are older children or aged parents allowed in and the category of 'distressed relatives' has been abolished. Admission of dependants is subject in some instances to adequate accommodation requirements and the ability to support them 'without recourse to public funds'. In effect a category of people has been created who are excluded from the rights and benefits of the welfare state.

Unlike British citizens, people settled in the UK do not have absolute freedom of movement. Commonwealth and other non-British citizens are excluded from the freedom of movement allowed within the EEC, and if they go abroad they lose their right to permanent residence unless they return within two years.

As the access to welfare benefits and citizenship by birth become increasingly dependent on immigration status, all those with foreign names or faces are becoming more and more subject to police and immigration surveillance. Officials who administer social security benefits and health care are being asked by the Home Office to report anyone they suspect might be in breach of immigration rules.

Belgium

Labour migration to Belgium started immediately after the second world war. From 1945 to 1963 it took the form of organised recruitment in what was called the *contingentensysteem*. Workers were recruited through bilateral agreements with Southern European countries, mainly Italy. Most of the migrants were needed for the coal mines and the iron and steel industry. In 1946 alone, 60,000 Italians were recruited. Although this was temporary labour migration of the guest worker type, Belgian regulations were fairly liberal about entry of family members, and many of the workers stayed on permanently.

After 1963, the *contingentensysteem* was abolished, but foreign work-seekers continued to come of their own accord. They came in as tourists without work permits, but were regularised (granted work permits and residence permits) once they had employment. In a period of rapid economic growth, such 'spontaneous' labour migration responded rapidly and flexibly to labour needs. Migrants found work in a much wider range of industries and enterprises than before 1963. In this period, the Italians were joined by large numbers of Spaniards, and then by Moroccans and Turks.[12]

In August 1974, the government decided to stop further immigration of workers (except from EEC countries). However, the ban took some time to become fully effective and clandestine immigration continued on a fairly high level until about 1976.

Regulations were made to stop this: some migrant workers without documentation were deported and their employers prosecuted. Some clandestine workers went on hunger strike in 1974 to protest against their treatment, but they were deported nonetheless.[13] At the time of writing, policies towards entry of migrant workers remain extremely restrictive. From 1978 to 1981 fewer than 4,000 initial immigrant work permits per year were issued to non-EEC migrants.[14]

On the other hand, policies towards admission of migrant workers' dependants remained liberal. Until 1977, the Belgian Government even paid up to 50 per cent of travel costs for spouses and children coming to Belgium. At present, migrant workers, who can prove that they have a job, can bring in their wife or husband. Children up to the age of 21 are allowed in if both parents are in Belgium. People coming in as dependants can easily obtain work permits.

So although labour migration was curtailed in 1974, family migration continued. The foreign population grew from 368,000 in 1947 (4.3 per cent of total population) to 453,000 in 1961 (4.9 per cent). Increase was more rapid in the sixties and early seventies, with a foreign population of 716,000 in 1970 (7.2 per cent of total population) and 851,000 in 1977 (8.7 per cent).[15] Since then the foreign population has become stabilised at around 900,000, making up just over 9 per cent of Belgium's total population.[16] Most growth in the foreign population in recent years has been through natural increase (the surplus of births over deaths) of around 14,000 per year. Very little recent data on the structure of the foreign population is available. It is known, however, that few migrants have settled in the more agricultural, Flemish-speaking areas, while more are to be found in the French-speaking industrial areas. The highest concentration is in Brussels, where around a quarter of the residents are foreigners.

Table 3.2 gives figures on the origins of migrants, from the 1970 census and the 1977 micro-census. No more recent data appears to exist. There appears to have been no appreciable immigration from Belgium's former colonies. The table does show a slight increase in the share of non-European residents between 1970 and 1977. Since then, migration flow figures show that more Italians and Spaniards have left Belgium than have entered, while the number of new entries from Turkey and Morocco has exceeded

Table 3.2. Foreign residents in Belgium, 1970 and 1977

Country of nationality	1970		1977	
	000s	% of foreign population	000s	% of foreign population
Italy	250	35.7	287	33.8
Spain	68	9.7	65	7.6
Morocco	39	5.6	81	9.5
Turkey	21	3.0	60	7.0
France	86	12.3	107	12.6
Netherlands	61	8.7	71	8.3
Britain	16	2.3	20	2.3
Germany	23	3.3	25	3.0
Greece	22	3.1	24	2.8
Poland	19	2.7	13	1.5
Others	92	13.1	98	11.5
Total	**701**	**100**	**851**	**100**

Source: Author's calculations from Wilfried Dumon, *Het Profiel van de Vreemdelingen in Belgie*, Leuven: Davidsfonds 1982, tables 5 and 6.

departures. This indicates that in Belgium, as elsewhere, there is a trend towards an increasing share of Third World migrants in the minority population.[17] The migratory process has now entered the third phase – settlement and formation of new ethnic minorities (see above pp. 14–15).

The current situation of foreigners in Belgium is marked by contradictory trends. On the one hand, favourable regulations concerning family reunification and residence status have given most immigrants a reasonably secure basis for settlement. A law against racism, discrimination and xenophobia was passed in 1981 (although the provisions of this law appear to be too weak to be effective). Another law passed in 1980 gave foreigners the right to form political associations and to demonstrate, so long as there is no disturbance of public order. Migrants also appear to have a fair amount of protection against deportation, with a right of appeal.

On the other hand, the fact remains that 9 per cent of the

population are disenfranchised and therefore second-class citizens. The right to vote does not exist for foreigners, except for municipal advisory councils, which have no real powers. In recent years, the government has promised to introduce the right to vote for local councils, but this has not yet been done. As unemployment has grown, there has been increasing public debate on the question of foreign workers, and administrative procedures concerning the issue of work permits for migrants' dependants have been made more restrictive. There is talk of making entry for workers' spouses and children more difficult, for instance only admitting children up to 18 and wives or husbands when the marriage has existed for several years. Some local authorities (especially in the Brussels area) are refusing to register foreigners as residents, which denies them rights to housing and social services.[18]

Belgium is no exception to the general trend towards increasing institutional discrimination and racism. The minorities will continue to remain identifiable by nationality, for naturalisation policy is highly restrictive, with high fees, long waiting periods and various other requirements. Only about 2,000 foreigners have been granted Belgian nationality annually in recent years.[19]

France

In 1945 the French government set up the Office National d'Immigration (ONI) to organise recruitment of foreign workers. Labour migration was seen as a solution to post-war labour shortages, and was expected to be mainly of temporary and rotating (including seasonal workers for agriculture). However, in view of low birth rates in France, a certain amount of family settlement was desired. Recruitment agreements were made with Southern European countries. French employers had to make a request to ONI and pay a fee. ONI organised recruitment and travel. There was continuous migration of workers to France from 1945 to 1974, with peaks in the late forties, 1956–8, 1964–5 and 1969–70. According to ONI statistics, about 2 million European migrant workers entered France from 1946 to 1970 and they were joined by 690,000 dependants.[20]

The impression of a highly organised system of recruitment is misleading. Prior to 1974 policies were pragmatic and unplanned, with various ministeries often pursuing contradictory aims.[21]

ONI's legal monopoly of recruitment of European workers became, more and more, a fiction. The proportion of migrants coming as 'clandestines' (on tourist visas or without passports) increased from 26 per cent in 1948 to 82 per cent in 1968.[22]

In the early years most workers were recruited in Italy. As competition for labour between Western European industrial countries increased, France had to look further afield, and ONI proved incapable of coping with recruitment. Patterns of spontaneous migration began to develop, from Spain in the early sixties, then from Portugal, later from Yugoslavia and Turkey.

Many Spaniards and Portuguese came as much to escape political repression as for economic reasons, and had no choice but to come illegally. They endured considerable hardships coming across the Pyrenees, and were often exploited by smugglers on the way. The repressive Salazar/Caetano regime of Portugal prohibited emigration and would not even grant passports to most of its citizens. Many young Portuguese left, not only to escape the appalling poverty, but also to avoid military service in the colonial wars. Here, as in many other countries, the economic and political causes of migration were closely linked.

Clandestine workers met employers' needs well. They were a flexible source of labour, which went where required, and their weak legal status compelled them to accept poor wages and conditions. Once they had jobs, clandestine workers were often 'regularised' by the authorities, which granted them work and residence permits. Unions and welfare organisations called for more control, to prevent exploitation of migrants by 'slave dealers' (labour-only sub-contractors), unscrupulous employers and landlords.

In any case, ONI was only responsible for migrants from European countries. Citizens of France's colonies and former colonies were able to enter freely until the late sixties. The largest group were the Algerians, and they played an active part in France in the struggle for Algerian independence. By 1970 there were over 600,000 Algerians in France, as well as 140,000 Moroccans and 90,000 Tunisians.[23] Increasing numbers of black workers were also coming in from Senegal, Mali and Mauritania (former French colonies in West Africa). Finally, there was considerable migration of black workers from the Overseas Departments of Guadaloupe and Martinique in the Caribbean and Réunion in the Atlantic.

These territories are considered part of France, so migration goes unrecorded. There were thought to be between 250,000 and 300,000 people from the Overseas Departments in metropolitan France in 1972, which meant that nearly a quarter of the population of these areas had migrated.[24]

By 1970 there were over 3 million migrants in France – over 6 per cent of the total population. About a million of them were non-Europeans. Migrant workers were highly concentrated in un-skilled and semi-skilled work in building, manufacturing and services. French agriculture employed over 100,000 seasonal labourers, mainly Spaniards. Migrants were beginning to bring in their families and there was a trend towards settlement, con-centrated in the industrial conurbations, particularly in the Paris region. Very little was being done to provide housing and other amenities and social strains were becoming evident. In the suburbs of Paris, Lyon and Marseilles, the housing shortage was so severe that migrants were forced to put up *Bidonvilles* (shanty towns) – all too visible signs of the Third World in the metropolis. Racially motivated attacks by French people on migrants (especially North Africans) were on the increase.

At this stage, attempts were made to tighten up immigration policies. The aim was to increase control on entries, and to introduce selectivity: demographic growth was to be provided by Europeans, while Africans were only to provide labour on a temporary basis.[25] Measures were taken to reduce entries from Africa, and restore ONI's monopoly of recruitment from non-EEC European countries.

The effects of these measures was limited. Immigration remained very high in the early seventies, and most of it was still spontaneous and uncontrolled. In 1973 fascist groups stepped up their campaign of racial violence against North Africans. No less than 32 Algerians were murdered in that year, mainly in Marseilles, Toulon and Nice. On 19 September 1973 President Boumedienne ordered the stopping of emigration to France – the only case we know in which migration has been stopped because of racism in the receiving country.[26] By now it was officially estimated that 90 per cent of immigration was uncontrolled, and that only 20 per cent of immigrant children in France were receiving 'normal' schooling.[27] The consequence was yet another 'new' immigration policy. In May 1974 Paul Dijoud was appointed Secretary of State for

Immigrant Workers. He announced tighter control on entries, deportation of illegals, and integration of those migrants legally in France through a long-term programme of naturalisation and assimilation.[28]

In July 1974, influenced no doubt by the stopping of labour migration to West Germany in November 1973, the French government banned the entry not only of workers but of family members as well (apart from those from EEC countries). The prohibition of immigrant workers seems to have been fairly effective – probably because opportunities were in any case poor during the recession. But it proved impossible to stop workers bringing in their dependants as tourists. The ban on family reunification contravened a number of international and bilateral agreements so in July 1975, a new decree permitted family immigration once again. Two years later Stoleru, the new Secretary of State for Immigrant Workers, announced that he planned to stop family entries for the next three years because of high unemployment and the alleged criminality of foreign youth. His decree of November 1977 did not in fact ban entries of dependants, but it denied them permission to take up employment. After a campaign by immigrant organisations, this measure was declared illegal by the Conseil d'Etat (the constitutional court) in December 1978.[29]

The Giscard government made efforts to send home unemployed migrant workers and to reduce the minority population. Deportations of workers without documents were countered by a wave of hunger strikes during the mid seventies. In 1977 a scheme was introduced providing financial inducements to leave the country. Foreigners were offered about 10,000 francs and a ticket home, if they renounced all claims on the French social security system. By publicly labelling migrants as a social problem, such measures fuelled racism, and attacks on North Africans continued to increase. A law prohibiting incitement to racial discrimination and violence had been passed in 1972, but it proved ineffective.

Measures introduced by Stoleru in the late seventies and codified through the Loi Bonnet (Bonnet Law) of 1980 combined work and residence permits, linked immigration with employment and extended the reasons for deportation. The aim was to export unemployment by getting rid of young migrants if they were unemployed, or if they committed an offence. The most minor delinquency was sufficient pretext for deportation. In one notorious case a 13-year-old boy who stole a pair of trousers was deported for the offence when he reached the age of 18.[30] By 1980 several hundred people were being deported every month. Many were young people who had been born and grown up in France. The main targets were North Africans and blacks. Most Europeans had protection through EEC citizenship (Italy) or impending EEC Association (Spain and Portugal).

All these measures may have made migrants feel insecure, yet they did not lead to a mass exodus, as the government hoped. Although the number of foreigners in the labour force fell from its 1973 peak of 1.8 million to a level of about 1.4 million in 1981,[31] the total number of foreign residents rose from 3.2 million in 1969 to 4.2 million in 1975, and then stabilised at about that level. Moreover, around a million people have obtained French citizenship under the fairly liberal naturalisation laws, so that the population of migrant origin totals over 5 million. Departures of workers was compensated by entries of dependants and by births of foreign children in France. The demographic structure of the foreign population was becoming more like that of the French.

At the same time, the composition of the foreign population by nationality has changed, as table 3.3 shows. In 1969, the Italians and Spaniards were the largest national groups. Together with the Portuguese and Yugoslavs, they made up 55 per cent of the foreign population. The biggest Third World group were the Algerians, but together with other Africans and Turks, they made up only 28 per cent of the foreign population. Between 1969 and 1981 the number of Italians and Spaniards fell considerably. Although the number of Portuguese and Yugoslavs increased, these four Southern European nationalities now made up only 43 per cent of the foreign population, while the Third World share had risen to over 40 per cent.

In May 1981 a new Socialist government was voted in, on a programme that promised a new deal for migrants. The Socialist Party declared that it was going to radically alter the conditions of life for the minorities, removing discriminatory measures and the power of the authorities to make arbitary decisions. Migrant and anti-racist organisations hoped for policies to give the minorities social and political equality in French society. In the meantime, it has become clear that the Mitterrand government is not going to fulfil all these expectations.

Table 3.3. Foreign residents in France, 1969 and 1981

Country of Nationality	31 December 1969		31 December 1981	
	000s	% of foreign population	000s	% of foreign population
Italy	612	19.3	452	10.7
Spain	617	19.4	413	9.8
Portugal	480	15.1	859	20.3
Yugoslavia	52	1.6	68	1.6
Turkey	9	0.2	118	2.8
Algeria	608	19.1	817	19.3
Morocco	143	4.5	444	10.5
Tunisia	89	2.8	193	4.6
Other Africa	55	1.7	115	2.7
Other EEC	512	16.1	176	4.2
Other			568	13.4
Total	**3,177**	**100**	**4,224**	**100**

Sources: 1969 figures from Ministère de l'Intérieur; 1981 figures from *OECD SOPEMI 1982.*

Note: Figures are based on police registers, and are thought to be overestimates, as some people may have left the country without deregistering. Migrants from Overseas Departments are not included.

Soon after coming to power, the government stopped deporting French-born foreign youths and declared an amnesty for illegal immigrants. New immigration laws controlling entry, stay and illegal immigration were passed in October 1981. Under these laws, foreigners born in France, aged under 18, married to a French person, or with a child of French nationality cannot be deported (except in exceptional circumstances concerning public order or the security of the state). The number of deportations has declined dramatically. Nonetheless the threat of double punishment (imprisonment and expulsion) does still exist for many migrants. There are fears that 'public order' provisions could still be used against migrant youth, especially in view of statements by officials and police accusing black youth of high criminality.[32]

The amnesty for illegal immigrants was directed at the 300,000 people estimated to be in France without work and residence permits. They were offered regularisation if they came forward and could show that they had a one-year work contract. In fact only about 140,000 came forward. Many lost their jobs, as employers did not want to offer regular conditions of employment. Others were refused permits. In some areas local authorities appear to have followed policies of discrimination, with rates of rejection as high as 45 per cent in Seine-Saint-Denis and the Rhône area.[33] Migrants who were refused regularisation or did not apply are liable to deportation, and live in complete insecurity, in constant fear of police checks and open to exploitation by employers and landlords.

The new immigration laws are designed to stop further entry of workers, although they do permit family reunification. Entry requirements are so stringent that the frontier police have in effect arbitrary powers to refuse entries. Even visits by family members require certificates from the town hall where the migrant lives.[34] It is reported that many foreigners are afraid to go abroad on holiday, for fear of not being readmitted.

One positive step was the repeal of statute of 1901, which restricted the right of foreigners to form associations. Migrants can now form organisations on the same basis as French people.[35] On the other hand, the government has not kept its promise to introduce voting rights for migrants in local elections. They remain disenfranchised, except for local migrants advisory councils, which have no real powers.

Despite the appointment of a new Minister of National Solidarity, migrants in France still experience discrimination and insecurity. Rising unemployment, fear of street crime and a number of terrorist attacks have led to a public outcry for 'law and order'. The police are often unwilling to implement anti-discrimination measures and press for a tough line against black and North African youth. France maintains its liberal naturalisation policy: virtually all children born to foreign parents in France can obtain French citizenship if they wish, as can spouses of French citizens. Other migrants can obtain naturalisation after five years. Over 50,000 foreigners annually have obtained French citizenship in recent years.[36] Yet it is becoming clear that even having French citizenship does not provide adequate protection against racism and discrimination.

The Netherlands

Like Britain and France, the Netherlands has had both immigration from colonies or former colonies and labour migration from the European periphery. The first and largest group of immigrants of the former type were the 'repatriates' from the former Dutch East Indies (now Indonesia), who came to the Netherlands between 1945 and the early sixties. The name 'repatriates' is misleading, for a large proportion had been born overseas. The group was estimated at between 250,000 and 300,000 people, many of whom were of mixed Dutch and Indonesian parentage. The repatriates were Dutch citizens who had the right to settle in the Netherlands. Official policy was the rapid assimilation of this group. Today they are considered to be on the whole well integrated into Dutch society. They appear not to experience prejudice and discrimination, and there is little information on their situation.[37]

A further group entering from South East Asia were Moluccan ex-soldiers of the Royal Netherlands East Indies Army and their families. When they arrived in 1951, their stay in the Netherlands was expected to be temporary, for they wanted to return to an independent Republic of the South Moluccas. They were therefore housed in camps, and no effort was made to integrate them into Dutch society. As time went on, it became clear that returning to the Moluccas was out of the question. Yet little was done to cope with the special problems of this group, who themselves rejected any form of integration. Matters came to a head with militant actions by young Moluccans in the mid seventies: occupations of government offices and hijacking of trains. In 1978 there were estimated to be around 32,000 Moluccans in the Netherlands, of whom about 60 per cent were classed as stateless, 30 per cent as Dutch citizens and 10 per cent as Indonesian citizens.[38]

Migration from the Dutch Caribbean territory of Surinam was low until the mid sixties, consisting mainly of students from the colonial elite. After 1965 an increasing number of Surinamese (mainly Creole black people) came to the Netherlands as workers. Net migration increased from 2,300 in 1966 to 5,500 in 1970. Then fears of impending immigration control led to a further jump in entries. A peak was reached in the two years leading up to independence; net immigration was 15,000 in 1974 and 36,000 in 1975. After independence, Surinamese living in the Netherlands maintained Dutch citizenship, while those living in Surinam lost it. Up to 1980 migration continued under a bilateral agreement, much of it taking the form of family reunification. Some new work-seekers entered too, especially in the period immediately preceding the expiry of the agreement in 1980. Since then, Surinamese have required visas to enter the Netherlands. Migration has dropped considerably, and seems to consist almost entirely of family reunification.[39] The total population of Surinamese origin in the Netherlands was estimated at about 160,000 in 1978.[40]

There has also been labour migration from the Netherlands Antilles to the Netherlands. This appears to have started in the mid sixties as a result of recruitment by Dutch employers. Net immigration from this area has been around 2,500 a year, and seems still to be in the pattern of temporary labour migration.

Recruitment of workers from Southern Europe did not get under way until the sixties. Indeed, in the immediate post-war years, the Netherlands had been officially regarded as over-populated and overseas emigration of Dutch citizens had been encouraged. Apart from movements connected with the end of the colonial era, the Netherlands was considered to be 'not a country of immigration'. Labour for post-war reconstruction and expansion was provided by internal migration, transfers from agriculture and drawing married women into the labour force. A policy of wage controls was used to prevent inflation and maintain profit rates. By the early sixties, however, all available internal labour reserves had been absorbed, and the unions were able to use this to break the 'guided wages policy'. The result was rapidly rising wages and a reduction in working hours. In order to reduce labour market pressure, keep down wages and maintain profits, industry started recruiting in the Mediterranean countries. The government made a series of bilateral recruitment agreements with Italy (1960), Spain (1961), Portugal (1963), Turkey (1964), Greece (1966), Morocco (1969), Yugoslavia (1970) and Tunisia (1970). The number of workers from the recruitment countries (excluding Italy) rose from a few hundred in 1960 to 46,000 in 1966.

The Mediterranean workers were regarded as temporary labour, who could be used as a buffer against economic fluctuations. The recession of 1967 demonstrated this function: the number of foreign workers was cut by about 7,000, so that a share of unemployment was exported to the migrants' countries of origin. However 39,000 migrant workers remained even though unemployment of Dutch workers rose sharply. Employed in jobs rejected by the Dutch, the migrants had become economically indispensable. When the recession ended, recruitment of foreign workers increased rapidly, so that there were about 90,000 by 1974. Nearly all workers from the recruitment countries came through the official system during this period. Recruitment of workers ceased from 1974, but this time the number of foreign workers did not decline, even though unemployment reached much higher levels than in 1967. From the beginning of the seventies, there had been a trend towards family immigration. Now this became more pronounced; by 1977 there were 105,000 workers from the Mediterranean countries (excluding Italy) in the Netherlands, and they were accompanied by 80,000 dependants.[41] By 1982 the number of citizens from the Mediterranean recruitment countries (excluding Italy) had reached 316,000.[42]

In 1947 the Netherlands had 104,000 foreign residents – 1.1 per cent of the total population. By 1982 the figure was 544,000 or 3.8 per cent of the total population. However this does not include the 'repatriates' from the Dutch East Indies, the Moluccans, the Surinamese and the Antillians. The size of these groups can only be roughly estimated. Table 3.4 shows that national composition of the foreign resident population in 1971 and 1982. In 1971, 29 per cent of foreign residents of the Netherlands came from the neighbouring countries of the UK, Belgium and West Germany. These people were for the most part qualified personnel, moving temporarily from one industrialised country to another. Twenty-one per cent of foreign residents in 1971 came from the Southern European countries, Italy, Yugoslavia and Spain. Twenty per cent came from the Third World countries, Turkey and Morocco. By 1982, the share from the neighbouring industrial countries had dropped to 20 per cent (although the number from the UK grew considerably). The share from the three main Southern European countries dropped to 11 per cent, while the share from the two main Third World countries jumped to 44 per cent. This confirms the trend already observed in Britain, France and Belgium.

Opinion polls have consistently indicated that the attitudes of the Dutch towards Mediterranean workers are less favourable

Table 3.4.   Foreign residents in the Netherlands, 1971 and 1982

Country of nationality	28 February 1971		1 January 1982	
	000s	% of foreign population	000s	% of foreign population
Britain	12	4.9	40	7.4
Belgium	24	9.2	24	4.4
West Germany	37	14.4	43	7.9
Italy	18	6.9	21	3.9
Yugoslavia	8	3.1	14	2.6
Spain	28	11.0	23	4.2
Turkey	30	11.9	148	27.2
Morocco	22	8.5	93	17.1
Other EEC	} 76	} 29.8	35	6.4
Other			103	18.9
Total	255	100	544	100

Source: Rinus Penninx, *Migration, Minorities and Policy in the Netherlands (Report for OECD SOPEMI 1982)*, Rijswijk: Ministry of Cultural Affairs, Recreation and Social Welfare 1982, tables 11 and 12.

than towards blacks from former colonies.[43] There were anti-Italian riots as early as 1959. Racist attacks on Moroccans were reported in 1969.[44] Street riots directed against Turks occurred in Rotterdam in 1972 and Schiedam in 1976. One explanation is that immigrants from former colonies have a wider range of occupations, while foreign workers compete with Dutch workers for increasingly scarce manual jobs. Another is the lack of overall planning of immigration policy, and the different treatment of the different groups. Colonial migrants were generally treated as permanent residents with full rights, while Southern European, Turkish and Moroccan workers were seen and treated as temporary migrant labour long after they had begun to bring in their families and settle. Accordingly, little provision was made for housing and schooling, and pressure on inadequate inner-city amenities built up.

In the mid seventies the government introduced restrictive policies in the hope of countering unemployment. Entry of workers was curtailed, border controls were tightened and illegal immigrants deported. Migrants' rights to unemployment benefit were cut. In 1974 the minister of social affairs proposed new legislation to control foreign employment. Employers were to be issued with employment permits for each foreign worker, and numbers were to be restricted according to labour market conditions. The effect would have been increased dependence of the migrant on the employer, and lack of freedom to change jobs. A departure premium of 5,000 guilders was also proposed, in order to encourage the rotation of the foreign labour force. This proposal – widely known as the 'piss-off premium' – aroused considerable opposition, and was dropped. The other proposals were amended to exclude workers legally resident for over three years, and had little practical effect.

In the last few years, Dutch policy has changed dramatically. In 1979 the Netherlands Scientific Council for Government Policy published its report,[45] showing that most Mediterranean workers were not likely to return home. They had become permanent settlers and should be recognised as ethnic minorities, within the framework of a general minorities policy. The government accepted this advice and gave an outline of its new policy in April 1981.[46] The minorities policy covers several groups (not all them immigrants) – Mediterranean workers and their families, people of Surinamese and Antillean origins, Moluccans, refugees, gypsies, and caravan dwellers. Chinese (of whom there are estimated to be 30,000) may be brought in later. The memorandum states:

> Minorities policy is aimed at creating a society in which the members of minority groups resident in the Netherlands, both individually and as groups, have an equal place and full opportunities for development.[47]

The memorandum admits that the government had previously misjudged the size and nature of migration:

> What was originally viewed as a temporary sojourn of a limited group of migrants proved to be a lengthy, if not permanent residence of large groups.

Measures to be taken to encourage the full participation of minorities include improvements in their legal status, housing, social services, and their situation on the labour market. Legislation against racism and discrimination is to be tightened up, and foreigners' political rights are to be improved. The new constitution of the Netherlands grants foreign residents voting rights in local elections.

The recognition of migrant workers and their families as permanent minorities is certainly a big step forward. Yet a question mark hangs over the implementation of the new policies. Virtually no funds are being made available to carry them out.[48] Improvement for settled immigrants is linked to a highly restrictive policy towards new entrants. This includes restrictions on the hitherto liberal policy concerning entry of migrants' dependants. Such policies are likely to increase migrants' insecurity, even if they are not intended to. Rising unemployment and increasing inner-city problems are leading to increased racism. Anti-immigrant parties have taken part in recent municipal and parliamentary elections. In 1982 one of these, the Centrum Party, won a seat in parliament on openly racist slogans.[49] The existence of a growing group opposed to improving the position of migrants may make the government hesitate.

Sweden

Sweden has experienced almost continuous immigration since 1945. Immigration provided around 45 per cent of total population increase between 1944 and 1978, and it is estimated that about a million of Sweden's 8 million inhabitants are either immigrants or children of immigrants.[50] The biggest single group are the Finns, who have enjoyed the right of free entry to Sweden since the setting up of the Nordic Labour Market (which also includes Denmark, Norway and Iceland) in 1954. Finnish migration to Sweden appears to be similar in many respects to Irish migration to Britain. In both cases an expanding industrial country has drawn in labour reserves from a predominantly agricultural neighbour, which was formerly a colony. Labour from the peripheral country has effectively become an integral part of the labour market of the industrial centre, institutionalised through free movement regulations. Finnish labour has been increasingly complemented by migrant workers from Southern Europe. Most recently refugees from outside Europe have formed an increasing share of immigrants.

In the fifties, net immigration totalled 106,000, with the majority coming from Finland. In the mid sixties, Swedish firms recruited increasingly in Yugoslavia, Greece and Turkey; at the end of the decade immigration reached an all-time high, with most workers again coming from Finland. Total net immigration in the sixties was 235,000. Rates of entry declined again from 1971. Since the mid seventies there have been extremely restrictive policies on the entry of foreign workers. Apart from citizens of other Scandinavian countries, who have the right of entry, only highly qualified workers have been admitted. The overwhelming majority of new immigrants are family members coming to join workers already in Sweden, or refugees admitted under special arrangements. The main refugee groups are Chileans and other Latin Americans, Vietnamese, Iranians and Turks, the latter mainly belonging to the Christian minority known as Assyrians. In recent years immigration to Sweden has gradually declined from 40,000 in 1976 to 27,000 in 1981. About half the entrants have been from Scandinavian countries. Total immigration has slightly exceeded total emigration (including that of Swedes).[51] The general picture is of a move from labour migration to family reunification in the 1970s with a trend towards permanent settlement.

This impression is born out by figures on total foreign population: the number of foreigners resident in Sweden increased from 124,000 in 1950, to 191,000 in 1960 and 411,000 in 1970. Since then foreign population has remained fairly constant, reaching 422,000 in 1980 and declining to 414,000 at the end of 1981. Foreign residents made up 1.8 per cent of the Swedish population in 1950, 2.5 per cent in 1960 and 5.1 per cent in both 1970 and 1980. However, the impression of a stable immigrant population is deceptive; the number of people of migrant origin has in fact grown during the seventies, both through immigration and natural increase. The effect of this has been counteracted by the very high rate of naturalisations. So the foreign population of Sweden has remained constant in numbers, while the population of migrant origin has continued to rise.

Swedish naturalisation policy is very liberal. Finns and other Scandinavians can apply for citizenship after two years in Sweden, nationals of other countries after five years. Children born in Sweden and persons marrying Swedes can obtain citizenship immediately upon application.[52] Altogether 404,000 immigrants were granted Swedish citizenship between 1948 and 1981. Of the total Swedish population of 8.3 million at the end of 1981, 632,000 (7.6 per cent) were born outside Sweden. If the second generation (children of at least one immigrant parent) is added, the total number of people of migrant origin totals over one million, one-eighth of the population.[53] It would be wrong to regard all these people as members of ethnic minorities, but such figures do indicate the way post-war migration has changed Sweden from an ethnically and linguistically homogeneous society into a multi-cultural society embracing several ethnic groups. Demographic projections indicate that, by the year 2000, 20–25 per cent of the Swedish population will consist of people closely linked by origin to other countries.[54]

Table 3.5 shows the composition of Sweden's foreign population by nationality in 1960, 1970 and 1980. The Finns were the largest single group throughout, their share increasing in the 1960s and declining in the seventies. The main reason for the decline was naturalisation: 91,000 Finns became Swedish citizens between 1970 and 1981.[55] Altogether the proportion of Scandivians among Sweden's foreign population declined from 65 per cent in 1970 to 57 per cent in 1980.

The proportion of Southern Europeans increased from 4 per cent to 15 per cent in the 1960s and then declined slightly in the seventies. The number of non-Europeans is fairly low, although it is on the increase. The share of Turks rose from one per cent to 4 per cent in the seventies. The number of refugees, mainly from Latin America and South East Asia, has also risen. Altogether, the Third World share in immigrant population is much lower in Sweden than in any of the countries dealt with so far.

Sweden has never followed a guest worker policy. Although migration to Sweden has mostly taken the form of labour migration, it has not been organised by the government, nor has there been any question of measures to get rid of foreign workers at times of recession. In the fifties and sixties labour migration developed spontaneously, with workers coming of their own accord, especially from Finland, although employers did carry out some recruitment abroad, especially in Southern Europe. In the seventies there was a move towards much more restrictive immigration policies. Apart from members of the Nordic Labour Market, few new workers have been admitted – although some

Table 3.5. Foreign residents in Sweden, 1960, 1970, 1980
(figures for end of year)

Country of nationality	1960		1970		1980	
	000s	% of foreign population	000s	% of foreign population	000s	% of foreign population
Finland	75	39.3	209	50.1	181	42.9
Other Scandinavia	50	26.2	61	14.8	59	14.0
Italy	5	2.6	8	1.9	5	1.1
Spain	1	0.5	4	1.0	3	0.7
Greece	–	–	14	3.4	15	3.6
Yugoslavia	1	0.5	37	9.0	39	9.2
Turkey	–	–	4	1.0	18	4.3
Germany	23	12.0	21	5.1	15	3.6
Poland	2	1.0	4	1.0	10	2.4
UK	2	1.0	5	1.2	9	2.1
USA	2	1.0	6	1.5	6	1.4
Chile	–	–	–	–	7	1.7
Others	30	15.7	38	9.2	55	13.0
Total	**191**	**100**	**411**	**100**	**422**	**100**

Sources: Statistisk Årsbok 1981 (Statistical Yearbook); Jonas Widgren, *Report of OECD (SOPEMI) on Immigration to Sweden in 1978 and the First Half of 1979*, Stockholm: Swedish Commission on Immigration Research 1979; *OECD SOPEMI 1981.*

have come illegally and been regularised later. In recent years, there has been some debate on proposals for stopping regularisations and deporting illegal immigrants.

Once in Sweden, immigrant workers have in general experienced better legal treatment than anywhere else in Western Europe. In the first year, they receive temporary labour permits, valid only for a specific job, but after that year they are granted permits valid for any occupation and receive permanent residence permits. Workers are allowed to bring in their family members and to settle. In the early seventies there was considerable discussion on policies for the integration of immigrants: should they be assimilated into the Swedish population, or integrated as groups with their own cultural identity? In 1975 parliament passed a law setting out guidelines for policy on immigrants and ethnic minorities. The new policy was officially characterised as having three objectives:

> *equality* between immigrants and Swedes; cultural *freedom of choice* for immigrants; and *co-operation* and solidarity between the Swedish native majority and the various ethnic minorities.[56]

A complex administrative framework was set up to administer this new policy. State grants are made to immigrants' organisations (about \$4 million per year). About \$65 million are allocated annually to the municipalities to finance special educational measures for immigrant children. Special classes are provided in 50 languages, to help maintain the cultures of the ethnic minorities. In 1973 a law was passed requiring employers to give immigrant workers 240 hours of paid leave per year to learn Swedish, and government finance is provided for these courses, many of them provided by trade unions and voluntary organisations. Since 1976 foreigners with at least three years' residence in Sweden have been permitted to vote and stand for office in local and regional elections. In the 1976 local elections, 60 per cent of the 220,000 foreign residents entitled to vote did so, and some 400 foreigners were elected to public office. It is now proposed to extend voting rights to parliamentary elections. It is easier for a foreign immigrant to obtain naturalisation in Sweden than in any of the other countries under consideration.

Nobody would claim that ethnic minorities of immigrant origin have achieved full equality in Sweden. Their labour market position is, on average, inferior to that of native Swedes. Informal discrimination takes place, and there are social tensions, judging by the spate of attacks by Swedish youths on immigrants in recent years. However, these problems are not being exacerbated by the institutionalised discrimination encountered in other countries.

Switzerland

A small country with a population of under 5 million in 1945, and with its economy intact from wartime neutrality, Switzerland was able to take full advantage of opportunities offered by the long boom. Swiss banks and investment trusts pulled in huge amounts of foreign capital, but it would have been impossible to make effective use of this if only Swiss workers had been available. From 1945 to 1974 Switzerland followed a policy of large-scale import of labour, in the framework of a rigidly controlled guest worker system. The number of foreign workers in Switzerland (including frontier and seasonal workers) rose from 90,000 in 1950 to 435,000 in 1960. Rapid growth continued until the summer of 1964, by which time there were 721,000 foreign workers. Then fears of 'overheating' of the economy led to the first measures to cut entries. The number of foreign workers declined slightly, but then increased again to 834,000 in 1970, and finally peaked at 897,000 in 1973. By that time, about a third of the labour force were foreigners, and about half of all factory workers came from abroad.

Foreign population in Switzerland rose correspondingly: from 279,000 in 1950 (6.1 per cent of total population), to 570,000 in 1960 (10.8 per cent), and 983,000 in 1970 (15.8 per cent). The peak figure was 1,065,000 in 1974 (over 16 per cent of the total population).

It is difficult to compare foreign population with foreign labour force in Switzerland, because not all workers are regarded as belonging to the population. Seasonal workers, of whom there were about 194,000 in August 1973 and about 120,000 in August 1981, spend eight to 11 months a year in Switzerland and are employed mainly in construction, hotels and catering and agriculture. They are not counted as residents, although they spend most of the time in Switzerland. Frontier workers – people who cross the frontiers from neighbouring countries every day to work – also do not appear in population figures. There were 105,000 of them in August 1973 and 109,000 in August 1981.[57]

Foreign workers were recruited abroad (mainly in Italy) by employers rather than government, but admission and residence was always closely controlled by the authorities. In the immediate post-war years, policy was extremely restrictive, because of fears of an impending economic downturn. The aim was to maintain a rapid turnover of foreign workers in order to prevent them from settling. The admission of dependants was kept to a minimum, and workers were granted residence permits that could be withdrawn at any time.

At the end of the fifties, people thought that the boom was going to last, and there was increasing competition for labour between Western European countries. A slight trend towards liberalisation became evident: workers were now generally permitted to bring in spouses and children after three years' residence in Switzerland. It also became official practice to improve foreign workers' rights of residence and labour market mobility, once they had been in Switzerland for 10 years (or five for certain nationalities). Such workers were granted 'establishment permits', conferring better status and security, in place of the annual permits. In the mid sixties attempts were made to cut immigration and to limit the number of foreign workers employed by each firm. The result was the beginning of a trend towards stabilisation of the foreign population, with a gradual increase in the share of non-working dependants. The migration agreement with Italy in 1964 contributed to this development, by making it easier for Italian workers to bring in dependants, and allowing seasonal workers to obtain annual residence permits after five consecutive seasons' work in Switzerland.

Severe restrictions were imposed on labour migration from the beginning of the 1970s. The number of foreign workers fell steeply from 1973, bottoming out at 650,000 in 1977. It increased again to 738,000 in August 1981; however, most growth after 1977 was provided by seasonal and frontier workers. If we count only workers considered to be residents of Switzerland (holders of annual permits and establishment permits), foreign employment dropped from 599,000 in 1973 to 500,000 in 1977, and then remained at that level until 1980, when it rose again, reaching 515,000 at the end of 1981. Foreign population did not drop as quickly or as much, falling from the 1974 peak of 1,065,000 to 884,000 in 1979 and then increasing again to reach 910,000 at the end of 1981. As in other countries, stopping labour entries led to a stabilisation of foreign immigrant population, with an increasing share of non-economically active dependants. By 1981 three-quarters of foreign residents in Switzerland held establishment permits – a clear indication of the long-term nature of their stay.[58]

Throughout the post-war period, Italians have been the largest migrant group, but their share in total foreign population has declined since the sixties, as table 3.6. shows. In 1960, Italians made up 59 per cent of the foreign population. By the end of 1981 their share was down to 46 per cent. In the early fifties the overwhelming majority of Italians came from the northern regions, which are relatively close to Switzerland not only geographically,

Table 3.6. Foreign residents in Switzerland, 1960, 1969 and
1981

| Country of nationality | 1960 | | 1969 (end of year) | | 1981 (end of year) | |
	000s	% of foreign population	000s	% of foreign population	000s	% of foreign population
West Germany	93	15.9	116	11.9	85	9.4
France	31	5.3	50	5.1	46	5.1
Austria	38	6.5	43	4.4	31	3.4
Italy	346	59.1	532	54.7	417	45.8
Spain	14	2.4	98	10.1	100	11.0
Portugal	n.a.	n.a.	n.a.	n.a.	13	1.4
Yugoslavia	1	0.2	21	2.2	49	5.4
Greece	n.a.	n.a.	n.a.	n.a.	9	1.0
Turkey	1	0.2	12	1.2	43	4.7
Others	61	10.4	100	10.3	177	12.8
Total	585	100	972	100	910	100

Sources: *Die Volkswirtschaft*, no. 4, April 1970; *Die Volkswirtschaft*, no. 3,
March 1982: United Nations Economic Commission for Europe,
*Labour Supply and Migration in Europe: Demographic Dimensions 1950–
1975 and Prospects*, New York: United Nations 1979, table annexe II–4.

but also in cultural and socio-economic terms. By the mid sixties
the great majority were coming from the underdeveloped south.[59]
There have always been a fair number of workers from the
neighbouring countries of West Germany, France and Austria,
but their combined share in the foreign population has also
declined, from 28 per cent in 1960 to 21 per cent in 1969 and 18 per
cent in 1981. These decreases have been compensated by the
growth in the number of migrants from more distant parts of
Southern Europe. Their share in foreign population increased
from 3 per cent in 1960 to 12 per cent in 1969 and 19 per cent in
1981. The largest groups are the Spaniards and Yugoslavs. The
only non-European group of significance in Switzerland is the
Turks, who now make up 5 per cent of the foreign population. In
recent years there has been an upward trend in entries of refugees.
In 1980, 3,102 Indochinese refugees were admitted to Switzerland,
and about 3,000 other foreigners from 65 countries also applied
for political asylum. A large proportion came from Eastern

European countries, but many were from Latin America and the Middle East. Most of those rejected were Turks, who were regarded as having come mainly for economic reasons.[60]

Switzerland is the classic case of the organised guest worker system. Migrant workers were recruited in large numbers in order to allow rates of growth and profit which would have been unthinkable otherwise. It was never intended that they should settle permanently. Yet just because they allowed most Swiss employees to move out of the undesirable low-pay and low-status jobs, they became indispensable to the Swiss economy. When foreign labour became scarce in the sixties, the authorities had no choice but to improve migrant workers' rights regarding labour market mobility, family reunification and long-term stay. Migrants had already started turning into settlers by the time of the economic downturn in the seventies, and could not be got rid of, or even significantly reduced in numbers. The immigrant population has become stabilised and is now even growing again slightly, both through immigration and births of foreign children in Switzerland.[61]

The government has refused to face up to the fact of permanent settlement, and has done little to provide the necessary housing and social facilities. Every effort has been made to control foreign residents and to restrict their rights. Immigrants lack political rights and are disenfranchised (although bodies for consultation on matters concerning foreigners have been introduced). Many migrant workers still have the status of seasonal or annual permit holders, which means they can be expelled at the discretion of the authorities. Even the growing number of establishment permit holders lack real security, for they can be deported for a variety of reasons. Naturalisation policy is highly restrictive, with a 12-year residence qualification, as well as requirements concerning language knowledge, character, and so on, which few migrants can meet. Even children born to foreign parents have no automatic right to Swiss citizenship and may be deported if they commit an offence. Nationality law discriminates against women: children born to a Swiss father with a foreign wife become Swiss citizens, while those born to a Swiss mother with a foreign husband do not.[62] At the present rate of naturalisation it would take over a hundred years for all foreign residents to obtain Swiss citizenship.

This restrictive policy reflects a widespread attitude of hostility among the Swiss towards foreign immigrants. There has been a series of campaigns to stop immigration and to expel foreign residents. The Schwarzenbach Initiative of 1970 led to a referendum in which Swiss citizens voted on a proposal for deporting a large proportion of the migrants. The proposal was only narrowly defeated. The pressure generated by such campaigns has been a major cause of official measures to limit immigration and to restrict migrants' rights. Since 1970 there has been discussion of the need to introduce new legislation to replace the Foreigners Law of 1931, and to give foreign residents a clear legal status. Legislation was finally passed by the Federal Assembly in June 1981. The new Foreigners Law was hardly more than a codification of existing administrative practices, with some modest improvements in the position of seasonal workers and family reunification rights. Yet even this was too much for many people. After a campaign by the *Nationale Aktion*, Swiss voters decided by a small majority in a June 1982 referendum to consign the new law to the wastepaper basket.[63]

West Germany

West German employers started importing foreign labour later than those of other countries, partly because post-war recovery started later (not until the Monetary Reform of 1948), and because there were large internal labour reserves (see above p. 25). The state drew on the system set up to utilise foreign labour in the Nazi economy and on the subsequent experience of other Western European countries, in devising a highly organised, official recruitment apparatus. The Federal Labour Office (Bundesanstalt für Arbeit or BfA) set up recruitment offices in Mediterranean countries. Employers requiring foreign labour had to apply to the BfA and pay a fee. The BfA then selected suitable workers, testing their occupational skills, giving them medical check-ups and screening criminal and political records. The workers were brought in groups to West Germany, where employers had to provide accommodation – usually in wooden huts on the work site. The first bilateral recruitment agreement was made with Italy in 1955. At that time temporary seasonal employment of workers for agriculture and building was envisaged. Soon large numbers of workers were being recruited for industry as well. The German government rapidly concluded recruitment agreements with Spain and Greece (1960), Turkey (1961 and 1964), Morocco (1963), Portugal (1964), Tunisia (1965) and Yugoslavia (1968).

The number of foreign workers in West Germany rose rapidly from 95,000 in 1956 to 507,000 by 1961 and 1.3 million by the middle of 1966. Then the recession of 1966–7 caused a cut-back in foreign employment to 904,000. West Germany was able to export a certain proportion of unemployment; but the majority of foreign workers remained, even though hundreds of thousands of Germans were out of work. After the recession, foreign employment shot up, reaching 2 million by 1970 and 2.6 million by the middle of 1973. This trend is clearly seen in figure 3.2.

Policies were shaped by the view that migrant workers were temporary mobile labour units, which could be recruited, utilised and disposed of according to market requirements.[64] Entry of dependants was discouraged, and every effort was made to ensure the rotation of the foreign labour force. Yet German employers had conflicting interests. They wanted a 'mobile labour potential', as they called it. On the other hand, at a time of labour shortages they needed to integrate foreign workers into their permanent workforces. So some foreign workers were encouraged to stay on, and they began to bring over their families – the wife usually being recruited as a worker herself. By the early seventies, tendencies towards family entry and settlement were becoming evident. As a result, foreign labour was losing its flexibility, and social costs were rising.

These tendencies became far more marked after the sudden ban on entries of non-EEC workers announced in November 1973. The ban was designed to reduce substantially both foreign employment and the foreign population, and it set a precedent which was followed by several other governments in the subsequent 12 months.

Foreign employment did indeed decline rapidly from its 1973 peak of 2.6 million (12 per cent of all employed workers in West Germany). By late 1976 the number of foreign workers was down to 1.9 million (9.5 per cent of the labour force). Some workers were forced to leave through withdrawal of work permits but most left because they were unemployed, or because earnings had dropped through loss of overtime or bonus payments. Some were encouraged to leave by offers of favourable redundancy payments by

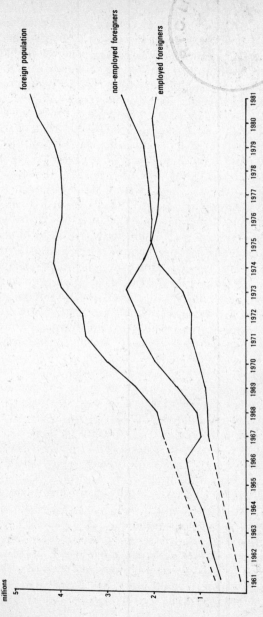

Figure 3.2. Growth of the foreign population in West Germany (by employment status), 1961–81

Source: Bundesanstalt für arbeit, 1974; Bundesminister für Arbeit und Sozialordnung, 1981; Bundesminister für Arbeit und Sozialordnung, 1982; *Statistisches Jahrbuch 1981.*

Note: Employed persons exclude the self-employed and unemployed. These are included as non-employed. In 1981 there were about 193,000 unemployed. No data are available from 1962 to 1966 for the total foreign population and hence for the non-employed population.

employers. Many foreign workers left because they had intended to anyway after a few years in West Germany. The rotation built into the guest worker system allowed export of unemployment and reduced social strains. After 1977 foreign employment started to increase again, as foreign workers' wives, husbands and children entered the labour market. By the middle of 1981 the number of foreign workers was again around the 2 million mark.[65]

The aim of reducing the foreign population was not achieved, as figure 3.2 shows. It did decline slightly from its 1974 peak of 4.1 million to 3.9 million in 1976. Then numbers started increasing again, topping 4 million in 1979 and by September 1982 there were 4.7 million foreign residents in West Germany. There were two major causes for this development. First, foreign workers were staying in West Germany for longer periods than originally planned and were bringing in their spouses and children. Secondly, as more wives and husbands were reunited, the birth rate of the foreign population rose as large numbers of foreign children were born in West Germany. These developments will be analysed in more detail in chapter 4. By 1975 there were more non-employed foreigners than employed. The old advantages of the guest worker system were gone now that the immigrants were making greater demands for housing, schools and other social amenities. West Germany had unintentionally acquired an ethnic minority population.

As late as 1960 West Germany had no significant number of non-European residents. During the sixties large numbers of Turkish workers were recruited, so that by 1970 469,000 (or 16 per cent) of the nearly 3 million foreign residents were Turks. After labour recruitment was stopped in 1973, most European nationalities tended to decline in number. Citizens of the more developed Mediterranean countries saw chances of finding employment or setting up businesses in their countries of origin, and many Greeks and Spaniards left after the demise of the dictatorships in their countries. In contrast, Turks saw little chance of finding work at home and therefore brought in their families. This trend became even more pronounced in the late seventies, as political terror and economic chaos in Turkey made return impossible and produced a stream of refugees. The situation was exacerbated by the draconian measures of the military junta, which seized power in 1980. By September 1982 there were 1,581,000 Turks legally resident in West Germany – a third of the total foreign population.[66]

Since 1979, 200,000–300,000 refugees have come to West Germany from outside Europe, considerably increasing the population of Third World origin. Countries of origin include Eritrea, Afghanistan, India, Pakistan, Vietnam, Chile, Argentina and Turkey. The impact of these refugees on German attitudes to immigrants is discussed in chapter 7. According to official figures, the number of Africans in West Germany rose from 69,000 in 1974 to 124,000 in 1982, while the number of Asians (excluding Turks) rose from 114,000 to 255,000. Most of this increase is attributable to the entry of refugees.[67]

Table 3.7 shows these developments. The proportions of the foreign population from neighbouring countries (Austria and the Netherlands) and from the EEC have tended to fall as have those from the Southern European recruitment countries. The share of Turks in the foreign population has risen steadily through the seventies. Turks and other Third World nationals now total nearly 2 million, over 40 per cent of the immigrant population.

At the end of the fifties, state migration policies were concerned only with short-term fulfilment of capital's labour requirements. Both employers and labour market authorities seem to have believed that the migrants would remain short-term temporary mobile workers, making no appreciable demands for housing and social infrastructure.[68]

The legal framework set up to deal with guest workers was therefore designed to give the authorities the greatest possible flexibility in recruiting and controlling the migrants. In the early years, regulations to control migrant workers were got simply by reactivating the appropriate decrees made by the Nazis to utilise foreign labour in the thirties.[69] These decrees did not confer rights on migrants, but merely permitted them to stay in Germany if 'their personality and the purpose of their stay' made them 'worthy of hospitality'. The vagueness of such provisions gave the authorities great latitude in granting or refusing residence permits, and kept migrants in a state of insecurity and dependence. As recruitment increased, the local authorities set up special departments, generally in the police force, to deal with foreign residents. These agencies, known as *Ausländerbehörde* (foreigners authority) or *Ausländerpolizei* (foreigners police) had considerable power

Table 3.7. Foreign residents in West Germany, 1970, 1974 and 1982

Country of nationality	1970		1974		1982	
	000s	% of foreign population	000s	% of foreign population	000s	% of foreign population
Austria	143	4.8	177	4.3	175	3.7
Netherlands	104	3.5	110	2.7	109	2.3
Italy	574	19.3	630	15.3	602	12.9
Spain	246	8.3	273	6.6	174	3.7
Portugal	54	1.8	122	3.0	106	2.3
Greece	343	11.5	406	9.9	301	6.4
Yugoslavia	515	17.3	708	17.2	632	13.5
Turkey	469	15.8	1,028	25.0	1,581	33.9
Africa	n.a.	n.a.	69	1.7	124	2.7
Asia (excluding Turkey)	n.a.	n.a.	114	2.8	255	5.5
Other EEC	482	16.2	142	3.4	205	4.4
Other			348	8.4	403	8.6
Total	2,977	100	4,127	100	4,667	100

Sources: *Wirtschaft und Statistik*, no. 5, May 1971 and no. 1, January 1983.

Note: Figures are for 30 September in each year.

over the lives of migrants – a situation which has not changed to this day.

Recruitment and control of migrant workers was seen as an administrative matter, and was not debated by parliament until the mid sixties, when a new law was introduced to replace the Nazi regulations. This *Ausländergesetz* (Foreigners Law) of 1965 did not do much to improve the situation of migrants. It did not give foreigners a right to residence, merely stating that 'a residence permit may be granted, if it does not harm the interests of the German Federal Republic'. This term is a key phrase in policies concerning migrants. It is so vague and elastic that it gives the foreigners police great power. 'The interests of the German Federal Republic' are whatever the government or the police care to define them as. A conservative legal expert commented:

According to the present legislation, the residence permit is brought close to being an act of grace. The authorities responsible for foreigners have extremely broad discretionary powers. These measures became necessary because the Federal Republic was being swamped by foreigners.[70]

The granting of political rights to foreign immigrants was certainly not seen as being in 'the interests of the German Federal Republic'. The law of 1965 specifically excluded not only the right to vote, but also other civil rights. The regulation that instructs officials on how to implement the law states baldly:

Foreigners enjoy all basic rights, except the basic rights of freedom of assembly, freedom of association, freedom of movement, and free choice of occupation, place of work and place of education, and protection from extradition abroad.[71]

The presence of foreigners was generally seen as being in 'the interests of the German Federal Republic' only if they were required by employers. Residence permits were linked with labour permits, and these were only issued by the labour offices if no West German workers were available. The rules guaranteeing primacy to West German workers (and after 1968 to workers from other EEC countries as well) were reiterated in the new labour law of 1969 (*Arbeitsförderungsgesetz*). Permits were to be of limited duration, could be restricted to a particular firm, occupation or area and could be withdrawn at the will of the authorities.

Thus the state established a system of institutionalised discrimination, through which temporary guest workers could be recruited, controlled and sent away, as the interests of capital dictated. The laws do not give rights to foreign residents. Rather, they give the authorities the power to confer or to deny privileges that can be withdrawn in the event of unemployment or if migrants do not conform to employers' requirements. Deportation is a permanent Damocles' sword.

As the shift from labour migration to settlement began to become apparent at the beginning of the seventies, conflicts between state and capital on future policy towards foreign workers emerged. These found expression in statements by employers' associations, political parties and various government departments, as well as through the deliberations and reports of a series of official commissions set up in the seventies and early eighties.[72] At first employers' associations demanded continued recruitment of foreign labour. They suggested that social costs should be kept down through enforced rotation; workers should be allowed to stay for a maximum of five years, and not to bring dependants or to settle.

This policy was impracticable, not only because of the various international agreements granting rights of family reunification, to which West Germany was a party, but also because many firms found that rotation led to problems of labour fluctuation and high training costs. State policies began to be shaped by concerns of increasing social problems and political tensions. From 1971 onwards steps were taken to restrict entries and to levy higher recruitment fees on employers. The ban on further entries of non-EEC workers in November 1973 was motivated not only by the economic situation, but also by political considerations, and was initially opposed by employers.[73]

In the period that followed, the authorities used existing discriminatory regulations in an attempt to cut drastically the foreign population. The Federal Labour Office decreed that work permits for migrant workers were not to be renewed if West German workers were thought to be available for the job concerned. This meant that in some cases foreigners were forced to leave jobs, although not dismissed by the employer.[74] The police then withdrew residence permits, forcing workers to leave the country. This type of compulsory repatriation does not appear to have been very frequent, but the threat of it led to insecurity, and encouraged migrants to leave 'voluntarily'. A further decree stipulated that work permits were not to be granted to spouses or children of migrant workers coming to West Germany after the 'key date' (Stichtag) of 1 December 1974. The idea was that this would discourage family reunification, and cause some migrant workers to leave.

Further discriminatory measures followed. The tax reform of January 1975 increased child benefits, but denied these to non-EEC workers, whose children remained in the country of origin. This measure backfired; many workers brought in children who had previously been looked after by grandparents or other relatives in the home country. In April 1975 a regulation was issued, forbidding migrants to take up residence in areas considered to be already 'overstrained': certain inner-city districts of Berlin, Frankfurt and other conurbations. The measure was dropped two years later, not because it contravened human rights, but because employers protested that it was making the labour market too inflexible, and because it was impossible to enforce effectively. The key date rule also proved to be a mistake. It created a class of youth who were not permitted to work and who had no rights to social security benefits – a perfect recipe for juvenile delinquency. The key date was first extended to the end of 1977, then dropped altogether in 1978. This was one reason for the upsurge in entries, in 1979 and 1980, of young people who were destined to enter the labour market without having received any schooling in West Germany.[75] The effect of all these measures was not to cut the foreign population, as intended, but to speed up the restructuring of temporary migrant labour into a more settled foreign population (see chapter 4 for more details).

The need for a co-ordinated, long-term approach was becoming inescapable, and the government set up a commission representing federal and state (*Länder*) authorities to make appropriate recommendations. This *Bund-Länder-Kommission* reported in February 1977, reiterating the old assertion that the 'German Federal Republic is not a country of immigration' and calling for the continuation of the ban on further labour immigration, and for measures to encourage repatriation. On the other hand, it did suggest steps for the integration of those foreign residents who wished to stay, and for policies to improve the position of second-generation migrants. The most important recommendation was to grant residence permits of unlimited duration after five years' stay in West Germany, and 'residence entitlements' after eight years, giving greater protection against deportation. However, these permits were to be conditional on possession of long-term work permits, proof of school attendance of the migrants' children, and having an 'adequate' dwelling (generally defined as at least 12 square metres of living space per grown-up and eight per child). At the same time, the commission called for restrictions of the right to family reunification, in particular the reduction of the maximum entry age for children from 20 to 17.[76] These measures were implemented in 1978.

By now there were about 700,000 foreign children under the age of 16 in West Germany. It was evident that most were going to stay, and that something was going to have to be done to clarify their situation and improve schooling and vocational training facilities.

The federal government appointed Heinz Kühn, a leading SPD member who had been prime minister of North Rhine Westphalia, as Ombudsman for Foreigners (*Ausländerbeauftragte*). His report, published in 1979, represented the first official attempt to come to grips with the reality of West Germany's new minorities. It stated:

> Future policy towards foreign employees and their families
> living in the Federal Republic must be based on the
> assumption that a development has taken place which can no
> longer be reversed, and that the majority of those concerned
> are no longer guest workers but immigrants, for whom return
> to their countries of origin is for various reasons no longer a
> viable option.[77]

Kühn recommended measures designed to offer foreign residents more secure legal status and to give them an opportunity of integration into West German society. He called for a restriction of the arbitrary powers of the foreigners police through the introduction of definite legal rights. In particular, children born to immigrant parents in Germany were to receive the right to a work permit, and entitlement to naturalisation. Kühn also recommended the introduction of the right to vote in local elections after eight to ten years' residence.

However, the federal government – at that time a coalition of the SPD and the FDP – did not implement these proposals. In a statement issued in March 1980, the government reiterated that permanent settlement was seen as the exception rather than the rule. The government expressed its support for integration of those who wanted to stay, but regarded the existing Foreigners Law as an adequate basis for this.[78] The government did accept the recommendation concerning easier naturalisation for second-generation youth, but its draft law to this effect was turned down by the Federal Council (Bundesrat), in which the conservative CDU–CSU was in the majority.[79]

In the early eighties the trend towards restrictive policies on migration and minority rights has continued. Rising unemployment and growing urban problems have led to increased racism. Matters have been further exacerbated by media campaigns against the alleged influx of refugees (see chapter 7). The government has introduced a range of measures to deter people seeking asylum. Entry visas have been made compulsory for several nationalities, including Turks. From the middle of 1980, those seeking asylum have had to wait for one year before being allowed to look for work in West Germany, and from October 1981 this waiting period has been extended to two years, except for those from Eastern Europe. Refugees are forced to live in isolated camps, where accommodation, food and hygiene are often poor. Many refugees have permits restricting them to certain districts, making it impossible to visit friends or relatives.[80] About 80 per cent of applications for asylum are turned down, after a wait of two years or more.

In December 1981, the federal government introduced rules reducing the maximum age of entry for children of foreign residents from 17 to 15 years. Immigration of wives and husbands was also restricted; the marriage must have taken place at least a year earlier, and the foreign resident concerned must have been in West Germany for at least eight years.[81]

There was a marked shift to the right in West German politics in October 1982 with a CDU–CSU–FDP coalition coming to power. Chancellor Kohl (CDU) emphasised that restricting immigration and encouraging repatriation was a major plank of his policy. Minister of the Interior Zimmermann (CSU) set up a working group of representatives from various ministries and *Länder* governments to work out a new policy. A few days before the federal elections in March 1983, the government announced that it intended to reduce the foreign population by at least one million in the next few years. This is to be achieved through severe restrictions on family reunification (the maximum age of entry for children will probably be reduced to five); departure premiums; deportation in the event of unemployment, claims for social security benefit or criminality; and a range of further measures designed to make the situation of foreign residents less attractive. By the summer of 1983 it was not yet possible to say exactly what form the new policies will take as changes in the law will take some time. Whether many will leave is uncertain; most foreigners remain in West Germany because they have no realistic alternative, and they will leave only if forced to do so. The CDU–CSU–FDP government is likely to stop short of a policy of mass deportation (if only because of international pressure), so that the main impact will be the increased marginalisation and isolation of the minority population.

Twenty-five years after the beginning of migration and ten years after the stopping of most labour migration, the state still chooses to regard the ethnic minorities as temporary residents who are expected to leave West Germany. The most visible aspect of the stigma of the minorities is not the colour of their skins, but the colour of their passports. Foreign residents are denied a whole range of civil rights. No wonder that West Germany (along with Switzerland) has no anti-discrimination law.

The lack of rights is not the same for all foreigners. Citizens of other EEC countries have the same rights as West Germans regarding employment and have reasonable security of residence, although they lack political rights and can be deported for offences to public order and security. Foreigners from other countries find themselves ensnared in a thicket of discriminatory regulations.

A non-EEC foreigner wishing to take up employment must apply for a work permit from the local labour office. If granted, this will initially be a 'general' labour permit, tied to a specific job and requiring annual renewal. After five years' uninterrupted employment, the foreigner may be granted a 'special' labour permit, valid for any job and renewable every five years. But even this gives no clear right to work. Every time a firm wants to take on a foreign worker, the labour office is supposed to check that no West German or EEC citizen is available.

Similarly, foreigners have no *right* to remain in West Germany. They have to apply for permission to stay. A permit 'may be granted' if the foreigners police think this will not harm 'the interests of the German Federal Republic'. The wide discretion of the police makes this regular application a source of fear and humiliation. Until 1978 it was general practice to issue and renew permits for only one or two years at a time. In 1978 the federal government introduced the *Verfestigungsregel* (consolidation rule) to give foreign residents a clearer legal status. Foreigners legally present in West Germany over five years were to be granted a residence permit of unlimited duration, while those resident over eight years were to get 'residence entitlements', giving much greater protection against deportation. Residence entitlement holders can only be deported for serious offences, but not because of unemployment or because of applications for social security benefits.

In fact, the *Verfestigungsregel* has not been implemented by the foreigners police. In September 1981, only 30,000 foreigners had been granted residence entitlements, although about 2.5 million foreigners had been in West Germany over eight years. Roughly one million foreign residents had a secure status as EEC citizens, while 1.2 million did not need residence permits because they were aged under 16. Well over 2 million foreigners had residence permits which permitted deportation in a wide variety of circumstances.[82] They have every reason to feel insecure, for in recent years official policy has been to make the fullest use of powers of deportation, in order to cut the immigrant population.

The right to protection of the family, which is guaranteed by Article 6 of the German constitution, is also severely restricted for foreigners. Discriminatory rules denying work permits to dependants, or subjecting them to long waiting periods before gaining permission to enter the country or to take up employment, have been used to discourage family reunification. Lowering the maximum age of entry for children in recent years and the rule that family members may only enter the country if a migrant worker can prove that adequate housing is available are also intended to cut immigration. With housing shortages, high rents and discrimination by landlords, few foreign workers can fulfil the requirements of space per person. The result is that many dependants are brought in as tourists, have no right to work, and live in constant fear of discovery and deportation. In the last few years, the foreigners police have taken to sending officials round to foreign workers' dwellings with tape measures. If they discover that the living space does not meet official norms, one or more family members may be threatened with deportation.[83]

Even children of foreign workers born in Germany do not gain an automatic right to live and work there. It is present policy to grant work and residence permits to them, but deportation in the event of conviction for a criminal offence or long-term unemployment is possible.

Only naturalisation gives real security to the immigrant, but West German law does not permit dual nationality and many people are unwilling to buy a clear legal status at the price of surrendering all hope of returning to their country of origin. In any case, naturalisation is extremely difficult to obtain. In 1980 1.7 million foreigners in West Germany fulfilled the residence qualification of 10 years, but only 15,000 (0.9 per cent) were in fact granted naturalisation. Only 387 Turks (0.1 per cent of those resident over 10 years) obtained naturalisation in 1980.[84]

Foreign residents do not have the right to vote, and none of the major parties is in favour of granting this, even in local elections. The official view, expressed by a leading civil servant in the Ministry of Labour and Social Order, is that the enfranchisement of foreigners would lead to:

> Groups with red and black flags marching through the streets and terrifying our population. The result would be that we would end up with the political party structure of the foreign countries, from communists to fascists in our parliaments, as a consequence of free electoral associations.[85]

The authorities have the power to forbid foreign associations and to stop any activity which 'threatens public safety or order', which 'hinders political decision processes' or which in any way threatens 'important interests of the Federal Republic'. These wide and vaguely defined powers have been used to imprison and deport foreigners who have demonstrated against the regimes of their countries of origin (including the Shah of Iran, the former Greek and Spanish dictatorships and the present Turkish military junta). They have also been used against foreign workers involved in unofficial strikes, or campaigns for social and political rights in West Germany.[86]

West Germany has maintained the laws and regulations designed to control a system of temporary labour migration, even though the situation has changed to permanent settlement of new ethnic minorities. The system was always discriminatory – it was meant to be – but it is all the more oppressive for people who have lived and worked in the country for over a decade, and who are beginning to see it as their home. The restriction of civil and political rights is a major cause of the isolation and marginalisation of the minorities, and is also tantamount to the disenfranchisement of a large section of the working class. The 3 million adults thus excluded from the political process have no choice but to seek other means of political expression, in their struggle against institutionalised discrimination and racism.

General trends

Patterns of migration

Post-war migration to the seven countries examined here has taken a variety of forms, which cannot always be clearly separated.

First: return migration of settlers from former colonies, such as the British from India, French 'pieds noirs' from Algeria, Dutch from Indonesia. A special case of entry of nationals was the immigration to West Germany of people expelled from the former eastern territories, lost to Poland and the Soviet Union after the second world war, and of refugees from East Germany. This type of migration may create social difficulties and shape attitudes, but it does not lead to the formation of ethnic minorities.

Second: immigration of ethnically distinct citizens of colonies, or former colonies, to the colonial power, in particular West Indians and Asians to Britain, North Africans and black Africans to France, Indonesians and Surinamese to the Netherlands.

Third: labour migration, mainly of manual workers, from Mediterranean countries, Finland and Ireland. Such migration has often, but not always, taken place through organised recruitment. In certain cases, free movement arrangements of regional economic organisations have eased migration: for example, migration of Italian workers to France and West Germany within the EEC; Finnish workers to Sweden within the Nordic Labour Market.

Fourth: migration of skilled employees between highly developed countries (often within multi-national companies). This migration is the only type which has remained mostly temporary. Again, the EEC free labour movement policy and the Nordic Labour Market have provided a framework in many cases.

Fifth: entry of foreign refugees seeking political asylum. Such movements were large after the second world war, then declined considerably, apart from periods following political upheavals in Eastern Europe. Since the mid seventies there has been a new upsurge, and a high proportion of the refugees now come from Third World countries. Although the number of refugees entering is low compared with entries of labour migrants in the sixties and seventies, the political impact of these new flows has often been considerable.

All the countries examined have had more than one of these forms of migration, some have had all five. Two forms have played the greatest role in the development of the new ethnic minorities: the migration of citizens of colonies or former colonies to Britain, France and the Netherlands; and migration of manual workers (followed by their dependants) to all seven countries.

In a sense, all forms of migration have been labour migration, for the newcomers have become part of the labour force. Similarly, whatever their original intentions, large numbers of both colonial migrants and foreign workers have stayed on, brought over dependants and settled down.

The period of primary migration (the first phase of migration, generally young single people, with a predominance of males) was 1945 to 1962 for Britain. For most other countries it was 1945 to 1974, but the peak was in the sixties and early seventies. West Germany was latest, with most labour migration between 1960 and 1973. The second phase – family reunification – was mainly in the sixties and early seventies in the case of Britain, mainly in the seventies in the other countries. Immigration is now on the decline everywhere (except possibly Switzerland). The phase of settlement and formation of minorities is well under way. Most growth in minority populations is now through births in Western Europe.

Growth in population of migrant origin
Table 3.8 shows the way population of migrant origin has grown in the post-war period. In all seven countries, the number of foreign residents, or (in the case of Britain) the number of people born abroad plus their descendants, was very much greater in 1980 than in 1950. In France the foreign population doubled, and the increases in the other countries were even greater. The most rapid growth in population of migrant origin was between 1960 and 1975. Since then numbers have become more stable, although, as will be shown in chapter 4, there have been changes in demographic structure. Workers have departed and been replaced by non-working dependants, including children born in Western Europe.

The figures in table 3.8 do not give a completely accurate picture of the size of minority populations. Except for Britain, figures are for foreign residents, and therefore omit migrants who possessed

Table 3.8. Minority population in the main West European countries of immigration (thousands)

Country[1]	1950	1960	1970	1975	1980
Belgium	354	444	716	835	904
France	2,128	2,663	3,339	4,196	4,148
West Germany	548	686	2,977	4,090	4,453
Great Britain[2]	1,573	2,205	3,968	(4,153)[3]	4,470
Netherlands	77	101	236	370	476
Sweden	124	191	411	410	422
Switzerland	279	585	983	1,012	893
Total	**5,083**	**6,875**	**12,630**	**(15,066)[3]**	**15,766**

Sources: UNECE 1980, table annexe II–4; OECD SOPEMI 1981; Die *Volkswirtschaft*, no. 3, March 1982; OPCS, Demographic Review 1977; GB Census 1971, 1981.

Notes: 1. Figures for all countries except Great Britain are for foreign residents and thus exclude people from the Dutch and French colonies; 2. Great Britain data are for 1951, 1961, 1971 and 1981. The 1951 and 1961 data are for the foreign-born population and thus exclude the children of immigrants. The 1971 figure includes children born in the UK with both parents born abroad; the 1981 figure is of the population living in households with a foreign-born head; 3. Figures in brackets are estimates.

citizenship of the immigration country before migration, or who have obtained it since. France has had several hundred thousand black migrants with French citizenship from Overseas Departments, while the Netherlands has also received large numbers of citizens of Asian and West Indian origin from former colonies. United Nations estimates put France's foreign-born population at 5.7 million in 1975, and the Netherlands' at 606,000 in 1971, but these figures include white descendants of colonial settlers.[87] Naturalisation has also reduced the apparent size of the population of migrant origin. This factor is particularly important for Sweden, but also significant for France, Belgium and the Netherlands.

Table 3.9 shows the population of migrant origin as a percentage of total population in the seven countries. In all cases there is an upward trend over the period 1950–80. The increase is particularly marked in the period 1960–75, after which the percentage becomes more stable, with slight increases in Belgium, West Germany, Britain and the Netherlands, and slight declines in France and Switzerland. Taking account of the fact that these figures actually underestimate the percentage of people of migrant origin, especially for Sweden and the Netherlands, Table 3.9 does give some indication of how Western European countries have become multi-ethnic societies since 1945.

Table 3.9. Minority population in the main West European countries of immigration as a percentage of the total population

Country	1950	1960	1970	1975	1980
Belgium	4.3	4.9	7.2	8.5	9.2
France	4.5	5.4	6.5	7.9	7.7
West Germany	1.1	1.2	4.9	6.6	7.2
Great Britain	3.2	4.3	7.4	(7.8)	8.5
Netherlands	1.1	1.0	1.8	2.6	3.4
Sweden	1.8	2.5	5.1	5.0	5.1
Switzerland	6.1	10.8	15.8	16.0	14.2

Sources and notes: as for Table 3.8.

Areas of origin

As labour migration developed between 1945 and the early seventies, migrants tended to come from increasingly distant areas. At the beginning of the post-war period, Italy was the main source of migrant labour for several countries, with Britain also recruiting in Ireland, and Sweden in Finland. In the late fifties and sixties other Southern European countries became major labour suppliers, while Britain, France and the Netherlands received large numbers of non-European migrants from former colonies. As the period of labour import drew to a close, more and more workers were coming from Third World countries, particularly as a result of large-scale recruitment by West Germany in Turkey. During the period of family migration and settlement after 1974, it was above all the non-Europeans who stayed on, while many Southern Europeans returned home. Table 3.10 gives the lastest available figures on the origins of ethnic minorities in the seven Western European countries.

The largest European minority group is the Italians: 1.9 million throughout the seven receiving countries. Next largest are the Portuguese (one million, mainly in France) and the Irish (950,000 almost all in Britain). Large numbers of Spaniards, Yugoslavs and Greeks also reside in the various countries. The largest non-European group is the Turks: 1.9 million, mainly in West Germany, but also in France, the Netherlands, Belgium and Switzerland. There are 1.7 million North Africans, mainly in France, and about one million people from the Indian sub-continent, mainly in Britain. A further large group of non-European origin are the 546,000 West Indians in Britain. It must be remembered that certain groups from Dutch and French colonies are excluded from the figures, as they hold citizenship of the country of immigration.

Table 3.11 summarises information on origin to reflect the socio-economic levels of the sending countries. About 8 per cent of residents of migrant origin come from industrialised EEC countries, which are very similar in socio-economic level and culture to the country of immigration. Thirty-eight per cent come from countries on the less industrialised European periphery (Southern Europe, Ireland and Finland). A further 38 per cent come from non-European Third World countries. Their socio-economic, cultural and ethnic backgrounds are very different from those of the indigenous populations of the receiving countries. Although Southern Europeans are regarded and treated as minorities, and suffer from institutional discrimination and ethnic exclusion, there is no doubt that rejection and racism are even more marked with regard to non-Europeans. In the three largest immigration countries, Britain, France and West Germany, over 40 per cent of the respective minorities are now of Third World origin.

Migration policies and minority rights

When post-war migration to Western Europe got under way, none of the states concerned anticipated or intended that it would lead to large-scale settlement and the development of new ethnic minorities. As one would expect in capitalist societies, migration and settlement have been shaped by market forces and by conflicting class interests, rather than by conscious planning.

The two most important forms of migration in volume have been the entry of citizens of colonies or former colonies and the recruitment of migrant labour through guest worker systems.

Table 3.10. Nationality or country of origin of Western Europe's ethnic minorities (thousands)

Country of nationality or origin	Country of immigration and year of data		
	Belgium 30.4.77	France 1.1.82	West Germany 30.9.81
Algeria	10	817	5
Finland			10
Greece	24		299
Ireland	1		
Italy	287	452	625
Morocco	81	444	39
Portugal	10	859	109
Spain	65	413	177
Tunisia	5	193	24
Turkey	59	118	1,546
Yugoslavia	7	68	637
India			
Pakistan and Bangladesh			
West Indies			
Other New Commonwealth			
Other Africa			
Other Asia			
Other EEC	231	176	308
Other	72	684	851
Total	**851**	**4,224**	**4,630**

These two forms imply quite different state policies, and legal and administrative frameworks. Yet, in the long run both types of migration have led to settlement, and in recent years the trend has been towards a convergence in their social and legal circumstances.

Imposing on subjected peoples the citizenship of the colonising power was an ideological instrument of domination used by Britain, France and the Netherlands in their respective empires. These states were not willing to rapidly abandon such citizenship laws

| Great Britain 5.4.81 | Country of immigration and year of data | | | Total |
	Netherlands 1.1.81	Sweden 31.12.81	Switzerland 31.12.81	
	1	1		834
		172		182
(12)	4	14	9	362
949				950
(98)	21	5	417	1,905
	93	1		658
(17)	9		13	1,017
(40)	23	3	100	821
	2	1		225
	148	20	43	1,934
	14	39	49	814
674				674
360				360
546				546
628				628
(111)				111
(151)				151
(207)	117	55	170	1,264
677	112	101	109	2,606
4,470	544	414	910	16,043

Sources: Belgium: *Enquête Socio-economique de l'Institut National de Statistique*, April 1977; France, Germany, Netherlands, Sweden, Switzerland: *OECD SOPEMI 1982*: Great Britain: 1981 Census.

Notes: Data are for foreign residents except Great Britain, which are for population living in households with a non-UK-born head.
Figures in brackets are for non-UK-born only and do not include their children born in the UK. Where no figure is given, data are unavailable, but the group concerned is usually small.

Table 3.11. Ethnic minorities in Western Europe by areas of origin

Area of origin	000s	% of ethnic minority population
EEC countries, excluding Italy, Greece and Ireland	1,264	7.9
Other Europe (Southern Europe, Ireland, Finland)	6,051	37.7
Non-European	6,121	38.2
Other	2,606	16.2
Total	**16,043**	**100**

Sources and notes: as for Table 3.10.

in the post-war period, for to do so would have been tantamount to accepting the breakdown of colonialism, which they were still trying to resist. So colonial citizens had the right of free movement to the 'mother countries' and came mainly of their own accord, in response to growing employment opportunities. Once in Britain, France or the Netherlands, these colonial migrants had the right to work and settle, were allowed to bring in dependants and enjoyed full political rights. This migration was certainly not planned by the states concerned, and reactions to it were ambivalent. On the one hand, it was seen as useful in meeting labour demands, and as politically necessary in order to maintain links with colonies and former colonies. On the other hand, there were fears of mass settlement, and its possible social and political impact.

Recent public records office research by Mark Duffield on the post-war period in Britain shows that there was much debate in the government about the undesirability of allowing large numbers of black citizens into the country.[88] The long-term implications were seen in the early fifties – and disliked – by members of the government. The British government has always been aware that migrants could form a long-term population, and on that account some people opposed colonial migration right from the beginning. Indeed government opposition to colonial migration has a history going back to at least the early part of this century.[89]

Similar debates were no doubt taking place in France and the

Netherlands. The free movement of Algerian workers was seen as a threat to public order during the Algerian war of independence in the fifties, but it could not be curbed because of the official ideology that Algeria was part of France. In the sixties there was growing concern about a possible upsurge of black workers from the newly independent African countries, which remained linked to France.

It was the British government that took the first step towards abolishing colonial migration, through the Commonwealth Immigrants Act of 1962, followed by further restrictions in 1968, and by limitations on the entry of dependants in 1971 (see above pp. 45–6). France took steps to restrict migration from Algeria and from other African countries in the late sixties and early seventies. Colonial migration to the Netherlands ceased to be significant after the independence of Surinam in 1975, although some labour migration and family reunification continued until 1980, when visas were made compulsory for Surinamese.

The majority of colonial migrants who came to Britain, France and the Netherlands before the introduction of immigration controls have maintained their citizenship (the main exception being the Algerians in France, who usually chose Algerian citizenship at the time of independence). Immigration controls have speeded the transition from temporary migration to permanent settlement, encouraging people, who have the rights to do so, to stay on and bring in dependants. The position of those few migrants still allowed in from colonies or former colonies has become virtually indistinguishable from that of foreigners in recent years, as immigration and nationality laws have been tightened up.

Citizenship has not guaranteed social equality; colonial migrants and their descendants still find themselves victims of racism and institutional discrimination. The ending of free movement makes it possible for police and other authorities to suspect any ethnically distinct person of being an illegal immigrant. The result is frequent harassment and victimisation of non-Europeans.

The legal status of guest workers corresponded with policies of short-term labour recruitment. The typical guest worker was recruited for a specific job, and his or her work permit was valid only for a specific employer for a fixed period (often one year). The residence permit was in turn tied to possession of a valid work permit, which meant that if a worker got involved in a conflict with the employer, the end result could be deportation. Residence permits could be withdrawn in the event of unemployment, so that migrants who lost their jobs could find themselves without the right to stay, and they could even be denied unemployment benefit. Foreign workers also had restricted rights with regard to family reunification and social services. Finally, foreign workers did not have the right to vote. In some countries they were also barred from forming political associations, from demonstrating and even from being trade union officials. The whole system of institutional discrimination was designed to keep foreign labour mobile, flexible and compliant, to deter settlement, and to make it easy to get rid of migrants in the event of a recession.

In the long run this system was unable to prevent family reunification and settlement. As the governments became aware of this, they began to reappraise their policies, and to weigh possible long-term social and political effects against short-term benefits to employers. The trend towards more restrictive immigration policies received further impetus from the ending of the post-war boom. Several states stopped most types of labour immigration in 1973-4. Some of the governments (especially the West German and French) appear to have expected that this would lead to a rapid decline in both the foreign labour force and the foreign population, and took various measures to encourage repatriation. Although the number of migrant workers dropped, family immigration continued, and the foreign populations declined little, or even increased. Just as restrictions on colonial migration had encouraged people to stay on in Britain, France and the Netherlands, the virtual stopping of labour migration speeded up the shift from temporary migration of foreign workers to family immigration and permanent settlement throughout Western Europe. Restrictive policies, shaped by fears of the possible impact of large-scale permanent settlement, did not achieve their aim of reducing the immigrant population. Indeed, their effect was rather to encourage the development of new ethnic minorities.

Although labour migration to Western Europe stopped for the most part a decade and more ago, and although the transition from migration to settlement is everywhere well advanced, most members of the developing ethnic minorities still suffer serious legal disabilities. Some states have maintained legal frameworks originally designed to manage temporary labour migration, and hence inappropriate to the current situation. In other countries, new restrictive policies have been introduced to control minorities. In both cases, the result is continued insecurity and restriction of rights for people who came as migrants and their descendants. Sometimes it is not just discriminatory laws and regulations, but the continual public debate on new restrictions, which makes it impossible for members of minorities to develop clear perspectives for their future. Campaigns for sending migrants away, state repatriation premiums, threats of deportation in the event of unemployment or committing an offence – these are some of the factors that tend to marginalise minority people. Their impact is particularly serious for minority youth, often born in Western Europe, who may face the prospect of being forced to leave for countries with which they have no real links. Discriminatory laws are often couched in such vague terms as to give the police and other authorities wide discretionary powers in dealing with members of the minorities. In a climate of growing racism, this makes enforcement of the law all the more arbitrary and repressive. Many members of the new ethnic minorities find themselves subject to institutional discrimination which makes them second-class citizens.

4. The formation of ethnic minorities

This chapter deals with some characteristics of the receiving societies and of the populations of migrant origin. The analysis here and in subsequent chapters concentrates on West Germany. Where possible, comparative material has been added for Britain, together with a limited amount of information from other countries.

Britain and West Germany are at opposite ends of a spectrum: at one end, post-colonial migration of black people possessing British citizenship; at the other, organised recruitment of what was seen as temporary foreign labour. In both cases the result was the development of large, identifiable ethnic minority groups in a generally subordinate socio-economic position. Common features observed in the situation of the minorities in Britain and West Germany are very likely to apply to the other countries too.

Defining ethnic minorities

Migrant groups entering a new country do not automatically or inevitably take on the position of ethnic minorities. Becoming a minority is a process whereby dominant groups in society ascribe certain (real or imagined) characteristics to the newcomers, and use these to justify the assignment of specific economic, social and political roles. In response to their experience, migrants and their descendants develop their own cultures and institutions, and perceive themselves as distinct groups within society. The following sociological definition by Wagley and Harris helps to clarify the term:

(1) Minorities are subordinate segments of complex state societies; (2) minorities have special physical or cultural traits which are held in low esteem by dominant segments of the society; (3) minorities are self-conscious units bound together

by the special traits which their members share and by the special disabilities which these bring; (4) membership in a minority is transmitted by rule of descent which is capable of affiliating succeeding generations even in the absence of readily apparent special cultural or physical traits; (5) minority people, by choice or necessity, tend to marry within the group.[1]

Why should the populations of migrant origin in Western Europe be examined in terms of ethnic minority status? When Godula Kosack and I wrote about migrant workers in Western Europe at the beginning of the seventies, we categorised migrants as a specific stratum of the working class.[2] At that time, the dominant role of migrants, especially in West Germany and Switzerland, was that of the worker. Since then labour migration has turned into settlement, temporary migrants have become settlers, and new communities are developing in most major cities. The former migrants are still mostly manual workers, but their involvement in social processes outside work is of growing significance. These are processes of community establishment, cultural change, political and social conflict, and of ethnic exclusion.

Minority status and class position are interrelated but far from identical aspects of foreign or black workers' lives. A person may cease to be a member of the working class, by, for instance, setting up a business, but remain a member of the minority because she or he is still subject to institutional discrimination and ethnic exclusion. Many workers not of migrant origin have the same position in the production process as minority workers, but do not share the stigmatisation arising from racism or from discriminatory legislation. This has important effects on social and political consciousness.

Of course there are other social groups subjected to various forms of discrimination and exclusion: the aged, the handicapped, sexual and cultural non-conformists, the long-term unemployed, welfare recipients. The largest such group is women, who are frequently pushed into inferior social and economic roles. The term minorities is problematic, for the majority of people belong to one or another of the groups subjected to racism, sexism, ageism, and so on. Discrimination is particularly severe when various criteria reinforce each other; black, working-class women are among the most exploited people in Western Europe.[3]

Most members of the new ethnic minorities are still manual workers (or dependants of manual workers), but their social situation cannot be adequately explained by this fact alone. Minority status is not reducible to a specific form of exploitation in the production process. It has historical, cultural and ideological dimensions of its own, which in turn help to determine position within the production process (or exclusion from it).

It is sometimes asserted that capital is 'colour blind', willing to exploit workers of any nationality or race. That is misleading; capital uses racial, national and sexual categorisation to differentiate between groups of workers, splitting the labour force, and permitting super-exploitation of certain sections. That is what lies behind the segmentation of the labour market. It is therefore necessary to look at the situation of people of migrant origin by considering both minority status and class position. The interrelationships and contradictions between these two aspects of their position in society are vital in determining economic, social and political behaviour, and interaction between various ethnic groups.

A social group becomes a minority mainly because it is defined as such by society. This definition takes many forms: stigmatisation of physical or cultural characteristics, racial exclusion, institutional discrimination, denial of civil rights, economic exploitation. One form of the definition is the names given to the minorities by dominant groups. In West Germany, the minority is officially called 'foreign employees and their dependants' (*ausländische Arbeitnehmer und ihre Angehörige*), a term that shows continuing emphasis on the economic character of migration. The migrants used to be popularly known as guest workers (*Gastarbeiter*), a term that was always problematic because guests are not usually invited to do the dirty work and because it implied that the 'guests' would leave when no longer wanted. Most Germans now speak of 'foreigners' (*Ausländer*), and this seemingly neutral term is becoming pejorative, just as the word 'immigrant' did in Britain two decades ago.

Many Germans opposed to discrimination (church representatives, for instance) now use the term 'foreign fellow citizens' (*ausländische Mitbürger*), but this is misleading. Foreigners are not 'fellow citizens', for they are denied many civil rights. Other progressive people are beginning to speak of 'immigrants' (*Einwanderer*), as a conscious way of rejecting the official line that West Germany 'is not a country of immigration'. Others use the expression 'ethnic minorities' (*ethnische Minderheiten*), which implies a decision to recognise that foreigners are permanent members of society. It means calling for an end to 'foreigners policy' (*Ausländerpolitik*), and its replacement by a 'minorities policy' designed to improve the situation of people of migrant origin.

Racists have a wide range of expressions to categorise members of the minorities. The most common is *Kanaken*. It refers to a people in the South Pacific called the Kanakas (although few racists realise this), and owes its origins to German attempts to establish a colony in the South Pacific in the late nineteenth century, a curious reminder of the links between colonialism and present-day racism.

In this book, the minorities in West Germany are in general referred to as 'foreigners' because this term best reflects their dilemma. They came as foreign workers, they remain foreigners after many years in West Germany, and their children are born as foreigners. Indeed members of the second generation are doubly foreign. They are not granted citizenship, and are treated as foreign by the country of birth but are foreign, in all but name, in their parents' countries of origin too. The legal, socio-economic and cultural status of 'foreigner' is the distinguishing mark of the minorities in West Germany, just as being black is the clearest sign of minority status in Britain.

Some foreigners are more foreign than others. Germans rarely refer to white residents of high occupational status from other West European countries or from North America as foreigners. (There is an exception: members of NATO forces stationed in West Germany encounter quite a lot of hostility – although the main targets are black US soldiers.) However, the foreigners who have minority status are essentially the labour migrants and their dependants from the six main 'recruitment countries' (*Anwerbeländer*): Italy, Spain, Portugal, Greece, Yugoslavia and Turkey. Together, these nationalities made up 3.4 million of the 4.7 million foreigners in West Germany in 1982 – that is, 73 per cent. In addition there are 124,000 Africans and 255,000 Asians, mostly refugees. So altogether 3.8 million people may be seen as members of new ethnic minorities, that is four-fifths of the foreign population, or 6 per cent of the total population of West Germany. By comparison, just under 4 per cent of the population of Great Britain were people of New Commonwealth and Pakistani ethnic origin in 1981.

Chapter 3 stressed the growing share of people of Third World origin in various Western European countries. Table 3.7 shows that the share of Southern Europeans in West Germany's foreign population has declined in recent years, while the share of Turks, Africans and Asians has increased. In 1970 there were 469,000 Turks, about 16 per cent of the foreign population, while the number of Africans and Asians was insignificant. By 1982 there were 1.6 million Turks, a third of the foreign population. If Africans and Asians are included, there are nearly 2 million residents of Third World origin in West Germany, 42 per cent of the total foreign population.

All the major Southern European groups have declined both absolutely and relatively since 1974, while the number of Turks has continued to grow, through family reunification and births in West Germany. *All* increase in the foreign population since 1974 can be accounted for statistically by growth in the number of Turks. Half of all foreign children born in West Germany are Turkish. In recent years, public opinion has shifted towards defining the minority problem as a Turkish problem. The Turks are highly visible, through both distinctive appearance and inner-city concentration. Germans appear to feel more threatened by Turks and blacks than by Southern Europeans, presumably because of greater differences in religion, culture, language and socio-economic background. There is no doubt that Turks are the main target of the growing racism (see chapter 7). The racist jokes that circulate widely are *Türkenwitze*, neo-Nazi propaganda is directed specifically against them, and most racist attacks have been on Turks. They are the minority within the minority, and experience hostility even from other foreign nationalities.

Demographic structure

West Germany

In 1961, when labour migration was in its early stages, 80 per cent of the relatively small foreign population were workers, as table

Table 4.1. Foreign population and foreign workers in West Germany, 1961–81

Year	Foreign population 000s	Share in total population %	Foreign employees 000s	Share in total employees %	Non-employed 000s	Rate of economic activity %
1961	686	1.2	549	2.7	137	80.0
1962	n.a.	n.a.	711	3.2	n.a.	n.a.
1963	n.a.	n.a.	829	3.7	n.a.	n.a.
1964	n.a.	n.a.	986	4.4	n.a.	n.a.
1965	n.a.	n.a.	1,217	5.7	n.a.	n.a.
1966	n.a.	n.a.	1,313	6.1	n.a.	n.a.
1967	1,807	3.0	991	4.6	815	54.9
1968	1,924	3.2	1,090	5.2	834	56.6
1969	2,381	3.9	1,501	7.2	880	63.0
1970	2,977	4.9	1,949	9.1	1,028	65.5
1971	3,439	5.6	2,241	10.3	1,198	65.2
1972	3,527	5.7	2,352	10.8	1,174	66.7
1973	3,966	6.4	2,595	11.6	1,371	65.4
1974	4,127	6.7	2,286	10.9	1,841	55.4
1975	4,090	6.6	2,039	10.1	2,051	49.9
1976	3,948	6.4	1,921	9.5	2,027	48.7
1977	3,948	6.4	1,869	9.3	2,079	47.3
1978	3,981	6.5	1,864	9.1	2,117	46.8
1979	4,144	6.8	1,947	9.3	2,196	47.0
1980	4,453	7.2	2,016	9.5	2,438	46.5
1981	4,630	7.5	1,930	9.2	2,670	41.7

Sources: Bundesanstalt für arbeit 1974, Bundesminister für Arbeit und Sozialordnung 1981, Bundesminister für Arbeit und Sozialordnung 1982; *Statistisches Jahrbuch 1981*.

Notes: Employees do not include the unemployed or self-employed. These are included with dependants in the non-employed category. This biases the rate of economic activity slightly downward. Data are for 30 September; except for 1981 employment figure which is for 30 June. Total population means indigenous and foreign residents.

4.1 shows. For labour from the recruitment countries, this proportion would have been even higher because citizens of these countries comprised less than half of the foreign population at that time. During the recession of 1967–8, the number of foreign workers fell, and economic activity rates were only slightly more than 50 per cent. The increase in activity rates after the recession suggests that workers with dependants in West Germany were more likely to remain during the recession than those with no dependants.[4] As recruitment was stepped up, the number of foreign workers increased rapidly, but the entry of dependants was also high so that activity rates reached no higher than two-thirds, compared to about 40 per cent for the German population. After recruitment was stopped and the next recession began, many foreign workers left the country, but others brought in their families in sufficient numbers to maintain the size of the foreign population. As a result, the proportion of workers amongst foreigners fell to below 50 per cent, and in 1981 was only slightly higher than for Germans.

These changes in the economic activity rates of foreigners have been accompanied and caused by considerable demographic changes in the structure of the foreign population. What was originally a highly abnormal demographic structure, consisting mainly of young male adults, became more balanced as wives, husbands, children and elderly dependants joined the breadwinner. Table 4.2 shows the broad extent of these changes: the proportion of children in the population has increased at the expense of the proportion of men, while the proportion of women has remained almost constant. Though the population has increased since labour migration was stopped in late 1973, the number of men has

Table 4.2. Broad demographic changes in the foreign population of West Germany, 1969–81

| | ——1969—— | | ——1974—— | | ——1981—— | | 1974–81 |
	000s	%	000s	%	000s	%	% change
Children (0–15)	364	15.3	768	18.6	1,166	25.2	+51.8
Women (16+)	680	28.6	1,240	30.0	1,385	29.9	+11.7
Men (16+)	1,337	56.2	2,119	51.3	2,079	44.9	−1.9
Total	2,381	100.0	4,127	100.0	4,630	100.0	+12.2

Sources: *Wirtschaft und Statistik*, No. 5, May 1971; *OECD SOPEMI 1982*.

declined, though it too is now on the increase again. Most of the increase since 1974 is attributable to children.

This broad pattern in the changing demographic structure of the foreign population does not hold for all nationalities. Indeed, the increase in the foreign population over the period 1974 to 1981 is a feature only of the Turks; the populations of all other significant minorities declined. This is seen in table 4.3, as are the relative sizes of the proportional changes in the six minority populations. The Greek and Spanish populations have decreased substantially, including reductions in the number of children. Whatever the direction of these proportional changes over time, their effect on the distribution of men, women and children has been roughly similar for all nationalities: to increase the proportion of children and to decrease the proportion of men, leading to more balanced demographic structures.

This process of 'normalisation' in the demographic structure of the foreign population is by no means complete. Considerable imbalances remain in the age and sex structure. There are still many more men than women, though the number of women per thousand men has increased from 509 in 1969 to 666 in 1981. Table 4.4 shows the extent of the variation in this ratio between nationalities in 1974 and 1981. The low ratio in the Italian population arises from the free movement of labour enjoyed by Italians as citizens from an EEC member state and the preponderance of males among mobile temporary labour.

In comparison with the total population of West Germany, the foreign population contains a high proportion of children. Table 4.3 shows that for all nationalities except the Turks this proportion is roughly equal to the average of 25.2 per cent for all foreigners. In all cases the proportion is greater than that of 17.9 per cent for the total population. For the Turkish population, the proportion of children is now very high, though this was not the case in 1974. The increasing number of Turkish children has contributed significantly to the growth of this population despite the fact that the proportion of Turkish women remains rather low. One reason for this is the relatively large family size among Turks.

The high proportion of children among foreigners is partly due to the very low proportion of elderly foreigners. Most of the young migrants of the sixties and early seventies are even now aged less than 45, and only 2 per cent are over 65, as table 4.5 shows. This

Table 4.3. Demographic changes in the foreign population (% unless specified otherwise) of West Germany, 1974–81

Country of nationality	1974				1981				1974–81: % change			
	000s	Children	Women	Men	000s	Children	Women	Men	Total	Children	Women	Men
Greece	406	22.7	35.5	42.1	299	27.8	32.8	39.5	−26.4	−9.4	−31.5	−31.1
Italy	629	21.5	25.0	53.7	625	23.4	26.6	50.1	−0.7	+8.1	+5.9	−7.4
Portugal	122	16.4	31.1	52.5	109	27.5	33.0	40.4	−10.0	+48.9	−3.8	−31.9
Spain	272	19.1	30.1	51.1	177	22.6	31.6	45.8	−35.1	−23.3	−31.0	−41.9
Turkey	1,028	22.1	26.6	51.4	1,546	35.9	25.4	38.7	+50.5	+145.1	+43.8	+13.3
Yugoslavia	708	11.4	31.8	56.8	637	22.3	32.3	45.4	−10.0	+74.8	−8.5	−30.0
All foreigners	4,127	18.6	30.0	51.3	4,630	25.2	29.9	44.9	+12.2	+51.8	+11.7	−1.9

Source: OECD SOPEMI 1982.

Note: children are defined as aged 0–15.

Table 4.4. Number of women per 1,000 men, West Germany, 1974 and 1981

Country of nationality	1974	1981	Change
Greece	843	836	−7
Italy	466	531	+65
Portugal	592	832	+240
Spain	589	699	+110
Turkey	518	658	+69
Yugoslavia	560	711	+151
All foreigners	**585**	**666**	**+81**

Source: *OECD SOPEMI 1982.*

Note: women and men aged 16+.

concentration of foreigners in the young adult age groups is, of course, highly advantageous to the German economy, but it also contributes to the relatively high birth rate and growth of the foreign population.

Table 4.5 also shows that males outnumber females in all ages except those 65 and over (who are mostly from industrialised countries and atypical of foreign workers) and that there is a steady progression towards fewer females at older ages. There are, in fact, considerably more single men than women in both adult age groups, as table 4.6 shows.

Whereas the numbers of married men and women aged 15 to 44 are roughly equal, there are about twice as many married men aged 45 to 64 as women. Part of this imbalance is due to the younger ages of wives than husbands, but it also indicates that older men are more likely than younger men to have families remaining in the countries of origin. The greater number of boys than girls in the foreign population reflects the tendency to leave girls rather than boys with grandparents in the country of origin.

The demographic differences between the total and foreign populations in West Germany are important. The German population was – and still is – ageing, with shortages of young adults caused by the low birth rate during the economic crisis of the thirties and after the second world war, and a deficit of males resulting from war deaths. In addition, the increased length of

Table 4.5. Age and sex structure of the foreign population (% unless specified otherwise) of West Germany compared with total West German population, 1981

	Total West German population	Foreign population			
Age		All	Female	Male	Number of females per 1,000 males
0–4	4.8	7.1	7.9	6.5	869
5–14	13.1	16.6	18.4	15.4	843
15–44	44.6	60.4	59.9	60.9	699
45–64	22.1	13.8	11.2	15.6	508
65+	15.5	2.1	2.6	1.8	1,037
Total	**100**	**100**	**100**	**100**	**708**

Sources: OECD SOPEMI 1982; Statistisches Jahrbuch 1982.

Table 4.6. Number of women per 1,000 men by marital status and age, foreign population West Germany, 1981

	Age	
Marital status	15–44	45–64
Single	376	358
Married	1,064	485
Widowed/divorced	1,255	1,659
All	**699**	**508**

Source: Bevölkerung und Erwerbstätigkeit, Reihe 1.4, Ausländer, 1981.

schooling, the withdrawal of men from productive employment for military service and the reduction in working hours all contributed to the labour shortage.

Though the demographic structure of the foreign population has changed considerably since the early seventies, the economic advantages to West Germany have not yet been eroded. There are very few foreigners of pensionable age in West Germany, so that foreign workers are still subsidising the pensions of elderly Germans. Table 4.7 shows the enormous disparity between the foreign and total populations in the ratio of elderly dependants to the population of working age. The higher proportion of children in the foreign population does not compensate for this; the total population has a dependency ratio of 747 per thousand of the population aged 15 to 44 compared to only 427 per thousand for the foreign population. When the older, less productive working age population is included, these ratios are reduced to 499 and 348 respectively. When only the labour force, rather than the entire population of working age, is considered, the foreign population has higher dependency ratios for children, but a lower dependency ratio overall.

Table 4.7. Number of dependants per thousand of adult population and per thousand of labour force (by age, total and foreign populations), West Germany, 1981

Age of dependants	Population 15–44		Population 45–64		Labour force	
	Total	Foreign	Total	Foreign	Total	Foreign
0–4	107	117	72	95	105	140
5–14	293	275	196	224	288	329
0–14	400	391	268	319	393	469
65+	347	35	232	29	341	42
0–14; 65+	747	427	499	348	734	511
All	–	–	–	–	1,203	979

Sources: OECD SOPEMI 1982; Statistisches Jahrbuch 1982.

The foreign population is thus supporting a disproportionately large proportion of the services for the young and the elderly. Perhaps surprisingly, table 4.7 reveals that when only the younger adult population is considered, the child dependency ratio is also lower for foreigners than for the total population, and it is only when the older population of working age is included that foreigners have a slightly higher child dependency ratio. This latter high ratio is a temporary phenomenon due to the low number of older foreign workers, and will obviously decrease as the population ages.

The higher birth rate of the foreign population compensates for the low birth rate of the German population. Foreigners currently comprise 7.5 per cent of the total population of West Germany, but account for about 13 per cent of births. Half of these foreign births are of Turkish nationality. Though there is a tendency for the number of children per family to decline after migration to industrialised societies, the total number of births is expected to remain high for a considerable period, especially since there is now a large number of young foreigners entering adulthood. The presence of the younger sections of the foreign population is advantageous in that they will prevent a substantial decline in the number of young people entering the labour market in coming years. The labour market advantages of the foreign population are thus prolonged by virtue of its youthful demographic structure. In the current situation of economic stagnation, however, these advantages are no longer appreciated and foreigners are seen as dispensable. Foreign workers suffer disproportionately in times of recession, and the current recession is particularly severe. What is more, the growing number of foreign school-leavers, with few prospects of employment, are beginning to be seen as a serious social threat.

Looking further ahead, population projections based on trends in 1980 suggest that the German population of West Germany will decline during the next 20 years, from its 1980 level of 57 million to 52 million in 2000, while the foreign population will increase from 4.6 million to 5.6.[5] By the year 2000, the foreign population would make up more than 10 per cent of the total population, with a continuing high growth rate due to the young age structure. This projection of the foreign population is based on the assumption that no further immigration to West Germany will occur, and must therefore be regarded as conservative since official estimates suggest that there are 600,000 children and 300,000 spouses of foreigners, remaining in countries of origin, who are entitled to enter West Germany under current regulations.[6] About half of these dependants are Turks. In addition, further labour immigration can be expected to occur when Spain, Portugal and Turkey join the EEC. It is with this knowledge, and in view of the present recession, that the West German government has announced its plans to repatriate millions of foreigners in the coming years.

Great Britain
The demography of settlement of minority populations has been similar in Great Britain to other countries of Western Europe. The

Table 4.8. Minority populations in Great Britain by whether born in the UK or abroad by birthplace or parents' or head of household's birthplace, 1971 and 1981

Birthplace	1971 Population 000s	Not UK-born %	UK-born %	1981 Population 000s	Not UK-born %	UK-born %
New Commonwealth and Pakistan	1,478	77.9	22.1	2,207	59.4	40.6
Old Commonwealth	146	97.5	2.5	n.a.	n.a.	n.a.
Irish Republic	1,071	66.2	33.8	949	46.9	53.1
Europe	784	80.7	19.3	n.a.	n.a.	n.a.
Other	402	86.4	13.6	n.a.	n.a.	n.a.
All	**3,881**	**76.9**	**23.1**	**4,470**	**56.8**	**43.2**

Sources: 1971 Census; 1981 Census.

Notes: The 1971 data include those born abroad plus those born in the UK to parents who were both born abroad in the same birthplace category. They exclude the UK-born with parents born in different broad categories (about 87,000 people). The 1981 data include all people living in households with a non-UK-born head. Both sets of data include some white British people who were born abroad (1971) or who live with a head of household who was born abroad (1981), and exclude some members of ethnic minorities living in Britain whose parents were born in Britain (1971) or who live in a household with a UK-born head (1981). Estimates for the New Commonwealth and Pakistani population in 1971 which take account of these factors indicate that 35 per cent were born in the UK, and by 1981 roughly half were born in the UK. Similar estimates for other groups are not available.

first to migrate were young men for employment, followed later by their dependants. Since many migrants, such as the Irish and many Commonwealth citizens, came to Britain without restriction, the process of settlement occurred more quickly than in West Germany, for example.

The increase in the number of people born outside the UK has been shown in table 3.1. Such residents comprised 6.2 per cent of the total population of Great Britain in 1981; roughly half were female and 10 per cent were children (aged 0 to 15 years). These data, however, do not allow comparison with other countries of Western Europe because they exclude children born in the UK to immigrant parents. The 1971 and 1981 Census data included these children in statistics of the minority population. Table 4.8 shows the proportions born in the UK for various minority populations. The available data show that these proportions are increasing as immigration is reduced and natural increase becomes the main determinant of the structures of the populations.

Table 4.9 shows the changes in the structure of the minority population. The proportion of children has increased, while the roughly equal proportions of women and men have both decreased slightly. Though the proportion of children in the minority

Table 4.9. Broad demographic changes in the structure of the minority population in Great Britain, 1971 and 1981

	1971		1981		1971–81
	000s	%	000s	%	% change
Children	790	22.1	1,250	28.0	+58.2
Women	1,383	38.7	1,604	35.9	+16.0
Men	1,397	39.1	1,615	36.1	+15.6
All	**3,570**	**100**	**4,470**	**100**	+25.2

Source: 1971 Census; 1981 Census.

Note: These data are not strictly comparable. In 1971 data refer to ages 0–14 and 15+; the 1981 data refers to ages 0–15 and 16+. No account is taken of this in the percentage change. Further non-comparability arises from the fact that the 1971 data refer to people born abroad and to people born in the UK with both parents born abroad, whilst the 1981 data refer to people living in households with a non-UK-born household head. Both sets of data include some white British people and exclude some members of ethnic minorities living in Britain. The 1971 data exclude UK-born people with both parents born in Ireland, and with both parents born abroad but in different places.

population is high compared to the total population, there has been a rough balance between the sexes for at least 10 years indicating the more settled nature of minority populations in Great Britain than in West Germany.

When children are included, the overall proportion of females is slightly less than half and has been so since 1971 at least. Table 4.10 shows the ratio of females per 1,000 males by birthplace or by parents' or head of household's birthplace. In 1971 all minority populations were fairly evenly balanced with proportions of

Table 4.10. Ratio of females per 1,000 males by birthplace or parents' or head of household's birthplace, Great Britain, 1971 and 1981

Birthplace	1971	1981	Change
New Commonwealth and Pakistan	853	956	+103
Old Commonwealth	1,159	n.a.	n.a.
Irish Republic	1,062	996	−66
Europe	1,164	n.a.	n.a.
Other	911	n.a.	n.a.
All	**983**	**980**	−3

Sources and notes: See table 4.8.

females ranging from 46 per cent for those of New Commonwealth and Pakistani origin to 54 per cent for those from Europe. By 1981 the two groups for which data are available had moved towards a more equal sex distribution.[7] The population of New Commonwealth and Pakistani origin experienced the greatest change over the 10-year period. This population is the most similar to foreign populations in other countries of Western Europe, but its proportion of females in 1971 was higher than those in West Germany in 1981 because of its more settled character.

Despite the earlier settlement of minorities in Britain than in other countries of Western Europe, the minority population is still very young compared to the total population. Table 4.11 shows the relative concentration of the minority population in the younger age groups and the marked sparseness of members of retirement age. There are also more males than females at all ages except post-retirement, though allowance must be made for the earlier age of retirement for women than men. This pattern is similar to, but less pronounced than, that found for foreigners in West Germany. The greater proportion of females in Britain arises partly from the earlier migration and settlement but also from the fact that many early migrants from the Irish Republic and the West Indies were young women.

The minority population in Britain has fulfilled the same functions as that in West Germany. The early migrants were mostly young adults who came without dependants to fill labour

Table 4.11. Age and sex structure of the population (% unless specified otherwise) living in households with a non-UK-born head with age comparison with those with UK-born head, Great Britain, 1981

| Age of household residents | UK-born head of household | Non-UK-born head of household | | | |
		All	Female	Male	Number females per 1,000 males
0–4	5.9	8.2	8.1	8.3	954
5–15	16.1	19.8	19.4	20.1	947
16–44	39.9	45.4	45.6	45.1	990
45–R	19.9	18.4	16.2	20.6	771
R+	18.1	8.2	10.7	5.8	1,802
All	**100**	**100**	**100**	**100**	**980**

Source: 1981 Census.

Notes: R denotes age of retirement, which is 60 for women and 65 for men. This difference between the sexes makes the last two age groups non-comparable. At ages 45+, there are 998 females per 1,000 males.

shortages created by the second world war and by the low birth rates of the twenties and thirties. As cheap labour with few dependants they contributed heavily to the economic growth of the country and to the welfare state. Today, the minority population still has lower overall dependency ratios than the indigenous population as Table 4.12 shows. Though the ratio of children to adults of working age is greater for the minority population than for those living in households with a UK-born head, the low dependency ratio for those of pensionable age more than compensates for this, resulting in considerably lower overall ratios. As in West Germany, the minority population continues to subsidise the welfare services of the indigenous population.

The higher dependency ratio for children among the minority population arises from the higher birth rate, which in turn arises partly from age structure and partly from higher fertility (i.e. number of children per family). In 1981, 13.1 per cent of births in England and Wales were to non-UK-born mothers, when the non-UK-born population comprised 6.6 per cent of the total population

Table 4.12. Ratio of dependants per 1,000 adult population by age and population living in households with UK-born head and non-UK-born head, Great Britain, 1981

Age of dependents	Population 16–44		Population 16 to retirement	
	UK-born	Non-UK-born	UK-born	Non-UK-born
0–4	147	181	98	129
5–15	404	436	270	310
0–15	552	617	368	439
R+	455	182	303	129
0–15; R+	1,006	798	672	568

Source: 1981 Census.

Note: R denotes age of retirement, which is 60 for women and 65 for men.

Table 4.13. Births and births per 1,000 women aged 16–44 by birthplace of mother, England and Wales, 1981

Mother's birthplace	Births		Births per 1,000 women
	number	%	
UK	551,400	86.9	62
New Commonwealth and Pakistan	53,200	8.4	116
Old Commonwealth	2,300	0.4	66
Irish Republic	8,300	1.3	67
EEC	5,700	0.9	66
Other	10,600	2.1	67
All	**634,300**	**100.0**	**65**

Sources: OPCS Monitor FM1 83/2, Births by birthplace of parent 1981; 1981 Census.

Note: Births to UK-born women of non-UK origin are included in UK data.

of England and Wales. About two-thirds of these births were to mothers born in the New Commonwealth and Pakistan as table 4.13 shows. The higher birth rate of the minority population is demographically advantageous to Britain in that it decelerates the ageing caused mainly by the fertility decline of the indigenous population. This higher birth rate is likely to persist for some time due more to the age structure of the population than to fertility rates.

The population of New Commonwealth and Pakistani (NCWP) origin receives a great deal more attention in Britain than do other minorities. This group is in the most similar position to minorities in other West European countries. In 1981 it made up almost half of the 4.5 million people living in households with a non-UK-born head, and within the group the largest minorities originate from the West Indies and from India.

Table 4.14 shows that a quarter to a half of the different minority populations were born in the UK, the highest proportion being among West Indians. This population also has the highest ratio of females to males, a result of the early migration of single women and the earlier settlement of dependants. In contrast, the population of Bangladeshi origin has the lowest proportion born in the UK and the lowest ratio of females to males, reflecting the

Table 4.14. Population living in households with NCWP-born head by birthplace of head of household, by whether born in UK and ratio of females per 1,000 males, Great Britain, 1981

Birthplace of household head	Population 000s	% born in UK	Females per 1,000 males
India	674	38.8	978
Pakistan	295	40.0	832
Bangladesh	65	26.2	614
West Indies	546	50.1	1,058
East Africa	181	26.9	972
Mediterranean	170	46.6	979
Far East	120	33.1	894
Other	156	37.0	948
All	**2,207**	**40.6**	**956**

Source: 1981 Census.

Note: This population is estimated to include 15 per cent white people and exclude 10 per cent of the actual population of NCWP origin. These biases vary according to birthplace.

later migration from Bangladesh and the extent to which dependants are still waiting to come to Britain.

The different stages of settlement are also reflected in the age distributions of the various populations, as table 4.15 shows. The population of Indian origin has the highest proportion of pensionable age, due partly to the migration of elderly dependants, especially those expelled from East Africa, many of whom were born in India. The population of NCWP origin has a younger age structure than in households with a non-UK-born head (see table 4.11), and has correspondingly higher dependency ratios for children and lower ratios for the retired.

Table 4.15. Age distribution of population living in households with a NCWP-born head by birthplace of head of household, Great Britain, 1981

Birthplace of household head	Age group				
	0–4	5–15	16–44	45–R	R+
India	10.1	23.2	45.8	15.2	5.8
Pakistan	18.5	26.8	41.3	11.6	1.7
Bangladesh	17.8	23.5	42.9	14.7	1.1
West Indies	6.7	24.8	46.9	18.7	2.9
NCWP	10.7	22.7	48.2	14.5	3.9
UK	5.9	16.1	39.9	19.9	18.1

Source and note: See table 4.14.

Overall, the population of NCWP origin has a lower dependency ratio when the population aged 16 to 44 is considered, but a slightly higher ratio when the entire population of working age is included. In comparison with the population living in households with a UK-born head, however, the population of NCWP origin has low overall dependency ratios. Table 4.16 shows dependency ratios by birthplace of head of household. For elderly dependants the ratios are very low and, except for the Bangladeshi and Pakistani populations, more than compensate for the higher child–adult ratios.

The variation in these dependency ratios mainly results from the different birth rates of different minority populations. These in turn depend on fertility. Table 4.17 shows births per 1,000 women

Table 4.16. Ratio of dependants per 1,000 adult population by age by birthplace of head of household, Great Britain, 1981

Age of dependants	Birthplace of head of household				
	NCWP	India	Pakistan	Bangladesh	West Indies
Population 16–44					
0–4	222	221	448	415	143
5–15	471	507	649	548	529
0–15	693	727	1,097	963	672
R+	81	127	41	26	62
0–15; R+	774	854	1,138	989	734
Population 16 to retirement					
0–4	171	166	350	309	102
5–15	362	380	507	408	378
0–15	533	546	856	717	480
R+	62	95	32	19	44
0–15; R+	595	641	888	736	524

Source and note: see table 4.14.

Table 4.17. Births, and births per 1,000 women aged 15 to 44 by birthplace of mother, England and Wales, 1981

Mother's birthplace	Births		Number of births per 1,000 women
	number	%	
India	12,400	23.3	109
Pakistan	13,300	25.0	248
Bangladesh	3,100	5.8	306
West Indies	6,200	11.7	65
NCWP	53,200	100.0	112

Source: OPCS MONITOR FM1 83/2, Births by birthplace of parent 1981.

Note: This NCWP rate differs slightly from that shown in table 4.13 because women aged 15 are included here. The data exclude births to women of non-UK origin born in the UK.

of childbearing age, and it is seen that the more settled populations have lower fertility. The higher fertility levels of the less demo-graphically settled minority populations are expected to fall, though the age structure will result in high birth rates for some time. Projections suggest that by the end of the century there will be about 3 million people of NCWP origin living in Great Britain.[8]

Concentration in the inner cities

Minorities make up 5 to 14 per cent of the total population in the industrial countries of Western Europe, but their regional distribution is very uneven, so their impact is much greater in certain areas. The original migrant workers came to the growing industrial conurbations, where their labour was needed, but where problems of urban stress, overcrowding and lack of amenities were greatest. In Britain, black communities have become established mainly in London, the west Midlands and the industrial areas of the north-west and north-east of England. In France, foreign residents are heavily concentrated in the Paris area, and around Lyons and Marseilles. Foreigners in Belgium are mainly in the Walloon industrial and mining areas, and above all in Brussels, where a quarter of the population are foreigners. In the Netherlands the highest concentrations of foreign residents are to be found in the four largest cities of the western conurbation: Amsterdam, Rotterdam, The Hague and Utrecht.[9]

The pattern in West Germany is similar. Few foreigners live in the rural regions of Schleswig Holstein, Rhineland Palatinate, Lower Saxony and northern Bavaria. In some districts foreign residents make up less than one per cent of the total population. Foreigners are concentrated in the industrial growth areas of the post-war boom; the Ruhr, the Rhine–Main conurbation around Frankfurt, the newer industrial areas around Stuttgart and Mannheim, and in southern Bavaria. Half of all foreign residents are to be found in cities (officially defined as towns with over 100,000 residents), where they often make up a large proportion of the total population: 24 per cent in Frankfurt, 18 per cent in Stuttgart, 17 per cent in Munich, 15 per cent in Cologne, Remscheid, Mannheim and Düsseldorf and 13 per cent in West Berlin.[10]

The distribution of nationalities varies. Over half the foreigners in Berlin, Cologne, Duisburg and Bremen are Turks, while Yugoslavs are the largest single group (but not the majority of the foreign population) in Frankfurt, Munich and Stuttgart. Sometimes these patterns result directly from employers' recruitment preferences; between 1960 and 1973 Volkswagen hired mainly Italians, so today over 70 per cent of the foreign population of Wolfsburg have that nationality. The Ruhr mines recruited mainly in Turkey, so Turks are now the most numerous group in towns like Gelsenkirchen, Hamm, Herne, Duisburg and Bottrop.

Within the cities, foreign residents are anything but evenly dispersed. In West Berlin, for instance, Turks have become so highly concentrated in the old working-class area of Kreuzberg, that politicians and the media speak of a 'ghetto'. In Frankfurt, the city with the highest foreign share in population (24 per cent on average), foreigners only make up 8 to 10 per cent of residents in outer suburbs like Nieder Eschbach or Harheim, or in the middle-class areas like Dornbusch and Eschersheim. In the district around the main railway station, foreigners make up 70 to 80 per cent of the population and, in the industrial districts, over a third of the total population.[11]

Concentration in the inner cities is typical for the new ethnic minorities throughout Western Europe. It is in part due to their recruitment by manufacturing industries sited in the major conurbations. It is also a result of the way the housing market has reacted to immigration. In Britain, as the white working class moved out of the inner cities into suburban estates (both council and owner-occupied), low standard inner-city accommodation became available. The newcomers had no choice but to accept such housing, initially as private tenants. Employment patterns, together with fears of racism and discrimination, have kept the minorities largely in such areas, even when they have been able to finance the shift to home ownership.

In West Germany, most foreign workers were initially housed by their employers, usually in huts or hostels on the work site. This accommodation had two major drawbacks: it allowed employers to control their workers' private lives, and it precluded family reunification. Indeed there were cases in which husband and wife, both recruited as workers, were forced to live in separate hostels.[12] Most foreign workers got out of employers' accommodation as quickly as they could. In 1972, 38 per cent of male foreign workers and 24 per cent of female foreign workers were still housed by employers.[13] Since then, this type of accommodation has declined considerably, although no figures are now available.

Most foreigners in West Germany are left with the option of either applying for housing through state subsidised 'social housing associations' (*Sozialwohnungsbaugesellschaften*), or trying their luck on the private market. Social housing generally consists of fairly modern flats of a reasonable standard, often in outlying suburbs. It appears that relatively few foreigners have found accommodation of this type. This may be partly due to discrimination in allocation, and partly to the fact that foreigners have not been resident in the area concerned for long enough to reach the top of the long waiting lists. Social housing also has certain drawbacks. Despite the name, it is often far from cheap; estates are often distant from workplaces, which means long travel times and the need to run a car; the outlying sites and the attitudes of German residents may socially isolate foreigners.

So most foreigners have to depend on the private market. Prices are so high that very few manual workers (German or foreign) can afford to purchase housing (although some foreigners are now trying to do so, whatever the financial sacrifice, as they simply cannot get adequate rented accommodation). Most people live in flats rented from private landlords, typically in blocks with five to ten dwellings. Post-war systems of allocation and rent controls have been removed, so landlords can pick tenants at will.

Foreigners find themselves the victims of a double process of discrimination. On the one hand, owners of better quality housing in areas with reasonable environmental conditions often refuse to rent to foreigners. On the other hand, landlords of poor quality housing in areas of urban stress exploit foreigners' weak position to demand extortionate rents. As a result, some inner-city streets and districts become predominantly minority housing areas. Overcrowding and pressure on social amenities in such areas further encourage better-off Germans to flee to the suburbs. Those remaining belong to socially disadvantaged groups. The West German inner cities are not purely foreign housing areas, but concentrations of the social groups at the bottom of the socio-economic ladder.[14]

Inner-city concentration has disadvantages for the minorities. Most obvious is the material deprivation. An officially commissioned survey in the late seventies showed that 15 per cent of the foreigners interviewed had no toilet in their dwellings (compared with 4 per cent of the Germans); 42 per cent of the foreigners had no bath or shower (6 per cent of the Germans had none); 45 per cent lacked running hot water (15 per cent of the Germans had none); and 58 per cent had no central heating (25 per cent of the Germans had none).[15] The survey also showed that foreigners pay more rent than Germans for comparable housing, and concluded that foreigners' inferior housing was in part due to discrimination and in part to foreigners' low occupational status.[16] Lack of such amenities as schooling, medical care and recreation facilities is most marked in inner-city areas. This is a special handicap for foreign children since their schooling and therefore their future occupational opportunities are severely jeopardised. The problem hardly affects Germans, for most of those remaining in the inner cities are elderly. The situation is growing worse in the current fiscal crisis of the cities which, in turn, is partly a result of the decline of the inner cities. As better paid Germans move out, the cities' tax income falls, while at the same time demands for social amenities and welfare benefits increase. There is less money to meet more needs, and the quality of inner-city life deteriorates yet further.

The trend towards concentration and semi-segregation in the inner cities also has advantages for the minorities. It offers them protection from racism and discrimination, and makes it easier for them to maintain and develop their own cultures, and informal networks of mutual aid that are vital both to newcomers and to other members of the community who find themselves in difficulties.[17] Ethnic shops, cafés, cultural centres, mosques, churches, sports associations, parents' groups, political organisations and the like can be set up. At present, such institutions are developing rapidly in West German cities. They are the focal point of growing minority communities, and although they improve cultural, social and political life they also confirm and reinforce segregation by West German society.

From temporary recruitment to non-intended settlement

Economic and social conditions in the country of origin, migrants' education, culture and motivations are all important determinants of subsequent experience and social position in Western Europe.

Recruitment systems, such as those run by the German Federal Labour Office, had a built-in bias towards selecting the most experienced and competent workers from the most developed regions. For instance, the Turkish recruitment agency of the Labour Office was in Istanbul, and a large proportion of the workers hired came from the more developed western regions. In 1973, 101,000 Turks were recruited through the Labour Office, and no less than a quarter of them came from the three major cities of Istanbul, Ankara and Izmir.[18] A survey carried out in the late seventies found that only 4 per cent of Turkish workers in West Germany came from the most economically backward areas; the figures for other nationalities were: Greeks 52 per cent, Spaniards 34 per cent, Yugoslavs 25 per cent and Italians 86 per cent. On the other hand, 68 per cent of Turks, 34 per cent of Yugoslavs, 24 per cent of Spaniards, 16 per cent of Greeks and 8 per cent of Italians came from the most developed areas of their countries.[19] However, some rural migrants did move initially to cities in their own country before being recruited to work in West Germany, so more foreign workers may have come from underdeveloped areas than the study suggests.

The same survey found that a large proportion of migrants had been skilled workers in their own countries: 55 per cent of Turks, 56 per cent of Yugoslavs, 58 per cent of Greeks, 38 per cent of Spaniards and 31 per cent of Italians. Significantly, only one-third of those who had had skilled jobs before migration were able to get skilled employment in West Germany.[20] Of course vocational training in the country of origin may differ from West German training in content and quality, but this is not sufficient to explain the extent of deskilling (especially in sectors like building), nor its persistence after many years. Foreign workers were also found to have standards of education and vocational training far above the average for their countries of origin, although not up to West German levels. Yugoslav workers were especially highly qualified, with lengths of schooling approaching German standards. No less than 40 per cent of Yugoslav workers had completed vocational training courses before migration, compared with around a fifth of the other four nationalities.

The survey came to the conclusion that the West German recruitment system led to the 'migration of an elite of the working class'.[21] This finding is underlined by the differences between Italian workers and those from the other countries. Since 1968, Italians have had the right to free movement within the EEC, and came of their own accord rather than through official recruitment. They were not selected by the Labour Office, they came from less developed regions, and had poorer educational and skill levels than other migrants. The West German authorities claimed that during the period of mass recruitment migration was helping to ease unemployment and encourage development in the countries of origin. The workers recruited were in fact the young, skilled, dynamic people needed for development, rather than the unemployed and underemployed rural masses. In the early seventies, when West German industry was drawing in hundreds of thousands of new foreign workers each year, loss of labour became a major constraint on the economies of the recruitment countries. Yugoslavia, Spain and Greece actually started taking measures to prevent emigration of skilled workers.

Recruitment was geared to West German employers' requirements, and took no account of workers' social needs. The consequences for family life were often serious. In early years, emphasis was on male workers, and many families were deprived of their men for years, seeing them only briefly during the summer holidays. In the mid sixties, as West German industry intensified production with increased division of labour and deskilling, employers requested more women workers. It became common for women to follow their husbands as workers, rather than as dependants. But the wife might be recruited by a factory in Hamburg, while the husband was in Munich, which could mean years of separation until one of them could get permission to take up employment in the other town.

At the height of the period of labour migration, a long waiting list developed. A Turkish man might have to wait six to eight years before getting the chance to come to Istanbul for medical and occupational tests prior to recruitment. The waiting list was shorter for women, and many women preceded their men to Germany. Once there, they could try to persuade the employer to recruit the husband by name, to avoid the long wait. But this form of migration also involved some years of separation, and sometimes had a disastrous impact on the families concerned. Turkish women were ill-prepared by their culture and socialisation for the role of family breadwinner in a strange land. Husbands lost their self-respect through living off their wives' earnings, and worried about what they were up to in immoral Germany. Many women who went through this experience were not willing to return to their old sex-role once their husbands arrived, and conflicts arose.[22]

Few foreign workers came to West Germany with the intention of staying for long, let alone settling permanently. The survey already referred to found that 70 per cent of those interviewed had originally intended to stay in West Germany for less than five years. Yet three-quarters of all respondents had in fact already been there over five years. Only 17 per cent had not changed their original plans.[23] These findings show how little the subjective intentions of migrants actually permit prediction of behaviour. The foreign workers' original plans coincided with the wishes of the West German employers and state: they wanted to work hard and live frugally for a few years, in order to save enough to improve their situation upon return to the country of origin. Indeed many migrants became temporary wage workers in West Germany in the hope of escaping permanent proletarisation in the home country. Some were farmers who wanted to save money to buy land or to improve their livestock and equipment. Others hoped to set up a small business, generally in the services sector: a shop, a bar or taxi.

Many migrants did achieve their aims and returned home with better economic prospects. Success depended not only on their own efforts, but on economic and political developments in the country of origin. Economic growth and the end of dictatorship in Spain and Greece have encouraged many workers to return, while crisis and military government have made it increasingly difficult for Turks to do so. Turks have found that their savings are insufficient to offer security upon return. Unemployment, the collapse of small businesses, increasing civil unrest and political repression have forced them to stay on in West Germany, especially since the 1973 ban on labour immigration, which made return irreversible.

In the sixties, some Turkish workers in West Germany started a scheme for investing their savings in the setting up of small and medium industrial enterprises, to provide them with jobs upon return. The scheme has received financial and administrative support from the West German and Turkish governments. It is estimated that 230,000 Turkish workers have invested over DM 700 million in such 'workers companies'. About a hundred firms of this type were said to be providing about 10,000 jobs for returned migrants in 1982[24] – only a small percentage of the number of workers who have invested in this way (and just this type of small company is now under great pressure from the monetarist policies of the military regime, which is opening up the economy to international capital). The Dutch government has supported similar projects in Turkey and Morocco. On the whole, it is reported, such schemes have not been successful.[25]

The foreign workers who remain in West Germany are those who have not been able to achieve their aims, or whose aims have changed in response to the experience of migration.[26] Apart from conditions in the countries of origin, the situation in West Germany has also played a part. Workers recruited abroad received no adequate preparation. They had heard of good wages, but nobody told them about large tax and social security deductions, or about high prices and rents. Many found it impossible to save enough to achieve their aims. As the hope of return receded into an uncertain future, many workers found it intolerable to spend the best years of their lives alone and isolated. So the wife or husband came too, and the children followed. As the children grew up and went to school in West Germany, links with the home village or town weakened. The area of origin became a place to be visited during the annual holidays. Remittances declined, and a higher proportion of income was spent on housing, household equipment and social life in West Germany. The decisive turning point in the transition from temporary migration to settlement is no doubt the decision to bring up children in a new country. But even then, most first-generation migrants still do not make a conscious decision to remain permanently. The realisation that migration is irreversible comes – if at all – when parents find their children speaking German better than Greek or Spanish or Turkish. Then they realise that their children will stay, and that if they themselves return, the family will be irrevocably broken.

The subjective side of the transition from temporary migration to settlement is not yet complete. When asked, the majority of foreigners in Germany still say that they plan to return home within the next four years. This answer was given in 1977 by 62 per cent of Greeks, 52 per cent of Italians and 44 per cent of Turks. On the other hand, 36 per cent of Turks saw that they were going to have to stay on for between five to 16 years longer, compared with 29 per cent of Greeks, 25 per cent of Italians, 33 per cent of Yugoslavs and 18 per cent of Spaniards.[27] Foreign workers who were asked about their future work plans in 1980 were less optimistic: only 17 per cent hoped to return to the country of origin. The figure for Turks was only 10 per cent. Hopes of returning to work in the country of origin were strongly correlated with age: only 11 per cent of 15–24-year-olds and 14 per cent of 25–29-year-olds saw their prospects in return, compared with 25 per cent of respondents aged over 45.[28]

The trend towards settlement is shown clearly by official statistics on length of stay. In September 1982, the average length of stay of all foreign residents in West Germany was 10 years, and 2.2 million foreigners had already been resident for over 10 years.[29] How many of them are going to stay permanently? Nobody can answer this important question, because it is impossible to predict the development of the world economy, which determines employment opportunities and social perspectives in both the countries of origin and the countries of immigration. Nor can accurate forecasts be made on political and ideological factors that cause racism, nor on the responses of minority communities. However it can be said with certainty that a large proportion of the former migrants and their descendants will stay permanently. Politicians and planners must recognise this fact.

5. Migrants and minorities in the labour force

Import of labour was a crucial factor in post-war economic growth throughout the capitalist world. Immigration of workers affected not only industrial growth, but also economic structure, levels of wages, profits and investments. It also played a part in the restructuring of the working class, and in shifting patterns of class consciousness. This chapter tries to answer two basic questions. What effect has the transition from temporary labour migration to permanent settlement had on the employment of former migrants who are becoming settlers? And, how has the role of migrant or minority labour changed during the period of economic stagnation which started in the early seventies?

Table 5.1 gives information on the number of economically active persons of migrant origin in seven Western European countries in about 1960, 1970, 1974 (the turning point in labour migration) and 1980. Care has to be taken in interpreting these figures, especially when making international comparisons, or comparisons with data on populations of migrant origin (for example, tables 3.8 and 3.9). Labour market data has been collected by different bodies, using different definitions, at different times. The figures merely indicate trends.

The general picture is of a big increase in the number of foreign or minority workers in the sixties and early seventies. After 1974, foreign employment continued to increase somewhat in Belgium, the Netherlands and Sweden, but declined substantially in France, West Germany and Switzerland. The trend towards stabilisation of the foreign labour force is in part due to the recession, in part to the demographic shifts described in chapter 4.

Table 5.2 shows the migrant or minority share in the total labour force of the seven countries. Again, the main growth period was 1960–74, with a trend towards slight reductions or stabilisation since. Minority workers now make up 5–10 per cent of the labour force in all the countries, except for Switzerland, where their share is over 20 per cent. But these global figures say very little about the structural importance of minority labour, or about the specific situation of minorities on the labour market.

Employment

By the late fifties, labour shortages in West Germany had begun to threaten inflation-free growth. The response of employers and the state was to recruit labour in Southern Europe. Foreign workers were *additional labour*; they allowed expansion of the labour force at a time when the number of German workers was stagnating or declining. The need for additional workers was especially great in the growth industries (engineering, vehicles, electrical products, chemicals, plastics, oil products), which were the driving force in expansion.[1] Foreign workers were also *replacement labour*; they entered the labour market at the bottom, where they replaced West German workers who were able to benefit from growing employment and training opportunities to move into better paid and pleasanter skilled and white-collar jobs. Moreover, foreign workers were recruited mainly by the secondary sector of the economy (manufacturing and building), at a time when West German workers were moving into the tertiary sector (transport, services and administration).

Table 5.1. Minorities in the labour force of West European countries (thousands)

| Country | Approximate year of data | | | |
	1960	1970	1974	1981
Belgium	170	257	278	332
France	n.a.	1,294	1,813	1,436
West Germany	461	1,729	2,287	2,082
Great Britain	1,233	1,773	n.a.	1,858
Netherlands	47	134	163	238
Sweden	95	174	200	234
Switzerland	641	787	810	689
Total	**(3,239)**	**6,148**	**(5,651)**	**6,869**

Table 5.2. Minority labour force as percentage of total labour force of West European countries

| Country | Approximate year of data | | | |
	1960	1970	1974	1981
Belgium	4.8	7.1	n.a.	8.7
France	n.a.	6.3	8.2	6.4
West Germany	1.7	6.5	10.9	9.5
Great Britain	5.1	7.1	n.a.	7.2
Netherlands	1.1	2.8	3.2	4.9
Sweden	2.9	5.2	5.2	5.4
Switzerland	21.8	25.2	25.4	22.9

Sources and notes: for Tables 5.1 and 5.2:

Belgium: 1961 and 1970 census figures from United Nations Economic Commission for Europe (UNECE), *Labour Supply and Migration in Europe: Demographic Dimensions 1950–1975 and Prospects*, New York: United Nations 1979, table annexe III–1; 1974 and 1981 from OECD SOPEMI 1982.

France: 1968 figures from UNECE, 1973 and 1981 from OECD SOPEMI 1982.

West Germany: 1961 and 1970 census figures from UNECE, 1974 Bundesminister für Arbeit, 1981 from OECD SOPEMI 1982.

Great Britain: 1960 from UNECE; 1971 from Census, Country of Birth, additional tables; part 2, table 15A (number of economically active persons, born outside UK, in Great Britain); 1981 Labour Force Survey data (April 1981) (economically active persons, born outside UK, in Great Britain).

Netherlands: 1960 and 1971 census figures from UNECE; 1974 and 1981 from OECD SOPEMI 1982.

Sweden: 1960 and 1970 census figures from UNECE; 1974 and 1981 from OECD SOPEMI 1982.

Switzerland: All figures from *Die Volkswirtschaft*, vol. 55 no. 5, May 1982. Figures are annual averages including seasonal and frontier workers.

Definitions of 'labour force' vary from country to country. Swiss figures refer to employed persons only. Other countries include the unemployed. British figures also include self-employed and employers.

Figures in brackets are estimates.

Table 5.3 shows the differences arising from this form of labour recruitment in employment patterns of foreign workers and of the total labour force. The figures show an overwhelming concentration of foreign workers in manufacturing and building. Two-thirds of the foreign labour force, compared with less than half the total labour force. Only about 30 per cent of foreigners are in the tertiary sector, compared with half the total labour force. Under-representation of foreigners is particularly marked in commerce, banking and administration, and in public authorities and social insurance.

There is a lack of comprehensive and recent data on employment for Britain, but it is worth comparing information from the 1971 Census with the West German material. Thirty-six per cent of all employed immigrants and 47 per cent of those from the New Commonwealth were working in manufacturing industries, compared with 33 per cent of all employed persons.[2] In the mid seventies the PEP survey found that 47 per cent of black men and 36 per cent of black women were employed in manufacturing, compared with 33 per cent of white men and 25 per cent of white women. Black workers were particularly concentrated in ship-building, vehicle production, textiles, construction and food processing. In services they were mainly in transport and communications, hotels and catering and the National Health Service.[3] The picture is surprisingly similar to West Germany.

It is now a decade since mass recruitment to West Germany stopped. Are foreign workers managing to move out of their original low-grade jobs as time goes on? In 1969, 16 per cent of foreign workers were in building (10 per cent in 1981) and 63 per cent in manufacturing (57 per cent in 1981). There has been an overall move of foreign workers to the tertiary sector: 17 per cent in 1969, 30 per cent in 1981.[4] A more detailed picture is given by the results of two official surveys, carried out in 1972 and 1980, which are summarised in table 5.4. The figures refer to workers from the six recruitment countries – Turkey, Yugoslavia, Italy, Greece, Spain, Portugal only (it is not comparable with the figures in table 5.3). The table shows the continued concentration of workers from these countries in manufacturing and building.

The shift to services has involved mainly foreign women. By 1980, 39 per cent of them were in the tertiary sector, compared with only 14 per cent of foreign men. The average for both sexes of

Table 5.3. Employment by economic sector of foreign
employees and all employees in West Germany, 1981, second
quarter

Economic sector	Foreign employees 000s	%	All employees 000s	%	Foreign employees' share in total employment %
Agriculture, forestry fishery	19	1	232	1	8
Energy, mining	36	2	485	2	7
Manufacturing	1,102	57	8,461	41	13
Building	202	10	1,677	8	12
Commerce, banking, insurance	136	7	3,676	18	4
Other services	314	16	3,965	19	8
Transport and communication	73	4	1,013	5	7
Public authorities, social insurance	47	2	1,353	7	3
Total	1,930	100	20,864	100	–

Source: Bundesanstalt für Arbeit, *Beschäftigtenstatistik* Ib4–4204,
March 1982.

Note: The figures exclude self-employed and unemployed persons.

19 per cent in the tertiary sector is considerably lower than the 30
per cent shown by table 5.3. This is because many workers from
outside the recruitment countries – from France, Austria, the
Netherlands and elsewhere – are in the services. Such workers have
employment patterns very like the Germans.

According to an official survey carried out in 1980, upon which
table 5.4 is based, the distribution from recruitment countries by
economic sector is fairly similar. The only significant differences
are underrepresentation of Yugoslavs in manufacturing and their
overrepresentation in building. Portuguese are more often in
'other manufacturing' and less often in 'metal manufacturing and
engineering' than other nationalities.

Table 5.5 shows some selected branches of industry with
particularly high proportions of foreign workers. On the whole,
these branches are characterised by heavy manual work and
unhealthy working conditions (plastics, iron and steel, foundries,

Table 5.4. Workers in West Germany from recruitment
countries, by sex and economic sector, 1972 and 1980 (%)

Economic sector	Men 1972	Men 1980	Women 1972	Women 1980	Total 1972	Total 1980
Agriculture, forestry, fishery	1	1	–	1	1	1
Mining, quarrying	5	4	–	–	3	3
Metal production and engineering	40	48	35	27	38	42
Other manufacturing	21	16	39	29	27	20
Building	20	16	–	1	14	12
Commerce, banking, insurance	3	1	5	3	4	1
Other services	2	5	8	18	4	8
Transport	3	3	–	1	2	2
Public services	2	5	8	17	4	8
Not classifiable	3	2	2	4	3	3
Total	**100**	**100**	**100**	**100**	**100**	**100**

Source: Bundesminister für Arbeit und Sozialordnung (ed.), *Situation
der ausländischen Arbeitnehmer und ihrer Familienangehörigen in
der Bundesrepublik Deutschland, Repräsentativuntersuchung 1980*,
Bonn: Forschungsinstitut der Friedrich-Ebert-Stiftung 1981.

Notes: The figures are for workers from the six recruitment countries:
Turkey, Yugoslavia, Italy, Greece, Spain, Portugal. In the 1972
survey, done for the federal Labour Office, 14,000 foreign workers
were interviewed. In the 1980 survey, done for the federal Ministry
of Labour and Social Order, 6,000 foreign workers were interviewed.

rolling mills, paper), repetitive monotonous work, shifts and
piece-work (vehicle and textiles), low pay and unsocial hours
(hotels and catering). Concentration is actually higher than these
figures suggest, due both to unequal regional distribution and high
proportions of foreign workers in low-skilled occupations.

There are a lot of parallels with the circumstances of black
workers in Britain. Concentration of black employees in textiles
and in foundries is well known. Black people in manufacturing
tend to be directly engaged in production work, rather than in
service or maintenance. They are also highly concentrated in

Table 5.5. Selected West German industries with high
 proportions of foreign workers, 1981

Industry	Foreign workers 000s	Foreign workers as % of all workers
Plastic manufacturing	64	19
Iron and steel production	50	15
Foundries	32	27
Rolling mills, etc.	49	18
Road vehicles	150	16
Electrical goods	150	15
Paper and cellulose	10	16
Paper products and bookbinding	17	16
Textiles	62	20
Building (main branch)	173	15
Hotels and catering	87	22
Average for whole economy		9

Source: Beauftragte der Bundesregierung für Ausländerfragen, *Daten und Fakten*, May 1982, appendix VII.

factories where shifts are worked.[5] Phizacklea and Miles draw attention to concentration of black workers in industries and services characterised by shortage of labour, shift-working, unsocial hours, low pay and an unpleasant working environment. They conclude that 'black labour tends to be replacement labour, employed in socially undesirable jobs vacated in the context of full employment by white indigenous labour'.[6]

Socio-economic status

Perhaps the best single indicator of minorities' position on the labour market is given by their socio-economic status, that is, whether they are employers or self-employed or, if employed, in what professional category. Table 5.6 compares the socio-economic status of economically active foreigners and Germans. It is based on the 1978 *Mikrozensus* (sample census). Foreigners are dramatically overrepresented in the manual worker category (81 per cent, compared with 40 per cent of West Germans). They are

Table 5.6. Economically active population of West Germany by
socio-economic status, 1978 (%)

	Foreigners	Germans
Self-employed and employers	3.8	9.1
Family helpers	0.6	4.3
Civil servants	0	9.4
Non-manual workers	14.5	37.5
Manual workers	81.1	39.7
Number of economically active persons, 000s	2,024	24,240

Source: *Mikrozensus* 1978, quoted from OECD, *Young Foreigners and
the World of Work*, Paris: OECD 1981, p. 30.

underrepresented in all other categories; only 15 per cent of
foreigners are non-manual workers, compared with 38 per cent of
West Germans. Virtually no foreigners are civil servants, because
German law bars them from this status, with very rare exceptions.
Less than 4 per cent of foreigners are self-employed or employers,
compared with 9 per cent of West Germans.

The development of minority businesses is important for
community development. Most are in the service sector: shops
offering food and other products of the home country, as well as
bars, cafés, restaurants and pizzerias. There is some specialised
manufacturing, most notably by Greeks, who play a major role in
the fur trade. One reason for the small number of foreign
businesses is that the authorities often refuse to allow them (except
in the case of EEC citizens). Residence permits generally state that
the holder is not permitted to set up independently. The authorities
can allow exceptions, but, especially for Turks, are reluctant to do
so. Turks who want to set up shops and cafés in their communities
often have to pay large sums to Germans or EEC citizens to get
them to act as formal owner.

Table 5.7 gives a more detailed breakdown of socio-economic
status by nationality and sex. (It refers to manual workers from the
recruitment countries only, and is not comparable with table 5.6.)
Since 95 per cent of men from recruitment countries and 90 per
cent of women are manual workers,[7] table 5.7 gives a reasonable
picture of their socio-economic status. The general impression is

Table 5.7. Socio-economic status of foreign manual workers in West Germany by nationality and sex, 1980 (%)

Socio-economic status	Turks	Yugo-slavs	Italians	Greeks	Spaniards	Portu-guese	Six recruit-ment countries
Men							
Skilled and supervisory	18	54	22	26	40	35	30
Semi-skilled	46	34	43	49	36	44	42
Unskilled	35	12	35	15	25	21	27
Women							
Skilled and supervisory	5	17	9	23	16	19	13
Semi-skilled	40	55	37	53	58	44	47
Unskilled	55	28	54	24	26	37	40

Source: as for table 5.4.

of very low status. Only 30 per cent of foreign male manual workers and 13 per cent of foreign women are classified as skilled. The largest group for both sexes is semi-skilled, but this generally means little more than brief on-the-job training, which does not impart a marketable skill. It is therefore appropriate to regard semi-skilled and unskilled persons together as the lowest stratum of the labour force. This applies to 70 per cent of foreign men and 87 per cent of foreign women. Even this is an improvement on their position in 1968 when less than one per cent of both male and female workers from recruitment countries were non-manual, and virtually none of the women were classified as skilled.[8]

In comparing nationalities, the most noticeable feature is the high skill level of Yugoslav men – no doubt a result of the high standards of education and training before migration. For male workers, the lowest average skill levels are those of Italians and Turks. For the former the cause is the continuation of temporary migration, due to membership of the EEC. For Turks the most likely cause is discrimination, for many Turks had relatively high levels of education and training before migration. As for women workers, Turks and Italians again have the lowest levels, with over 90 per cent semi-skilled and unskilled.

Information on the socio-economic status of minority workers in England was provided by the National Dwelling and Housing

Table 5.8. Distribution by socio-economic group, aged 16 and over, in England, 1977–8 (%)

Socio-economic group	UK-born		Not UK-born			
	White	West Indian	White	West Indian	Indian	Pakistani, Bangladeshi
Men						
Non-manual	40	10	43	12	35	16
Skilled manual	40	60	32	49	35	31
Semi-skilled	14	19	16	26	20	37
Unskilled	6	12	9	13	10	16
Women						
Non-manual	58		56	46	41	
Skilled manual	9		7	4	12	
Semi-skilled	26		30	40	34	
Unskilled	8		8	9	8	

Source: Ann Barber, *Labour Force Information from the National Dwelling and Housing Survey*, Department of Employment Research Paper no. 17, May 1981.

Note: The number of West Indian, UK-born, Pakistani and Bangladeshi women included in the sample is too low for accurate comparison.

Survey of 1977–8 (table 5.8). The figures show that white people born abroad have a socio-economic status very close to that of UK-born whites. This may be misleading, as it averages out the relatively high status of pre-1950 refugees and the low status of recent labour migrants from Southern Europe, Latin America and the Philippines. Black men have considerably lower socio-economic status than whites, even those of West Indian parentage born in the UK. West Indian and Indian women are over-represented in the semi-skilled manual category.

The figures indicate overrepresentation of black workers in manual employment, and confirm that about two-fifths of black workers are classified as semi-skilled or unskilled, compared with only about one-fifth of white workers.[9] More detailed examination would be needed to show the extent and character of minority subordination on the British labour market, such as the employment of Asian and Cypriot women (usually at very low wages) as

Table 5.9. Occupational promotion in West Germany by
  nationality and sex, 1980 (%)

Promotion	Turks	Yugoslavs	Italians
Men			
From unskilled to semi-skilled	30	20	26
From unskilled to skilled or supervisory	4	10	9
From semi-skilled to skilled or supervisory	4	10	6
Total gaining promotion	**39**	**40**	**41**
Women			
From unskilled to semi-skilled	29	36	22
From unskilled to skilled or supervisory	1	6	5
From semi-skilled to skilled or supervisory	2	6	1
Total gaining promotion	**32**	**47**	**28**

Source: as for table 5.4.

home workers.[10] Concentration of minorities in the manual
working class is less marked in Britain than in West Germany.

Members of ethnic minorities in Britain also seem more involved
in running their own businesses than foreigners in West Germany,
no doubt due to the greater maturity of migration and to the lack
of legal barriers. According to the 1971 Census, 2.4 per cent of
West Indians, 6.7 per cent of Indians and 5.1 per cent of Pakistanis
were self-employed or employers, compared with 9.3 per cent of all
economically active persons in Britain. The National Dwelling
and Housing Survey of 1977–8 indicated considerable increases in
minority self-employment and business since 1971.[11] But most of
the people concerned were self-employed craftworkers (for
example, West Indian builders) or owners of small retail or service
enterprises, sometimes catering mainly for their own ethnic group.
Going into business often simply meant exchanging a position as

Greeks	Spaniards	Portuguese	All workers from these countries
41	28	27	28
20	30	21	10
7	3	6	6
67	**60**	**54**	**44**
44	42	30	33
15	9	15	6
4	1	2	3
63	**52**	**46**	**42**

marginal worker for that of marginal proprietor, rather than high income and social status.[12]

Social mobility

Have former migrants been able to win higher-status employment with increasing length of residence? Table 5.9 shows the extent to which foreign workers have achieved promotion during their stay in West Germany. Forty-four per cent of foreign men from recruitment countries and 42 per cent of foreign women have gained advancement, but mainly only from unskilled to semi-skilled. This is hardly real upward mobility for it generally means only on-the-job training which is not officially recognised as a skill. Only 16 per cent of foreign men and 9 per cent of foreign women have achieved the more significant shift from unskilled or semi-skilled employment to skilled or supervisor level. The extent of promotion varies considerably by nationality; again, Turks and Italians are at the bottom of the scale. Yugoslavs do not show very high rates of promotion, probably because a high proportion of them started off as skilled workers anyway. The highest rates of promotion have been achieved by Greeks, Spaniards and Portuguese.

On the whole, foreign workers in West Germany do not have very much chance of getting out of their original circumstances as industrial manual workers or doing the least desirable service jobs. This is not surprising since they were recruited for such jobs and policies have on the whole aimed to keep them there.

There is certainly a national hierarchy. The employment of workers from European Community countries (apart from Italy and Greece) is similar to that of Germans. Yugoslavs – 18 per cent of foreign workers – make an important contribution to the skilled labour force, especially in building (rather like Irish migrants in Britain). Greeks, Spaniards and Portuguese are often skilled industrial workers, but together these nationalities make up only 13 per cent of the foreign labour force, and their share is declining. The biggest group, the Turks (30 per cent of foreign workers), has the lowest status and the lowest rate of promotion. Their situation is most comparable to that of black workers in Britain. The Italians (15 per cent of foreign workers) have a low occupational status, related to their continued mobility as European Community citizens.

For Britain, the evidence is that the 'concentration of black labour in the manual working class is being reproduced, partly because of racial discrimination'.[13] The PEP survey produced evidence of discrimination at the point of employment, and with regard to promotion. Such discrimination applies even to blacks who have obtained educational qualifications in Britain. The National Dwelling and Housing Survey of 1977–8 showed that the occupational level of people of West Indian origin, born and educated in Britain, was no better than that of their parents, and was much worse than that of whites.[14]

A survey by the French Ministry of Labour is summarised in table 5.10. It refers to changes in the structure of the foreign labour force, rather than to individual promotion (as in table 5.9).

The figures show the continued very high concentration of

Table 5.10. Socio-economic status of foreign employees in industrial and commercial firms with ten or more employees, France (%)

	1971	1973	1976	1979
Supervisory staff	1.1	1.3	1.7	2.1
Foremen, forewomen and technicians	1.7	1.7	2.1	2.6
Clerical employees	3.6	5.1	6.7	9.2
Skilled manual	20.8	30.5	34.8	37.9
Semi-skilled manual	40.1	42.6	38.3	34.5
Unskilled	26.7	18.8	16.1	13.4

Source: OECD SOPEMI 1982, p. 61.

foreigners in manual employment. But there has been a slight growth in non-manual employment. Within the manual sector, there has been a steady increase in skilled employment at the expense of semi-skilled and unskilled employment. The general picture looks fairly similar to West Germany.

Deskilling and work intensification

The evidence so far indicates that most migrant or minority workers still have a subordinate position on the labour market. This corresponds with the specific roles played by most such workers in the labour process. Firstly, they provide particular types of labour required by employers to fit in with changes in technology and the division of labour. Secondly, they provide a flexible source of labour at times of expansion, or a relatively easy and politically acceptable way of cutting the labour force at times of recession. This section deals mainly with the first aspect, the following one with the second aspect.

For West Germany, the *Forschungsverbund* study provides useful data on this theme. The authors divided labour processes into three broad categories, and then carried out a survey of 1,696 factories. They determined which type of labour process pre-dominated, and related this to the share of foreign workers in the labour force.

The first category was relatively flexible workshop production with a fairly low level of mechanisation. One-off products or small series were produced by workers with relatively high skill, usually each carrying out a variety of tasks. In such factories 16–17 per cent of workers were foreigners.

The second category was highly mechanised production of medium and large series, often using conveyor-line methods. Such work is characterised by high levels of specialisation of workers, with monotonous tasks and low skills. Here the proportion of foreign workers was very high: 22 per cent for medium series production, 28 per cent for large series production. The proportion of women workers (both foreign and German) was also high.

The third category was highly automated and continuous process production. Such work embraces both repetitive unskilled jobs and highly skilled maintenance and control tasks. In such factories 20–21 per cent of the workers were foreigners.[15]

These findings correlate with information on methods of payment. Seventy-one per cent of German production workers were paid hourly, compared with 60 per cent of foreigners. Eighteen per cent of Germans were on piece-work and 11 per cent on bonus payment schemes, while 26 per cent of foreigners were on piece-work and 15 per cent on bonus schemes.[16] Payment by results is, of course, particularly common in factories of the second category using mass production methods, where foreigners are most highly concentrated. These findings are confirmed by the 1980 survey, which found that 35 per cent of foreign men and 36 per cent of foreign women were paid by results.[17] Turkish and Portuguese men, and Turkish and Greek women were most frequently on piece-rates. A study at the Hanover Volkswagen factory found that 91 per cent of foreign male wage-earners were on piece-rates compared with 57 per cent of their German equivalents. No less than 99 per cent of foreign women were on piece-rates, compared with 75 per cent of German women.[18]

Foreign workers are also frequently employed on shifts. According to the *Forschungsverbund* study, 47 per cent of foreign production workers were on shifts, compared with 39 per cent of Germans. Shift work was most common in factories of the third category (highly automated and continuous process production), where no less than 77 per cent of foreigners and 71 per cent of Germans were on shifts.[19] The 1980 survey found that 44 per cent of all foreign men and 28 per cent of all foreign women were on shift work.[20]

There is little detailed data on the relationship between production technology and minority labour in Britain, but findings on shift-working do point in the same direction. The PEP study found the proportion of black workers on shift work to be much higher than that of whites. Thirty-two per cent of the factories in which ethnic minorities were the majority of the labour force had permanent night-shifts, compared with only 12 per cent of those firms employing only white workers.[21] Some textile factories in Lancashire and Yorkshire have night-shifts manned almost exclusively by Indian, Pakistani and Bangladeshi workers. Black workers and foreign workers from Southern Europe, Latin America and the Philippines are highly concentrated in occupations with unsocial hours in the health service, hotels and catering.[22]

Some of the findings of a Swedish survey on immigrants' work are summarised in table 5.11. The overrepresentation of foreign workers – in particular of Finns and Southern Europeans – in jobs with monotonous and unhealthy working conditions indicates a position in the labour process similar to that of immigrant workers in Britain and West Germany.

Such findings do not merely demonstrate the disadvantaged position of minorities at work. They also tell us something about the function of these workers in the labour process: providing a special form of labour for types of production involving deskilling and unpleasant working conditions. In periods of growth and full employment, some indigenous workers have been able to reject such work. But employers have had a strong interest in introducing working methods with increased division of labour and intensification of work, in order to maintain growth, raise productivity and secure control of the labour force. This historical dimension is crucial to understanding the relationship between economic growth, changes in the labour process and use of migrant or minority labour.

In West Germany, expansion in the fifties took a largely labour-intensive form, using readily available, internal labour reserves (although productivity did increase as new plant came into service). In the sixties, labour shortages began to develop, so employers recruited foreign workers, and at the same time speeded up the shift from one-off or small series production to mass production using conveyor-line methods.[23] This trend gained in

142 / Here for good

Table 5.11. Workers subject to unpleasant working conditions
  in Sweden, 1975 (%)

	Swedes	Naturalised immigrants	All foreigners	Finns	Southern Europeans
Deafening noise	12	16	27	29	34
Dirt	15	12	20	18	21
Heavy lifting	21	19	22	22	24
Repeated and one-sided movements	31	38	51	53	60
Hectic and monotonous work	10	14	26	24	32

Source: Statistik Årsbok 1981, table 22.

momentum during the very rapid expansion following the 1966–7 recession. To maintain growth in this period, the West German state organised the fastest mass labour recruitment to take place anywhere in post-war Western Europe.

The rapid capital accumulation of this period was but a prelude to further changes in the labour process, which became evident in the period commencing with the recession of 1974–5. Now the main emphasis has shifted to automation and continuous process production, in which the quantitative need for labour is lower, but the qualitative requirements (education and skill) are often higher. In this current phase, there is far less demand for the type of labour provided by migrants and minorities. Hand in hand with such changes goes the development of the 'new international division of labour' (see pp. 33–5 above). The very industries that expanded so fast in the sixties and early seventies through the use of foreign workers, are now in the forefront of the drive to export labour-intensive branches of production to low-wage areas. The foreign workers were vital to the accelerated capital accumulation that is now making them redundant.[24]

Such trends are not specific to West Germany. Asian workers have played a similar role in the British textile industry. In the sixties, their enforced willingness to work night-shifts made possible the introduction of new expensive machinery, which only paid if used continuously. In the meantime, many of the factories modernised at that time have been closed down, because it is even cheaper to produce abroad.

Similar patterns are to be found in the French building industry, where about one-third of the labour force are foreigners. Recent studies indicate that French workers have left building not just because of unpleasant working conditions, but also because of the deskilling of labour. Employers' efforts to rationalise production and save labour through increased mechanisation have undermined traditional training structures and increased the proportion of dead-end jobs. Employers have seen the short-term employment of migrants as the solution.[25] This applies particularly in huge industrial construction projects such as the Fos steel complex near Marseilles, where 70 per cent of the workers were immigrants, mainly Algerians.[26] Working conditions and safety standards are often lowered through the use of labour-only sub-contractors, who concentrate on employing illegal migrants, paying extremely low wages and ignoring social security regulations. At the Fos site no less than a third of all workers were employed by such sub-contractors, who frequently recruited in the bars of Marseilles' 'Arab quarter'. Now that this phase of structural change and deskilling has been completed, employers are embarking on a policy of 'renationalisation of building and civil engineering'.[27] As a result, the number of foreign workers in building firms with 10 or more employees has declined from 408,000 in 1973 to 310,000 in 1979.[28]

Unemployment

Where the state pursues a policy of temporary recruitment of migrant labour, the intention is to use foreign workers to regulate the labour market. They are supposed to provide additional labour during growth periods and to leave if there is a recession. In a guest worker system, unemployment of foreign workers should never be a problem. One might therefore expect to find considerable differences between the unemployment rates of foreigners in West Germany and minorities in Britain. But, in fact, this is not the case.

A basic tenet of the guest worker system was that migrants were 'target earners', that their motivation for migration was the desire to earn a certain sum of money to improve their position in the country of origin. The system therefore had rotation built into it: workers came for a few years and would return home once they had saved enough. They could then be replaced if labour was still needed. In case of recession, they would simply not be replaced, so that unemployment could be exported without even dismissing anybody. This idea was a major element of labour market policy in several countries in the fifties and sixties. The condition for its success was the prevention of family immigration and settlement. As a leading representative of the German Employers' Federation put it:

> In case of a decline in the employment situation . . . the foreigners would therefore have to expect to be the first to lose their jobs. For this reason it would be absurd to encourage utopian ideas about the large-scale settlement of families.[29]

Of course, the matter was not left to chance – the whole system of work and residence permits, of precedence for Germans on the labour market, was designed to prevent permanent settlement of foreign workers, and to keep them mobile.

The failure of the guest worker system is best seen by looking at patterns of employment and unemployment in the various economic cycles. In the first phase of expansion of migrant labour from the end of the fifties, the number of foreign workers grew to a peak of 1.3 million in 1966. Then came the first significant recession since the 'economic miracle'. The number of foreign workers declined by 400,000 to reach about 900,000 in 1968. Few foreign workers were actually dismissed – the rotation built into the system seemed to be working. There were never more than 29,000 foreigners drawing unemployment benefit during this recession, so the West German state was able to save considerably. But things must have looked different from the perspective of the many Germans (especially older workers) who lost their jobs at this time. Although there were half a million Germans out of work, nearly a million foreign workers remained. They had become so fully integrated into the labour process that it was impractical to dismiss them to make way for Germans. The limitations of the function of foreign workers as a cushion against unemployment were becoming evident.

But the 1966–7 recession appeared to be a mere hiccup in the expansion of the German economy. Growth rates leapt after 1968, and foreign workers were recruited faster than ever. However, it was in this period that the trend towards family entry and

Table 5.12. Unemployment in West Germany (annual averages), 1965–82

	Total labour force 000s	unemployed %	Foreigners 000s	unemployed %
1965	147	0.7	2	0.2
1966	161	0.7	4	0.3
1967	459	2.1	16	1.5
1968	323	1.5	6	0.6
1969	179	0.9	3	0.2
1970	149	0.7	5	0.3
1971	185	0.8	12	0.6
1972	246	1.1	17	0.7
1973	273	1.2	20	0.8
1974	582	2.6	69	2.9
1975	1,074	4.7	151	6.8
1976	1,060	4.6	106	5.1
1977	1,030	4.5	98	4.9
1978	993	4.3	104	5.3
1979	876	3.8	93	4.7
1980	889	3.8	107	5.0
1981	1,272	5.5	168	8.2
1982	1,883	7.5	246	11.9

Source: *Amtliche Nachrichten der Bundesanstalt für Arbeit, Jahreszahlen 1982*, Nuremberg 1982.

settlement became more pronounced. Unemployment remained very low in this last burst of glory of the post-war boom: the rate for the whole labour force was around one per cent until 1973, and the rate for foreigners was even lower, as table 5.12 shows.

Unemployment shot up in 1974–5 during the recession that heralded the beginning of the long period of stagnation. Significantly, unemployment of foreign workers rose far more rapidly than that of Germans. In fact the number of foreigners who lost their jobs is far higher than the unemployment figures suggest, for several hundred thousands left the country after the ban on new entries in 1973. The total number of foreigners in employment fell by over 600,000 between 1973 and 1978, but the number registered as unemployed was about 100,000 in the latter year. In other words, West Germany was able to export about half a million unemployed persons, considerably reducing the social costs of the recession.

Labour market conditions improved somewhat in the late seventies, though now foreign workers' unemployment rate remained relatively high. Unemployed foreign workers were staying in the country, no doubt because the rest of their families were there. In the early eighties, unemployment hit new peaks. By February 1983, 2.5 million people were out of work (10 per cent of the labour force). Of the unemployed, 318,000 were foreign (15 per cent of the foreign labour force). An unknown but considerable number of foreigners looking for work were not registered as unemployed for fear of losing their work permits and being deported. An official survey in September 1981 showed that 41 per cent of unemployed foreigners were industrial workers (compared with 30 per cent of German unemployed). Seven per cent were building workers and 11 per cent service employees. Unemployment of foreigners grew fastest in the year preceding the survey in the textile industry, foundries, the electrical industry and building; it more or less doubled in all these branches. Thirty per cent of foreign work-seekers were not assigned to specific industries, as they had not worked before (young people and refugees) or had been unemployed for long periods.[30]

The pattern observed in the 1966–7 recession has continued. Foreign workers are hardest hit by the recession, and their rates of unemployment have risen faster than those of German workers, but clearly only a certain section of the foreign labour force has remained flexible and mobile enough to serve as a shield against unemployment for German workers. A larger section has become part of the basic labour force of essential industries, and cannot be dismissed to make way for German workers, even when over two million are out of work. The situation is not the 'dual labour market' postulated by certain observers,[31] in which indigenous and immigrant workers hardly compete. Rather, the labour market is segmented: groups of foreigners remain flexible and potentially disposable, while others have become established and are hardly more mobile than indigenous workers.

In Britain total unemployment doubled between November 1973 and February 1980, but the number of blacks registered as unemployed quadrupled. Black people made up just over 2 per cent of all unemployed in 1972, but nearly 4 per cent in 1980. Unemployment of minority groups grew about three times as fast as average unemployment for the whole labour force between 1974 and 1980.[32] Table 5.13 shows unemployment rates of various ethnic groups according to the National Dwelling and Housing Survey. The figures show that unemployment was significantly higher for black workers than for whites. The unemployment rate for people of West Indian origin born in the UK is dramatically high. This is of course mainly youth unemployment.

Table 5.13.   Unemployment rates in England, 1977–8(%)

| | UK-born | | Not UK-born | | |
	White	West Indian	West Indian	Indian	Pakistani, Bangladeshi
Men	5.3	21	9.2	7	8.6
Women	4.6	24.1	7.5	10.5	–

Source: Ann Barber, *Labour Force Information from the National Dwelling and Housing Survey*, Department of Employment Research Paper no. 17, May 1981.

Note: The number of Pakistani and Bangladeshi women included in the sample is too low to permit comparison.

The pattern is similar throughout Western Europe. The rates of unemployment of foreign or minority workers are higher than those of indigenous workers and, in periods of recession, their unemployment rises faster. In France, 12 per cent of foreign workers were unemployed in March 1982. In 1981 the rate of unemployment of foreigners increased by 35 per cent, compared with 22 per cent for French workers. The highest and fastest-rising rates of unemployment were those of North African workers. In the Netherlands, 13 per cent of foreigners were out of work in 1981, compared with 9 per cent of the total labour force. The highest rates of unemployment were for recent immigrants from Surinam, Turks and Moroccans. In Sweden, the unemployment rate for foreign workers was twice as high as the average for the whole labour force in 1981 (4.8 per cent as against 2.4 per cent).[33]

Why can certain groups of workers be more readily eliminated from the labour force than others at times of recession and structural change? A variety of explanations have been proposed.

First, shorter average duration in employment of migrant workers makes them vulnerable to 'last in, first out' rules, when redundancy occurs. This factor was certainly significant during the phase of mass labour migration, but should not be so a decade or more after entries were stopped. The 1980 survey showed that foreign workers in West Germany are far less mobile than generally believed: over half had been in the same job for over four years in 1980. Over one-third had been in the same job all the time they had been in West Germany.[34] Where the fluctuation of immigrant workers is high, this is generally because their jobs are insecure, or because poor working conditions make them seek other work.[35]

Second, it is always workers in the less skilled jobs who lose their jobs first. For instance, 87 per cent of unemployed foreign workers in West Germany in September 1981 did not have a recognised skill.[36] However, lack of skill often relates to discrimination. It has been shown that skilled migrants often do not get skilled jobs, and that chances of promotion are small. Lack of education and training of the second generation is a result of social disadvantage and discrimination.

Third, migrants found work mainly in the sectors that have declined most rapidly in the recession: in building and in unskilled and semi-skilled mass production sectors like textiles, the electrical industry, metal manufacture. Dohse has shown how West German employers have cut back their labour force mainly by dismissing foreigners. Between 1974 and 1977 the workforce in West German manufacturing was reduced by 765,000, of whom 319,000 were foreigners, so, 42 per cent of the cutback was achieved by sacking foreign workers. The absolute number of foreigners dismissed was highest in the electrical industry, chemicals and plastics, engineering and textiles. Particularly in vehicle building, rolling mills, precision engineering and optics, the reduction in the number of foreign workers was greater than the reduction in the total labour force – that is, foreigners were being replaced by West German workers.[37]

Fourth, migrant workers have been employed in 'declining centres of capitalist production'.[38] In other words, migrant labour was brought in to older industrial areas in the fifties and sixties, to forestall their decline at a time when indigenous workers were moving to other areas. When the decline accelerated in the recession, migrant workers were hardest hit. The hypothesis applies to Britain to a considerable extent, and also fits the Ruhr and West Berlin, and older industrial areas of northern France and Belgium. It certainly does not apply to all immigrant workers in West Germany, France, Switzerland and Sweden, for many have been recruited by growing high-productivity sectors.

Fifth, migrant and minority workers have high rates of unemployment due to discrimination in hiring, promotion and firing. In Britain there is evidence of widespread informal racial discrimination.[39] In West Germany and other Western European countries, there is both informal discrimination by employers, and a state system of institutionalised discrimination. The guest worker system, controlled and implemented by the state, with the co-operation of employers and unions, was based on the restriction of migrant workers' rights. The shift from migration to settlement has brought some improvements in some countries. But in West Germany, for example, the current trend is towards increased restrictiveness; since 1973 successive governments have chipped away at foreigners' rights in the hope that it will pave the way for repatriation.

Trade union responses

The recruitment of migrant labour tends to cause a rift within the labour force. Language and cultural differences make communication difficult. Some migrants lack industrial and trade union experience, and employers exploit these to force down wages and conditions and to weaken the labour movement. 'Target earning' can be divisive: if migrants want to earn a lot quickly to be able to return home, they may become 'rate busters', pushing production norms up. Trends towards segregation at work, the concentration of migrants in certain jobs and departments, hinder communication and deepen mutual mistrust.

The split is also caused and exacerbated by nationalist and racist attitudes, arising from the colonialist traditions and cultures of Western European countries. These problems are not new: ever since the industrial revolution, employers have tried to use migrant workers to dilute labour, keep down wages and hinder union organisation. Workers and trade unions have often opposed recruitment of migrant workers, because they saw them as tools of the bosses.

The unions in post-war Western Europe have therefore found themselves in a dilemma. On the one hand, employers have used migrant labour in an effort to stop wages rising at the expense of profits. Officially this is described as 'maintaining the elasticity of the labour market'. So unions might regard it as being in the best interests of their members to oppose immigration. On the other hand, the unions claim to represent the whole working class, and see that failure to bring migrants into the labour movement will lead to the very split they fear. Moreover, the unions have always declared internationalism to be one of their basic principles.

Trade union responses to this dilemma have varied. Some unions have supported restrictions on immigration and the limitation of foreign workers' rights (Switzerland, France in the fifties, Britain with regard to European Voluntary Workers in the forties). Unions following such policies have found that migrants are unwilling to join and do not trust union officials. In other cases, unions have welcomed migrants and expressed solidarity, but done little to integrate them into the labour movement, as special measures were seen as a sort of discrimination in reverse. Such were the policies of the British TUC towards Commonwealth immigrants. The TUC has done little to fight discriminatory immigration legislation, or to combat racism, although local union bodies have sometimes taken action.[40] A third strategy has been to accept the inevitability of labour migration, and to make special efforts to organise the newcomers (West Germany and France in the sixties and seventies).[41]

In West Germany, just under 8 million workers are organised in the 17 unions linked in the DGB (Deutsche Gewerkschaftsbund) which corresponds to the TUC in Britain. Although officially without party allegiance, the DGB is in fact close to the SPD. However, the DGB has on the whole supported state policies on labour migration, both during the CDU–CSU–FDP coalition up to 1969, and later when the SPD and the FDP were in power from 1969–82. When recruitment of foreign workers was started in the late fifties, the DGB expressed fears about effects on full employment and wage levels. The DGB agreed to the entry of foreign workers, once state and employers accepted three basic principles: equal pay for equal work according to collective agreements, provision of initial accommodation by employers, and a monopoly on recruitment abroad by the federal Labour Office. The DGB then followed a largely acquiescent policy throughout the period of mass recruitment, and did little to press for state measures to combat discrimination and exploitation.[42]

By the early seventies migrants were over 10 per cent of the total labour force and a far higher proportion of the manual workers in industry. Union policies began to change; the DGB called for a ban on further recruitment of foreign workers in 1972, ostensibly because of lack of social infrastruture.[43] When the federal government stopped entries of foreign workers in November 1973, the DGB expressed strong support. As unemployment grew in the mid seventies, leading DGB officials declared that the unions would not tolerate a situation in which millions of Germans were out of work, while foreigners still had jobs.[44] Edmund Duda, a DGB official who represented the unions on the board of the Labour Office, was quoted as saying:

> In order to protect German employees, all legal possibilities must be utilised to send home foreign workers who are no longer needed. If they do not go voluntarily, regulations which permit their expulsion will just have to be applied more stringently.[45]

However, in practice the unions have not called for mass deportations, nor for dismissal of foreign workers to make jobs available for Germans. They have simply gone along with existing government policies, and with the application of regulations that give Germans priority in job allocation. In December 1982, the DGB expressed support for discriminatory measures, most notably the restrictions on labour market access for foreign workers' children, and the restrictions on entry of children and spouses. The DGB issued a press statement on the latter measure, praising it as 'socially responsible' and demanding its full implementation. It remains to be seen whether the DGB will go along with the further restrictions on entry of dependants currently planned by the CDU–CSU–FDP government.

On the other hand, in the early seventies the unions started calling for measures for the social integration of migrants and their children. But the concept of integration was limited to improvements in welfare rights and did not extend to civil and political rights. The DGB has consistently and categorically refused to accept the concept of permanent immigration – even during the brief period when this seemed to be becoming the policy of the SPD at the time of publication of the Kühn Memorandum (see p. 80 above). The DGB has called for measures to encourage foreigners to return to their countries of origin.[46] It continues to reject voting rights for foreigners in local elections, and opposes the European Trades Union Congress's demand for full social and labour market equality of foreign workers and their dependants.

A second aspect of the trade union response concerns the integration of migrant workers in the unions and in workers' representative bodies. The unions have made very considerable efforts to encourage foreign workers to become members. Special measures include advisory offices staffed by foreign officials, foreign language leaflets and newspapers, provision of interpreters, courses for foreign members and shop stewards. The DGB has also established links with unions in the countries of origin, largely confined to unions of a social-democratic complexion which are often not the most significant organisations in the countries concerned.

These efforts have met with considerable success. It was estimated in 1977 that the DGB unions had 611,000 foreign members – one-third of all foreign workers. However the rate of unionisation for German manual workers is over 50 per cent.[47] Over half the foreign trade unionists are members of the enormous *IG Metall* (Metal Workers' Union) which has 2.6 million members in all. There are 73,000 foreign workers in the *IG Chemie* (Chemical Workers' Union) and 41,000 in the *Gewerkschaft Textil–Bekleidung* (Clothing and Textile Workers' Union). In each case, around 60 per cent of foreigners working in the industry are union members. In the mines and on the railways, rates of union membership are even higher: over 90 per cent of both German and foreign workers. Membership of DGB unions varies according to nationality. The Turks have the highest rate (46 per cent in 1980), followed by Spaniards (39 per cent), Greeks (38 per cent), Portuguese (34 per cent), Italians (31 per cent) and Yugoslavs (29 per cent).[48]

Mere membership says little about involvement in the unions

and commitment to them. An important indicator is the extent to which foreigners become shop stewards (*Vertrauensleute*), but not much data is available on this. Figures are available for the metal industry: in 1973, 5,633 foreign shop stewards were elected. That was 4.7 per cent of the total number of shop stewards, although foreigners were over 16 per cent of the labour force. The number of shop stewards in other industries is said to be generally low, so that foreign workers are seriously underrepresented.[49] As for foreign full-time union officials, the number is very low, although exact figures are unobtainable. Moreover, it appears that foreign officials are mainly employed to deal with specific problems of their own national groups, rather than to do union work in general.[50] The tasks of foreign officials are often more akin to social work than normal union activities.

Another important field is participation in the works councils (*Betriebsräte* or – in the public services – *Personalräte*) which West German labour law permits in all but the very smallest workplaces. These councils have important functions, such as co-determination in hiring and firing. They are not union bodies, but the unions play a large part in them. The number of foreign works councillors has steadily increased since the 1972 *Betriebsverfassungsgesetz* (Works Constitution Law), which gave foreigners the right to stand for election. In 1972 3,824 foreigners were elected; in 1974 4,985; in 1978 5,962; in 1981 6,556.[51] However, foreigners are still considerably underrepresented. In 1981 about 4 per cent of works councillors elected in the metal industry were foreigners, compared with about 15 per cent of the workers. Figures for other industries were similar. In the metal industry, only 1 per cent of works council chairpersons and 2 per cent of deputy chairpersons were foreign.[52]

This shows a low level of active participation in the unions, which is reflected in foreign workers' attitudes. A survey found that only 10 per cent of male foreign workers thought the unions represented their interests well, and a further 37 per cent found them adequate. Twenty-one per cent of the male foreign workers thought the unions only represented the interests of Germans, while 27 per cent said they were not informed about the activities of the unions. Foreign women had an even more negative view of the unions. Seven per cent found them very good, 25 per cent adequate, 15 per cent thought they only represented Germans and

46 per cent lacked information. Union membership is higher among foreign men (51 per cent) than women (30 per cent). Qualifications also play a part: the higher the skill level, the higher the rate of union membership.[53]

Attitudes towards works councils were also far from positive. Only 36 per cent of foreign men and 33 per cent of foreign women thought that the works council represented their interests adequately. Thirty-seven per cent of foreign men and 34 per cent of foreign women said that the works council represented the employers' interests, while 16 per cent of foreign men and 17 per cent of foreign women saw the works council as representing only the interests of Germans. Nearly half the foreign workers interviewed did not even know that foreigners had the right to stand for election to works councils, which shows how little relevance the work of the councils had for them.[54]

Why do many foreign workers play a passive role in the unions despite formal membership? The most telling reason is probably the widespread feeling that the unions are an organisation of the German workers, controlled by them and representing their interests. This attitude depends not only on the national division of the labour force but also on stratification by sex and skill. The leadership of the unions at enterprise, district and national level is largely held by skilled male German workers. Whether consciously or not, this group tends to equate its own interests with those of workers in general, and ignores conflicting interests of other groups. So foreign workers, women and unskilled workers remain uninvolved in union activities. This is a major problem for the unions when there is a trend towards deskilling. The skilled section of the industrial working class is shrinking and its sectional interests are less and less representative of the class as a whole.

This factor is also important when looking at a third aspect of union activities concerning foreign workers: representation in disputes about wages, conditions and redundancies. Since foreigners make up a large percentage of the workforce in the overwhelming majority of factories, they are inevitably involved in most labour disputes. In our 1973 study Godula Kosack and I described cases in various countries in which employers had tried to make use of the specific position of migrant workers to split the labour force during conflicts. We also gave examples of disputes in which migrants had taken action against specific forms of exploitation and discrimination, and had received little support from indigenous workers and the unions.[55]

Foreign workers took a leading role in the two most important West German strike movements of recent times, in 1969 and 1973. Their part was of special significance in the 1973 movement which arose from the demands of unskilled and semi-skilled workers. The largest single strike in 1973 was at the huge Ford motor works in Cologne, where the leadership was mainly in the hands of semi-skilled Turkish production-line workers. This strike was broken by employers and police with the active co-operation of German union leaders and works councillors, causing a great deal of bitterness and anti-union feeling among foreigners.[56] International solidarity was achieved in some factories during the 1973 strike movement, with remarkable successes, most notably at the Pierburg motor component works, where foreign semi-skilled women managed to secure the support of German male skilled workers and won substantial pay increases.[57]

The militance of foreign workers was an underlying cause of the decision to stop entries of foreign workers in November 1973. The DGB's support for the ban may have been in part motivated by fears of losing control of foreign workers, for after the strikes many migrants felt they were not adequately represented by the German unions, and discussed establishing their own.

Since 1973 there have been few spectacular labour struggles in West Germany (except for the printers' strike of 1978 which involved mainly German skilled workers). Foreign workers' struggles have been mainly local and defensive: battles against redundancies and plant closures. West German labour law gives works councils (and, indirectly, the unions) an important role in helping to decide who gets sacked first, and what compensation is offered. Many German employers have followed the strategy of using dismissals of foreign workers to cushion German workers from the effects of declining employment. On the whole, unions and works councils seem to have gone along with this policy. Indeed it could hardly have been carried out without their co-operation.[58] There is no doubt that redundancies are an area where potential conflicts of interests between German and foreign workers are at their greatest.

On the other hand, as the crisis deepens, there is growing awareness that plant closures can only be effectively combated by a united labour force. In 1981 and 1982 there were major struggles against mass redundancies at three Frankfurt factories – Adler office machines, VDM metal works and Rockwell–Golde engineering works. In all three, foreign workers played a major part, and a high degree of international solidarity was achieved. It proved impossible to stop closure of VDM, but there was a partial success at Adler, and almost all redundancies were prevented at Rockwell–Golde.[59]

In the UK the record of the TUC in relation to supporting or defending the interests of black workers shares many features of the situation described in detail for Germany. The struggles of black workers in the UK are many and have been well documented in Miles and Phizacklea (*Labour and Racism* and 'The TUC and black workers'), Moore (*Racism and Black Resistance in Britain*), and most recently for female workers in *One Way Ticket*. Briefly, while the TUC is committed in theory to opposing all forms of racism and racial discrimination, in practice it has often denied the existence of widespread racism and so has taken no steps to combat it.

During the late 1960s and early 1970s when the British government was involved in passing restrictive and racially defined immigration laws (the 1968 Commonwealth Immigrants Act and the 1971 Immigration Act) designed to prevent further immigration of black workers into the UK, the TUC did not oppose them. It was only later, when the threat of organised white racism in the form of the National Front appeared, that the TUC reorganised itself actively to combat racism and address itself to issues of 'race relations'. Yet they have focused more on the threat of organised racism than on the disadvantages suffered by black and migrant workers, and have not been noticeably involved in fighting for the improvement of the specific material conditions of black workers. The Mansfield Hosiery strike and that at Imperial Typewriters in the 1970s were initiated by black workers who were complaining about discrimination on the part of white workers and trade union officials, as well as on the part of the employers. The historic dispute at Grunwick Film Processing Laboratories, London, in 1976 did involve trade union support at the grassroots level for the migrant workers participating in the strike, but the two-year struggle ended in defeat. The women failed to get union recognition at their place of work, they experienced unemployment as a result of the dispute, and they felt that ultimately they had been betrayed by the trade union bureaucracy.

Trade union policy did change in the mid-1970s and there was a commitment to combat white racism among the working class, and to pressing for 'equal opportunities' for all workers. In practice, however the record of some individual unions are better than others, and in many ways the TUC has not grasped the nettle of black disadvantage.

Conclusions

For the most part, while increasing numbers of indigenous workers move into white-collar and service employment, black and foreign workers remain within the manual manufacturing working class.

The circumstances of the new ethnic minorities in the various countries are intrinsically similar: they were compelled to enter the labour market at the lowest levels, and they have remained there, because that is where the capitalist economy needs them. There are some variations between different minority groups in each country. In Britain it is mainly black workers who occupy the most disadvantaged positions, although recent foreign workers from Southern Europe and elsewhere are often just as badly off. In France, it is the North African and black workers who are at the bottom of the pile. In West Germany, the Turks and the Italians have the lowest positions on the labour market.

As mass production is replaced by automation, or exported to low-wage countries, the demand for the type of labour provided by migrants during the growth period declines. Migrant workers were needed to create the pre-conditions for a new shift in the labour process, which in turn is eliminating them. So what role remains for migrant or minority labour in the current economic situation?

Black and foreign workers continue to provide manual labour in manufacturing, building and parts of the service sector. Despite the recession, the point has not (yet) been reached at which enough indigenous workers are available for these jobs. Also, because of their special vulnerability to dismissal, black and foreign workers can be used to partially cushion other workers from the effects of the crisis. This reduces the social and political strains of the process of restructuring for capital and the state.

This role lies behind the ideological offensive against the minorities: an attempt to blame them for the crisis, and to justify continued discrimination. In West Germany, politicians, employers and the media continually hammer home the message that there would not be 2 million unemployed in the country if the 2 million foreign workers were sent home. Many German workers are convinced that the foreigners are somehow to blame for unemployment, and that forced repatriation would create jobs for Germans. The call for dismissal of foreign workers first leads to splits in the struggle against plant closures and redundancies.

Racist ideology boomerangs on those workers who accept it. The state is trying to force German workers back into the unskilled production jobs that many left during the boom years. Since the mid seventies, politicians have repeatedly called on the unemployed to abandon 'unrealistic' expectations and accept deskilling. New regulations issued to the labour exchanges since 1976 compel white-collar and skilled workers to accept downgrading to unskilled employment after a period of unemployment. Those who refuse lose the right to unemployment benefit.

A decade after the curtailment of labour migration to most Western European countries, the former migrant workers, who are now settling, still play an important role in the strategies of capital and state. The labour movement has not been able to solve the problems presented by a divided working class.

6. Ethnic minority youth

The 'second generation problem'

As the migratory process matures, and labour migration develops into settlement, there is a corresponding shift in the way society perceives the minorities. During the period of mass recruitment, the foremost issue in ruling-class debate was how best to utilise and control migrant labour. Government commissions were set up in Switzerland, West Germany and elsewhere to study the 'problem of foreign workers'. It was, of course, the workers who were defined as the problem, rather than the discriminatory system set up to recruit them and restrict their rights. Now the issue is how to deal with minority youth, who are seen as a growing threat to social order and security. A spate of government reports on 'the integration of the second generation', has appeared in recent years. Again, it is the youth who are defined as the problem, rather than institutionalised discrimination and racism that keep them in a minority position and prevent equal participation in society.

Working-class youth is always a problem in capitalist society. It bears the potential for refusal to take on subordinate roles in the production process, for rejection of cultural domination, for violent revolt against prevailing norms and values. Youth is seen as a threat, whether its protest takes an individual or collective form. Powerful institutions – the family, school, social services, vocational training, work itself, police, the courts, prison, the army – have been developed to 'socialise' working-class youth and educate them to accept wage labour and social subordination – and to criminalise those who do not conform.

Even in prosperous times, socialisation cannot be completely controlled by the state and capital. Some young people develop sub-cultures of refusal and protest. But in periods of crisis, like the present one, the problem is far more acute. Large-scale unemployment and urban decline prevent school and work from functioning as effective agents of socialisation for working-class youth. The result is increasing non-conformity and unrest. The state responds by defining youth protest as criminal and by increasing social control, above all through the police.

Black and foreign working-class youth are particularly hard-hit by the crisis, both economically – unemployment, housing problems, and so on – and ideologically – for example, racism and campaigns for deportation. At the same time, the institutions of socialisation are far less effective in their case. The family is disrupted by migration and by insecure legal and socio-economic circumstances; the education system discriminates against minority children, giving them neither useful knowledge nor the certificates needed for access to the occupational system, decent work opportunities are closed. So the potential for rebellion among minority youth is even greater than among other groups.

Having unintentionally acquired new ethnic minorities, the states and media of Western Europe are now waking up to the fact that a second generation is growing up and that they will not automatically fill the class position of their parents. There is growing recognition that the schools are failing to cope. As Hans Krollmann, the minister of education of the West German *Land* (state) of Hesse put it:

> If we put the foreigners in national classes today, in which they cannot obtain German school certificates, we will have to cope with the social effects in a few years time, in the form of unemployment, ghetto-formation and criminality.[1]

The media have defined foreign youth in West Germany as a 'social time bomb'. Reports of criminality, riots and risings of black youth in the USA and Britain are receiving increasing attention as portents of what is to come. The message is rubbed in by sensational headlines on street crime in West German cities. Politicians use such reports to justify calls for stronger policing and more deportations of foreign offenders.

The underlying fear is that, given the choice between 'shit work' or no work at all, increasing numbers of minority youth are going to reject the social values and institutions that define them as inferior. (This trend has gone further in Britain than in the other Western European countries. The reasons lie in the greater maturity of the migratory process in Britain, and in special characteristics of black colonial migration to a declining imperial power.) This chapter will focus on the situation of foreign youth in West Germany. The underlying question is whether educational disadvantage, lack of occupational opportunities, and experience of racism and discrimination are taking the same forms they have in Britain.

One obvious and important difference should be mentioned at the outset: most children born to immigrant parents in Britain can obtain British nationality, so the overwhelming majority of black youth have citizenship. In West Germany and Switzerland children born to foreign parents do not gain the nationality of the country of birth, and naturalisation policies are highly restrictive. Almost all descendants of migrants therefore have foreign nationality. In other countries, citizenship policies are less restrictive, and many children of migrants are not foreigners. In Sweden, the foreign population is 422,000, but the number of people of migrant origin is put at over a million. A French government report estimated the number of 'young people of foreign origin' aged 0–25 years in 1980 to be at least 2.2 million. Three-quarters were said to have been born in France, and one-third had French nationality. The number of young people of foreign origin was growing at a rate of 115,000 per year (95,000 children born in France and 20,000 new entrants).[2]

What is the significance of nationality? Possessing citizenship of the country of residence does not mean that young people of migrant origin enjoy equal political, economic or social rights. It does not mean that their language and culture are the same as those of the majority of the population. But it would be wrong to regard citizenship as unimportant. People who lack security of residence, civil and political rights are prevented from participating fully in society. They do not have the opportunity of deciding to what extent they want to interact with the rest of the population, and to what extent they want to preserve their own culture and norms. The choice is pre-empted by legal disabilities, which lead to isolation, separatism and alienation. The option of becoming a citizen may not automatically lead to equality and full participation, but it is a pre-condition for it. That is why naturalisation and citizenship is a major issue throughout Western Europe.

Youth of migrant origin in Western Europe

The waves of labour migration in the fifties, sixties and early seventies were followed, after a lag of some years, by family reunification or the establishment of new families in the immigration countries. Most of the original labour migrants were young adults, predominantly men. The curtailment of labour migration and the shift to family migration and settlement have led to a shift in demographic structure. As shown for West Germany and Britain in chapter 4, populations of migrant origin still show a bulge in the 0–15-year-old group. Because the overwhelming majority of migrants were of child-bearing age, family reunification has led to relatively high birth rates, and a new generation of descendants of migrants is now growing up throughout Western Europe.

In Britain, it was estimated that 7 per cent of all births in 1980 were to black mothers, and that 40 per cent of the black population was British-born.[3] The overwhelming majority of black school-children were born in Britain. Half the foreign population of Belgium were aged below 25 in 1977. The 1975 French census counted 1.3 million foreigners aged less than 25 – 39 per cent of the total foreign population. In Sweden, under-25s made up 45 per cent of the foreign population; for Switzerland the corresponding figure was 38 per cent.[4] Everywhere, foreigners are underrepresented in the higher age groups, and overrepresented among the youth. In France and Belgium, foreigners are around 7 per cent of the total population, but around 10 per cent of the under-25 population. In Sweden, foreigners are 5 per cent of the total population, but 7 per cent of the under-25s, and in Switzerland, around 14 per cent of the total population, but 16 per cent of the under-25s.[5]

The most dramatic change in the demographic structure of the foreign population of West Germany has been the increase in the number of children and young people. The number of under-16s rose from 364,000 in 1969 to 768,000 in 1974, and 1.2 million in 1981. A quarter of the foreign population were children in 1981 (see table 4.2) and 54 per cent of them had been born in West Germany. If the 16–24-year-olds are added, then 1.8 million of the 4.6 million foreigners were under 25 – about 40 per cent of the total foreign population.

Table 6.1 shows the number of children of various nationalities; 555,000 children are Turkish, nearly half of all foreign 0–15-year-olds, although Turks altogether make up only one-third of the foreign population. Of the Turks, 36 per cent are aged 0–15 compared with 22–28 per cent of the other nationalities. It is on this basis that the 'second generation problem' is increasingly being defined by the state and the media as a 'Turkish youth problem'.

Table 6.1.   Foreign children in West Germany by nationality, 1981

Nationality	Children aged 0–15	
	000s	%
Italy	146	13
Spain	40	3
Portugal	30	2
Greece	83	7
Yugoslavia	142	12
Turkey	555	48
Others	170	15
Total	**1,166**	**100**

Source: *OECD SOPEMI 1982*, p. 41.

Foreigners make up 7.5 per cent of the total population of West Germany, but 13 per cent of births are to foreign mothers. Foreign birth rates are likely to remain high because of the age structure of the foreign population, while the German birth rate is declining. But migrants have settled mainly in inner-city areas, where a large proportion of the remaining German population is elderly. In many such areas, births to foreign mothers make up 50 per cent or more of the total. For instance, 45 per cent of children born in the city of Frankfurt in 1974 had foreign parents, but the percentage in the inner-city districts was far higher.[6]

Migration and the family

The experience of migration has a profound effect on foreign workers' families, and hence on the conditions of socialisation of the children, whether they are born before or after the move. This very real problem is often overstated by sociologists to give the impression of a sudden move between two totally different kinds of society; the background of the migrants in Southern Europe and Turkey is described as being characterised by pre-industrial forms of production and social organisation. The central institution of social life is seen as the extended family, which is responsible both for production (agriculture or handicrafts), and for re-production (nourishment, child care, socialisation, health care and provision for old age). Community life is dominated by the patronage of landowners and other dignitaries, and by traditional religious (either Catholic or Muslim) norms for family structure, gender roles and social behaviour. The situation in West Germany, on the other hand, is characterised as an isolated, individual existence in an anonymous society, dominated by the ration-ality of industrial production, and regulated by bureaucratic, impersonal administration.

This dichotomy gives rise to the idea that migrants suffer a 'culture shock', which makes it hard for them to cope in the new country, while their children are 'torn between two cultures'. However, these notions are misleading, for they imply that migrants move between two intact, coherent and homogeneous societies. The reality is different. In response to the spread of capitalist farming and industry, the social and economic frame-work of the countries of origin is going through dissolution and change. Traditional forms of production are collapsing, and family farms and handicraft enterprises can no longer provide a livelihood. Internal migration, political conflict and shifts in family and social structures correspond with this process. Also, many of the migrants come from the more developed areas of the countries of origin, and have already experienced such trans-formations.

Recent research indicates that the extended family is no longer dominant in Turkey. It is being replaced by the nuclear family, so that many Turkish workers have decided to bring their children to West Germany for lack of child-care facilities in Turkey.[7] While traditional family and community structures dissolve, their modern counterparts – social insurance schemes, health care, pensions – are developing only slowly, if at all. Emigration is indeed the most obvious expression of this process of economic and social change.

It is highly misleading to think that migrants have intact, extended families to return to in case of need. A specific sort of migrant or 'guest worker family' develops, leading a marginalised existence during the migratory process.[8] This insecure family is a temporary phenomenon, but it has been the essential unit of primary socialisation for the foreign children now growing up in West Germany.

The guest worker family is temporary because migrants are rapidly developing new communities in the inner cities where they settle. These help to overcome the isolation and insecurity implicit in the experience of migration. New relations and institutions are being established in a struggle against the institutional discrimination of the guest worker system, against exploitative landlords, and against the day-to-day racism of West German society.

Rather than being 'torn between two cultures', migrant youth are part of a new and evolving 'culture of migration'. This is not just a combination of various aspects of the culture of the countries of origin and of immigration. It embodies the dynamic response of migrants to the experience of migration, and to the problems of working-class existence in the inner city. The culture of migration is contradictory and volatile at this formative stage, for it has to try to incorporate elements of experience which are in themselves irreconcilable.[9]

At the present time, the situation of many foreign children is still characterised by a high degree of mobility and insecurity. When the father or mother originally migrated, the children were often left with relatives in the country of origin, and only brought in after some years. Later on, children (including those born in West Germany) are frequently sent back to the country of origin to attend school. When children reach school-leaving age (11 in Turkey) they are brought back to West Germany and continue schooling there. Yet others are left with grandparents until they get close to working age, or until they reach the maximum age for entry as dependants (15 at present). Young men often return to the country of origin to do their military service, and then return to West Germany (if permitted to do so).[10]

Movement between country of origin and West Germany may be for more personal reasons. There are more foreign boys than girls in West Germany, indicating a preference to leave girls in the country of origin. In other cases, girls are brought over to look after younger brothers and sisters. Some children are sent home because the family cannot find an adequate dwelling, and may be sent for later on if better housing is found.

It is impossible to say how many children have experienced this oscillation between the two countries, but it is far from unusual. The effects on children's mental development, social relationships and school success are often negative. Underlying the problem is foreigners' lack of security of residence, and the resulting impossibility of making clear plans for the future of the family. Most migrants still want to return to the country of origin at some time, or expect that they will be forced to do so. So they are not sure whether it is more important for children to learn German and succeed in the German education system, or to maintain full knowledge of the language and culture of the country of origin. Insecurity is a constant source of worry for both parents and children.

Migration and the conditions of inner-city, working-class life often lead to considerable stress for foreign families. The parents' own upbringing has rarely prepared them adequately to cope with this situation. Marital relationships are often strained by long periods of separation, or by the need for both parents to go out to work. Cramped housing conditions and lack of social amenities make matters worse. Where foreign families live in isolation, lack of support from relatives and the community can be a serious problem. Often the need to work long hours means that parents have little time and energy left for their children, who are left to their own devices in a strange and sometimes hostile environment.

Family strain is exacerbated by the breakdown of the gender-roles of the countries of origin, especially where migrants come from strongly patriarchal societies, like Turkey. Where the father is no longer the sole breadwinner, his dominance over wife and children is weakened. Working mothers may demand more say in family affairs and begin to reject male authority, especially when the husband is unemployed and the wife becomes the sole earner. Some men try to reassert their authority through emphasis on traditional values, through return to patriarchal religion, and sometimes through violence towards wife and children. Wives who do not work, on the other hand, are frequently isolated, do not learn the language, and can do little to guide their children in

the new environment. Children often take on the role of interpreters and mediators between parents and bureaucratic institutions, weakening parental authority.

Despite these strains and conflicts, it would be wrong to see the
foreign family in West Germany as a 'pathological family', which
is somehow responsible for foreign childen's educational failure.
The idea of the 'pathological black family' has been advanced in
Britain as a convenient explanation of continued social disadvantage of black youth.[11] There is no evidence that foreign
families break down more frequently than German families. On
the contrary, the rate of divorce among Germans is higher.
Foreign families are at least as likely to be able to provide
emotional support and refuge for the children. It is not the family
that is pathological, but the conditions under which migration and
settlement have taken place, and the constant pressure of discriminatory laws that often split families. The establishment of
closely knit, inner-city minority communities and the trend
towards cultural separateness are mechanisms of defence against
such conditions.

One of the most obvious problems of the foreign child is
language. If left in the country of origin until school age, children
have serious language problems upon entering a German school.
Even children born in West Germany have difficulties, for German
is rarely spoken at home, and most playmates in inner-city areas
are likely to be of the same nationality. Foreign children's
language problems are often highly complex. If the child is of
Kurdish parentage, which is frequently the case, she or he also has
to learn Turkish to manage in the preparatory class and the
mother-tongue class (see below). She or he also has to learn the
local dialect to be able to communicate with German children, as
well as high German for normal classes. So it is a matter of
learning not just one language, but three. Young Macedonians,
Sicilians, Catalonians, Basques and others have similar difficulties.

Young foreigners also share the problems encountered by all
working-class children in an educational system geared to the
language, norms, values and behavioural patterns of the middle
class. Success in education for working-class children often means
rejecting their origins and accepting middle-class cultural dominance as a pre-condition for selection for higher levels of education.
This class selection system is highly effective in West Germany;

less than 10 per cent of university students come from working-class homes.

Foreign children in education

The 'dual strategy'

In Britain, the fact of permanent settlement of black immigrants was recognised early. The education system was regarded as having an essential role in making the newcomers' children into Britons, with the same values and behaviour as the rest of the population. Hazel Carby describes this policy:

> We can characterise initial educational policy as embodying the philosophy of assimilation. Schools were viewed as the primary site for successful assimilation. Black parents were referred to only as potential or actual inhibitors of this process. In commonsense terms the system was seen as capable of absorbing black children; 'race problems' would literally die away with the older generations.[12]

By the late sixties, however, it was becoming evident that policies of individual assimilation of black children through imbibing English language and culture at school were failing. The result was a shift towards policies of 'multi-culturalism', based on the principle of 'pluralistic integration'. Blacks were to be integrated into society as members of distinct ethnic groups. Certain aspects of their cultures were to be encouraged as a potential enrichment of social life, while others were rejected as threatening to British society. It was argued that black children were failing at school because of 'complex disabilities', arising from language, 'cultural shock' and 'pathological' family structure. The result was a shift towards direct intervention, linking the social services, the schools and even the police in involvement in the education of black children.[13]

Policies have taken a very different course in West Germany. Large-scale entry of foreign children was not anticipated nor desired by the state, and the fact of settlement is still not officially recognised. Policies towards foreign youth have therefore been fragmentary, contradictory and belated, and apparently guided by the hope that they would go away if life were made uncomfortable for them. The official principle of policy towards foreign youth is generally known as the 'dual strategy', as formulated by the *Bund-*

Länder-Kommission (a commission of enquiry linking federal and state governments) in 1977. This consists of measures designed to encourage the legal, social and economic integration of foreigners, while at the same time encouraging them to go back home (see p. 79 above).

When foreign children unexpectedly started entering the schools in large numbers in the sixties, there were no clear policies. In West Germany education is not the responsibility of the federal government, but rather of the 11 *Länder* (state) governments, which differ considerably in political complexion. At first, the *Länder* adopted quite different courses. There was not even agreement as to whether schooling should be compulsory for foreign workers' children, or whether the governments of the countries of origin should be permitted to set up national schools – a course much favoured by dictatorships as a means of political and cultural control. By the late sixties most of the *Länder* had made attendance at West German schools compulsory, and were beginning to take special measures to tackle the problems of foreign children. A general policy for the whole country was proposed in 1971 by the Standing Conference of Education Ministers (*Kultusministerkonferenz*) – a consultative body linking federal and state authorities. Policy was revised and updated in 1976 although most substantial points remained unchanged. In many respects West German policies are similar to those laid down by the 1977 EEC Directive on the Education of Migrant Workers' Children. However, measures are implemented by the *Länder* governments, and there are important variations.

The aims of the 1976 Decision of the Standing Conference of Education Ministers were defined as follows:

> It is a question of enabling foreign pupils to learn the German
> language and to obtain German school-leaving certificates,
> as well as allowing them to keep and improve their knowledge
> of their mother tongue. At the same time, educational
> measures should contribute to the social integration of the
> foreign pupils during the duration of their stay in the German
> Federal Republic. They also assist in the maintenance of their
> linguistic and cultural identity.[14]

Again we see the 'dual strategy': schools were to help foreign children integrate into West German society and at the same time prepare them for return to the country of origin. The Decision was to be implemented through setting up special 'preparatory classes' to give intensive language instruction to prepare foreign pupils for entry to normal classes, and 'native-language classes' to maintain knowledge of the language and culture of the country of origin. The contradictory aims of the dual strategy and the isolation and strain caused by the special classes are at the root of many of the difficulties experienced by foreign youth.

Pre-school and after-school facilities

Pre-school education could play an important role for foreign children, by helping them to become familiar with the German language and culture, and preparing them for the demands made by school. It is officially claimed that about half of all foreign children aged 3–6 years attend nurseries, compared with four-fifths of German children. Nursery attendance is lowest for Turks (39 per cent), compared with 43 per cent for Greeks, 46 per cent for Italians, 56 per cent for Spaniards, 68 per cent for Yugoslavs and 75 per cent for Portuguese.[15] However, other sources indicate far lower rates of nursery attendance: between 16 and 30 per cent in some areas.[16] In any case, there is no doubt that nursery attendance is far lower than for German children.

Why do children who need pre-school education most attend least? One reason is the unfamiliarity of foreign parents with nurseries, which are less common in the countries of origin. Another is the concentration of foreign families in inner-city areas, where nurseries are least adequate, in both number and quality. Many foreign workers are unable to pay the high fees charged by some nurseries. Parents are afraid of the cultural and ideological influences their children may be exposed to – especially in view of the fact that about two-thirds of nurseries in West Germany are run by church bodies. This is of special importance for Muslims, who also worry about the food served, which often contains pork. Another reason for low nursery attendance of Turkish children is the relatively low rate of employment for Turkish women – a factor common to Muslims throughout Western Europe. There are also cases of discrimination, with preference given to Germans where there is a shortage of places.[17] If both parents have to work and cannot find a nursery place, children are sometimes left alone all day. Others are cared for by older sisters, whose own schooling is hampered. Some children are cared for by unregistered child-minders, usually of the same nationality.

Even when foreign children do attend nurseries, little is done to respond to their special needs. There are a few national, bilingual or multi-lingual nurseries, designed to try out various strategies for the cultural integration of immigrant children. But the overwhelming majority of foreign children are at nurseries designed to meet the needs of German children. Despite official recommendations, it is rare for staff to have any training on the special problems of foreign children, and there are virtually no special educational programmes in use (although some have been worked out and tested in recent years). In general, nurseries do little to prepare foreign children for success at school.

Foreign parents' child-care problems are far from over when their children start school at the age of six. West German schools seem to work on the assumption that there is always a mother at home, ready to care for the children. School generally runs only in the mornings, starting at eight o'clock. The timetable varies from day to day, and in the first few years may consist of only two or three lessons. After-school care is urgently needed and official facilities are far from adequate. Voluntary organisations have tried to fill the gap, providing after-school play facilities and help with homework for foreign children. It is official policy to provide financial and organisational help for such efforts, but in recent years voluntary groups have found themselves severely hit by cuts in social expenditure and many have had to close down. Many foreign children are on the street after school. Moreover, homework is required from the age of six onwards, and foreign children are further handicapped, for their parents often lack the time and the educational background to help them.

Preparatory classes
When they reach the school age of six, foreign children take the same tests of maturity and ability as German children. Children not considered mature enough for school may be sent to 'preliminary classes' (*Vorklassen*), where they receive special instruction for a year, before being sent to join the first class of a normal primary school, or of an educationally sub-normal school (*ESN, Sonderschule*), if still backward. Preliminary classes are not only for foreign children, but they are overrepresented in them. Around

30 per cent of children in such classes in Hesse in 1979–80 were foreign. On the other hand, foreign children are not significantly overrepresented at ESN schools.

This is different from Britain, where there has been considerable evidence of discriminatory practices that send large numbers of black children to ESN schools. In 1972, the last year for which statistics are available, children of West Indian origin were 1.1 per cent of all children in state schools, but 4.9 per cent of all children in ESN schools.[18] Bernard Coard's study showed how culturally biased tests, low teacher expectations, and poor self-esteem and self-concept led to black children being classified as sub-normal.[19] This does not happen in West Germany, presumably because there is a system of separate preparatory or national classes for foreign children.

Foreign six-year-olds, whose knowledge of German is considered inadequate, do not start school in normal classes, but in preparatory classes (*Vorbereitungsklassen*). These are meant to prepare them for transition to normal schooling through intensive instruction in German, as well as through teaching of general subjects in the mother tongue. Children who come to West Germany over the age of six also generally start school in preparatory classes, which exist at all age levels in primary and secondary modern schools. Transition to normal classes is supposed to take place as soon as the pupil is ready for it, at the latest after two years. The class teacher is generally a compatriot of the children, while intensive language instruction is supposed to be given by a German teacher.

Transition to normal classes is rarely as rapid and smooth as it should be. The reasons lie in the cultural problems of migration and in the socio-economic position of foreign teachers and children. A high proportion of school-beginners are foreign. In Hesse, 19 per cent of 5–6-year-olds were foreign in 1980.[20] In many towns, foreign children make up a quarter or more of school entrants. In Frankfurt, for instance, the figure was 38 per cent for the whole city in 1980, going up to 80 per cent in some neighbourhoods.[21] Official policy in most *Länder* is to keep the share of foreign children in normal classes below 20 per cent.[22] This level is almost unobtainable, unless foreign children are kept out of normal classes for as long as possible, by concentrating them in preparatory or national classes. In West Berlin, school law was amended in 1982 to lay down a maximum of 50 per cent foreigners in a class. If there are too many foreign children, foreigners-only classes are to be set up.[23]

The easiest way out for the school authorities is to gather foreign children together in a few central schools, which may mean busing children from outlying areas. The official rationale for this course is that centralisation allows for special remedial and language teaching facilities. Often there appears to be pressure from German parents, who fear that their children may be at a disadvantage in schools where most pupils are foreign. The result is the development of schools with a high share of preparatory classes, and with low educational standards. In effect this means partial segregation in the school system.

In some *Länder*, authorities are now responding to this danger by trying to phase out preparatory classes and replace them with intensive German courses for foreign children who spend most of their time in normal classes.[24] In Bavaria, on the other hand, the maintenance of national classes is official policy, and it is possible for foreign children to spend their whole school life in a so-called bilingual class. Teaching is supposed to be partly in the foreign language and partly in German, with the proportion of the latter increasing as time goes on.[25] But in fact children in such classes frequently learn little German, and have no chance of success in the German school system.

The number of children in preparatory classes varies in the different *Länder*. In Hesse in 1981 the figure was 5,186 out of all 70,441 foreign pupils – a relatively low proportion of 7.4 per cent.[26] In Bavaria, on the other hand, no less than 47 per cent of foreign children were in bilingual classes in the 1980–81 school year.[27]

Children encounter considerable difficulties in the preparatory classes. A Kurdish or Macedonian child, for example, entering a preparatory class may be confronted with a teacher and children of the same nationality, but whose speech she or he cannot understand. Another problem is the wide range of age and experience in the class. A six-year-old Turk born in Berlin may be sitting next to a nine-year-old straight from Anatolia. Even the best teacher is likely to have trouble maintaining interest and discipline in such diverse classes.

An important cause of the problems of preparatory classes is the insecure situation of the foreign teachers. The use of foreign teachers is one of the main planks of the dual strategy. Most West German education authorities have left teacher-recruitment to the governments of the countries of origin. These in turn have rejected use of the teachers already in West Germany, whose political loyalty is suspect. Instead they send out 'politically reliable' teachers. The special training they receive before coming (if any) is inadequate, so many foreign teachers know little about West German society and hardly speak German. In Hesse, an official survey found that 43 per cent of foreign teachers did not speak enough German to carry out their duties effectively.[28] Foreign teachers are supposed to attend staff meetings and to teach the normal curriculum and textbooks. But if they do not speak enough German, they are left to their own devices, generally using textbooks from their home country which are inappropriate to German conditions, and which do not prepare children for entry to normal classes.

Foreign teachers are employed by the German authorities, but they are paid neither for their qualifications (which vary widely) nor by normal teachers' salary scales. Employed specifically to teach foreign workers' children, their contracts are inferior in pay and conditions to those of German teachers. Unlike German teachers who normally have tenure for life, immigrant teachers have no security of employment. They appear to themselves and their pupils as 'second-class teachers for second-class pupils'.[29] Indeed, an unwitting premium is put on failure to meet declared policy aims. Foreign teachers who successfully prepare pupils for entry to normal classes are working themselves out of a job. As soon as the number of pupils in the preparatory class falls below 12, the class may be dissolved and the teacher dismissed.

Data on foreign children's length of stay in preparatory classes appears to be unobtainable, but there is considerable evidence that very few children manage the transition after just one year, and many stay for two years or longer. Often the term 'preparatory class' is simply a euphemism for permanent one-nationality classes – ghettos within the schools – which prevent rather than facilitate integration into normal classes. The Frankfurt branch of the Teachers' Union (GEW) has called the special classes 'an illegitimate but firmly established national school system'.[30]

Native language classes

Special classes, set up to develop and maintain fluency in the language of the country of origin and knowledge of its culture, also have the effect of segregating children on a national basis. The declared aim of these classes is to keep the option of repatriation open by preventing alienation from the area of origin. Basic instruction in language, history, geography and 'national norms and values' is given by a teacher of the appropriate nationality. Such classes are administered and financed by German school authorities and are held in schools, often in the afternoon or on Saturday, and, as a rule, for five hours a week. They are compulsory, where available, but in fact do not cover all foreign children. In 1980 about 40 per cent of foreign children in Hesse attended native language classes.[31]

Attendance at such classes has been criticised because of the added strain it puts on foreign children, taking up time needed for doing homework, and hindering normal schooling. Little attempt is made to co-ordinate the content of the native language classes with normal schooling. Foreign teachers generally use the curricula and textbooks of the countries of origin – a desirable practice from the point of view of aiding future reintegration. But can education that is irrelevant to a child's actual life lead to successful learning?

Native language classes are a focus for the battle for ideological control of foreign children. Authoritarian regimes select the teachers and put pressure on them to follow the correct line. The Turkish military regime forces teachers to use militarist and fascist material. Turkish parents are often put under pressure by consulates and teachers to send their children to Koran schools, in addition to the normal native language classes. There they have to learn in yet another language, Arabic. Many Koran schools are not only bearers of religion and culture, but also spread reactionary ideologies.

Foreign trade unionists have repeatedly protested at the indoctrination carried out with official sanction in the native language classes. Some social-democratic *Länder* governments have taken steps to control teaching in such classes, and to curb the use of Koran schools by far-right organisations. These measures have been ineffective, partly because the authorities are incapable of monitoring what is going on, but also because the West German state is anxious to co-operate with the governments of the countries of origin, however reactionary they may be. In an attempt to overcome these difficulties, some *Länder* have introduced Islamic religious instruction as a regular school subject.

Throughout Western Europe interest in bilingualism has grown in recent years. Swedish and Finnish educators have pointed to the importance of fluency in the native language for a child's intellectual and social development. They believe that children should receive initial schooling in the native language, and learn the language of the immigration country as a second language, before entering normal classes after some years. This debate has also been taken up in Britain, where minority communities have tended to develop their own native language schools outside the state system.[32] The debate on the pedagogical merits of bilingualism is overshadowed by the political implications. As long as native language classes are an instrument of cultural domination and an element of state repatriation policies, they cannot serve the interests of foreign children and parents.

Normal schooling

The foreign children most likely to succeed in education are those who start their school career in normal classes together with German children, or at least enter such classes after a brief period in a preparatory class. Overcoming foreign children's special difficulties requires well-trained teachers in adequately staffed and equipped schools, but such conditions are all too seldom available.

In 1980–81, 637,100 foreign children were enrolled at West German schools (an increase of 1.5 per cent on the previous year). On average they made up 12 per cent of primary school pupils and 10 per cent of secondary modern school pupils. But regional distribution was very uneven: a third of all primary and secondary modern pupils in West Berlin were foreigners. In Hamburg 40 schools had over 30 per cent foreign pupils.[33] Many inner-city schools have more foreign than German pupils; sometimes the foreign proportion is as high as 80 per cent.

Many German teachers find it hard to cope with large classes containing several different nationalities, especially in the old, overcrowded and poorly equipped schools of the inner cities. The variation in ages of children transferred from preparatory classes does not help matters. A 10-year-old in a class of 7-year-olds presents serious problems for the teacher. Bored by the subject matter and ashamed at being put on a level with much younger children, the 10-year-old is likely to react with aggression and disruption or inattention and truancy. The teacher has little time to devote to the specific problems of each pupil, as 30 or more others need attention.

Very little has been done to prepare teachers for the task of teaching foreign pupils. Until recently, teachers' training colleges did not provide any special instruction on this topic. Now courses are being introduced, usually as voluntary options. But these measures affect only new staff, of whom there are few, since falling birth rates and expenditure cuts mean that schools are not taking on many new teachers. Older teachers have no special training. The Teachers' Union has demanded special in-service training for all teachers of foreign pupils, but this is unlikely to be introduced because of the cost of replacing teachers during the training period. Nor has much been done to provide special teaching materials for the needs of immigrant children, although some research and development projects in this field are being completed.

These deficiencies are all the more disturbing, considering that the 'bulge' of foreign children is only just entering the schools. In Hesse, 16 per cent of children in the first school year were foreign in 1980–81; the figure for the eighth year of school was only 6 per cent. As the bulge moves up through the age-groups, the foreign share in schools will go up to 12–15 per cent in the next few years.[34] The best solution to foreign children's educational problems would be to employ more teachers, to provide intensive language and remedial courses, and more individual attention. This has been official policy in Hesse since 1978. There is supposed to be one extra teacher for every 75 foreign children. It was said that 1,000 extra teachers were employed in this way in 1980–81, plus another 54 paid for by the European Social Fund. However, half these extra teachers were foreigners employed for preparatory and native language classes. The other 500 were often not specifically engaged in teaching foreign children.[35]

The situation in the normal schools is complex. To describe it adequately would require examining reports by individual teachers in various types of schools.[36] Here it is possible only to identify certain problems. When (and if) children are transferred from preparatory classes to normal classes, their knowledge of German is often too poor for them to learn well. Most studies rely on verbal communication, so that foreign children are at a disadvantage not only in German but also in geography, maths, history, social studies and scientific subjects. The only classes where foreign children are less hampered by language are those involving manual or artistic skills, but such subjects play a minor part in the curriculum, and are not significant for passing exams or finding employment later on. Most school authorities regard remedial classes and intensive language teaching as essential for foreign children who attend normal classes, but such facilities are rarely available in practice. The result is that many children are designated failures in normal classes and sent back to preparatory classes; the proportion is as high as 40 per cent in some schools.[37]

Where there are many children of a particular nationality in a normal class, they tend to spend most of their time together speaking their own language. Such groups do not become integrated into the class, and conflicts between them and Germans or other nationalities may develop. Of course, the presence of strong national groupings within a class can also be a benefit, if the teacher is able and willing to bring their culture into learning, and to use it as a basis of communication with other children.[38] But few teachers are capable of doing this. All too often, teachers feel helpless in the face of the problems of large multinational classes. They end up merely trying to maintain discipline, and give up all hope of securing an adequate educational level for their pupils. Many teachers try to get transferred out of inner-city areas.

Parents react too. Some foreigners come to the conclusion that their children have no chance in West German schools, and demand the right to set up national schools. There have been considerable conflicts on this issue. National schools may be used by reactionary governments and political groups to indoctrinate children with nationalist and fascist ideologies. The German far right, and some CDU and CSU politicians, support national schools because they encourage repatriation. On the other hand, national schools help children to develop their cultural identity and protect them from racism. It is certainly cynical when the West German authorities forbid national schools in West Germany, but encourage and finance German schools wherever there are German settlers abroad. The move towards national schools is most marked among parents who hope to be able to return to their own countries reasonably soon, especially Greeks and Spaniards.

Many German parents withdraw their children from inner-city schools, and demand that they should be enrolled in suburbs with low foreign populations, even if it means travelling considerable distances. Other German parents put pressure on teachers to concentrate on their children, and not spend too much time on the special problems of foreign pupils. But there are also many instances of German and foreign parents joining in struggles for better school conditions, and carrying out campaigns for more teachers and improved facilities. Some multinational parents' groups have organised after-school clubs, providing play facilities and help with homework. In other cases German parents give individual assistance to foreign children.[39]

The consequences

The special educational problems of foreign children and the inadequacy of official measures to cope with them lead to severe educational handicaps. One is *under attendance at school*: many foreign children go to school for a few years only, or not at all. This applies particularly to the so-called 'late entrants' (*Späteinsteiger*), the foreign children brought over only a few years before reaching working age. Many can see no point in going to German schools for a short period only, especially as they rarely speak the language. They hang about until they are working age, or work illegally in the informal economy. Their chances of getting a reasonable job are almost nil. Another group which does not attend school are children brought in illegally because the parents cannot get permission for them to enter as dependants. The current tightening of rules on family reunification is likely to lead to the growth of this group. These children cannot attend school; to do so would invite deportation and, for obvious reasons, there are no statistics on them.

Many legally resident children do not go to school either. It is officially claimed that school attendance of foreign children aged 6–15 (the years of compulsory education) has increased from 50 per cent in 1970 to 75 per cent in 1978 and to 92 per cent in 1980.[40] The latter figure should be taken with a large pinch of salt, as it conflicts with data provided at the local and *Land* level. In Hesse, for instance, a survey showed that only 77 per cent of 8- to 14-year-old children attended school in 1980–81.[41] School attendance appears to decline with increasing age, partly because of 'late entrants', partly due to children leaving school earlier than school-leaving age. On the whole it seems likely that about one-fifth of foreign children do not attend school – a disturbing figure even if it represents an improvement over previous years.

Another education handicap is *underrepresentation* in the upper levels of selective secondary education. West Germany still has a tripartite system: the *Hauptschule* corresponds to the British secondary modern; the *Realschule* is a sort of middle school, ending with a certificate that gives access to intermediate vocational training as well as white-collar employment; the *Gymnasium* corresponds to grammar school, giving access to university. Less than 3 per cent of students are at the experimental *Gesamtschule* (comprehensives).

Table 6.2.   Students by type of school, West Germany, school year 1980–81 (%)

| | Type of school | | | | |
	Primary and secondary modern	ESN	Middle	Grammar	Comprehensive
Foreigners	83	4	5	6	2
Germans	53	4	16	25	3

Source: *Statistisches Jahrbuch* 1982, p. 346.

Table 6.2 shows distribution of German and foreign students by school type. These figures show a very substantial concentration of foreign children in primary and secondary modern schools, and underrepresentation in middle and grammar schools. However they do not measure underrepresentation precisely, because primary and secondary modern schools are lumped together, and because no account is taken of variations in age structure of German and foreign children.

Tischler gives a more accurate comparison, by comparing school types attended by foreign and German 14-year-olds (table 6.3). The figures refer to the *Land* Hesse only, but may be regarded as reasonably typical of the whole of West Germany. About 60 per cent of foreign students aged 14 attend secondary modern schools, compared with around a third of German students. Only 11 per cent of foreign students attend grammar schools, compared with

Table 6.3. 14-year-old students at various types of schools in Hesse (%)

| | Type of School | | | | | |
	Secondary modern	ESN	Middle	Grammar	Comprehensive	Vocational
Foreigners						
1976–7	60	3	10	13	12	1
1980–1	59	6	12	11	12	1
Germans						
1976–7	28	5	23	25	16	3
1980–1	23	5	26	29	16	2

Source: Lothar C. Tischler, *Ausländerreport Hessen 1982*, Wiesbaden: HLT Gesellschaft für Forschung, Planung, Entwicklung 1982, p. 101.

29 per cent of Germans. The situation of foreign students in selective secondary education is greatly inferior to that of Germans; moreover the position of foreigners did not improve between 1976–77 and 1980–81, while the percentage of Germans in middle and grammar schools increased.[42] The *Hauptschule* is fast becoming a school for foreigners, while Germans move into the *Realschule* and *Gymnasium*, which offer far better job prospects and access to higher education.

Attendance at selective schools varies considerably for the different nationalities. In 1980–81 only 11 per cent of 14-year-old Turks were at grammar or middle schools. The figures for other nationalities were: Yugoslavs 38 per cent, Spaniards 33 per cent, Greeks 26 per cent, Italians 20 per cent and Portuguese 18 per cent. Of the Germans, 59 per cent were at grammar or middle schools.[43] One reason for the poor performance of Turkish children may be that this is the nationality with highest percentage of recent entrants, so that many of the children have only been in West Germany for a short time.

The third education handicap is *underachievement at school*. About half the foreign children who attend secondary moderns leave without obtaining the *Hauptschulabschluss* – the school-leaving certificate that corresponds to the British Certificate of Secondary Education (CSE).[44] This certificate is generally the minimum requirement for getting an apprenticeship or any other form of vocational training. Young foreigners without the

Hauptschulabschluss have very little chance of finding employment. Success varies according to nationality: in Hesse in 1979–80 only 36 per cent of Turks left the *Hauptschule* with a certificate, compared with 72 per cent of Greeks, 64 per cent of Italians, 77 per cent of Yugoslavs, 55 per cent of Portuguese, 73 per cent of Spaniards and 86 per cent of Germans.

In summary, many young foreigners find that West German schools provide them with neither useful knowledge nor formal qualifications needed for getting vocational training or finding a decent job, so they attend sporadically or not at all. Teenage girls are often kept at home to look after younger brothers and sisters, and boys are sent out to work in the informal sector, at exploitative wages and without insurance. Many of those who do attend school regularly still do not obtain certificates, so their fate is sealed: a future of insecure unskilled labour, alternating with unemployment. Nor do young foreigners get an adequate grounding in the language of their parents' country of origin, so they are likely to have difficulties if they do return. No wonder that schooling for foreign workers' children has been called 'education for bilingual illiteracy'.[45]

According to Hazel Carby:

> The expectations of what schooling in Britain would mean for the black community were shattered by the end of the sixties. The social-democratic rallying cry of 'equality of opportunity' became demonstrably bankrupt. The research of Bernard Coard into the over-representation of black children in Educationally Sub-Normal (ESN) schools presented what many black parents were already experiencing – formal schooling was not going to provide an alternative future for their children.[46]

Foreign parents and youth in West Germany are coming to a similar realisation, setting the stage for coming struggles concerning education.

Vocational training and access to employment

The knowledge, social skills and – above all – the certificates provided by schools are the main determinants of work opportunities. If youth of migrant origin are severely handicapped by the school system, then their job chances are also going to be poor. There is strong evidence for this in West Germany.

Young people who leave school at the age of 15 or 16 are supposed to enter work through what is called the 'dual system': an apprenticeship with an industrial, commercial or handicraft firm which provides practical on-the-job training, combined with one day a week at a vocational school (*Berufsschule*) which gives theoretical trade instruction as well as some general subjects (German, maths, social studies). Vocational school is compulsory for all 15- to 17-year-olds, unless they are still attending normal schools. Youths no longer at school, but without employment, are supposed to attend vocational school full time.

In fact most 15- to 17-year-old Germans are still at school: the figure in Hesse in 1980–81 was 65 per cent, but only 31 per cent for foreigners. Of the young Germans no longer at school, 96 per cent were attending vocational school, but the figure for foreigners was only 37 per cent.[47] Taking West Germany as a whole, something like half the 15- to 17-year-old foreigners are neither at normal schools nor at vocational schools.[48]

Even those young foreigners who are at vocational schools are often not on an equal footing with Germans. In 1980, only 45 per cent of foreigners at vocational schools in Hesse were employed as apprentices; the figure for Germans was 89 per cent. The majority of foreign vocational school students were either unskilled workers, or unemployed. Vocational schools provide special full-time courses for unemployed youth, known euphemistically as the 'occupational preparation year'. In Hesse in 1981–2, 34 per cent of participants in such courses were foreigners, compared with an average foreign share in vocational school students of 6 per cent. The proportion of foreign students in commercial and technical courses leading to higher qualifications was 2–4 per cent.[49]

Altogether young foreigners make up less than 3 per cent of apprentices in West Germany, although foreign workers are about 9 per cent of the labour force.[50] Employers give preference to Germans when taking on apprentices. Despite the crisis, the overwhelming majority of German youth receive vocational training, while most young foreigners remain unemployed or have to take unskilled jobs. In Hesse in 1980–81, 87 per cent of all young Germans no longer at school had apprenticeships, compared with 20 per cent of foreigners.[51] For the country as a whole, only 19 per cent of foreigners aged 15 to 18 were receiving vocational training in 1980 – a decline since 1976 when the figure was 25 per cent.[52]

Moreover, foreigners lucky enough to get apprenticeships tend to learn trades with poor prospects, generally in the handicrafts sector rather than in industry or commerce. For instance, 15 per cent of foreign apprentices in Berlin in 1979 were training to be hairdressers.[53] Most foreign apprentices are being trained for manual jobs, while the majority of Germans are in non-manual work.[54] In West Germany it is common practice for firms (especially in the handicrafts sector) to take on far more youngsters than can be employed after training: the apprentices provide a source of cheap labour. So, many of the foreigners who do manage to get training find themselves without a job after three years, and end up as unskilled labourers. According to a survey of workers aged 15–25 in 1979–80, about two-thirds of the foreigners were employed as unskilled workers, compared with only about one-fifth of the Germans.[55]

It is hard to assess the rate of unemployment for foreign youth. The number of foreigners reaching working age is growing rapidly, although the real bulge will not enter the labour market until the beginning of the 1990s. Official figures put the rate of foreign youth unemployment at around 6 per cent in 1980, compared with 3.7 per cent in 1974.[56] However these figures greatly underestimate actual unemployment. Young foreigners are only counted as unemployed if they hold a work permit; but these are granted only if they obtain a job – and even then, only if it is a job for which no German or EEC citizen is available. So most young foreigners who cannot find a first job are not classed as unemployed. Even young foreigners who do hold work permits often do not sign on at the employment exchanges, because they have not been employed long enough to qualify for benefit, they know that the employment exchange is unlikely to find them a job and they fear deportation in the event of long-term registration as unemployed.

There have been attempts to calculate youth unemployment by comparing the number of foreigners in each age group with the number in employment or still engaged in education. Dohse estimated a rate of unemployment of 33 per cent for foreigners aged 15 to 20 for the whole of West Germany in 1975. The rate for young woman was 41 per cent, 26 per cent for young men. Schober calculated the rate in 1978 at 31 per cent. The *Prognosinstitut* estimated that 'well over 50 per cent' of young foreigners in Berlin were out of work in 1978.[57] Most recently, Tischler calculated a rate of unemployment of 46 per cent for 15–17-year-old foreigners in Hesse. For the whole of the Federal Republic, a sample survey indicated that only about 24 per cent of foreign 15–17-year-olds were in employment. Assuming that about 30 per cent of the age group were still at school (as in Hesse), that indicates unemployment of about 45 per cent. Altogether between a third and half of young foreigners are out of work, and the figure has risen steeply in recent years.

Another disturbing trend is the growth of informal employment: irregular and insecure, often part time, without contract or social insurance – for example, helping in shops and bars or working 'the lump' (labour-only sub-contracting) on building sites. It is hard to estimate the size of this sector, although Tischler puts it at nearly a quarter of the 45,000 young foreigners aged 15–17 employed in West Germany in 1980.[58]

The system of schooling and vocational training designed to prepare working-class youth for wage employment is clearly failing in the case of young foreigners. In recognition, the state has introduced special courses known as MBSE (*Massnahmen zur Berufsvorbereitung und sozialen Eingliederung* – measures for vocational preparation and social integration). They combine language instruction with classes in reading, writing and maths, as well as 'social and life skills' (how to apply for jobs and fill in forms) and some basic technical instruction. MBSE courses last one year and do not provide any recognised vocational certificate, although it is hoped that employers will be more willing to take on young foreigners who have completed such courses.

The programme has strong similarities with the British Youth Opportunities Programme (YOP), although the latter is much larger and not exclusively for members of ethnic minorities. In both cases, the aim is to keep youth off the streets, to discipline young people rejected by the educational system in order to make them employable and to steer them towards the sort of low-grade jobs open to them.[59]

The official target group of the MBSE is young foreigners who leave secondary modern schools without certificates, but in fact the majority of participants are late entrants – foreign workers' children entering West Germany just before reaching working age

– because the federal government has decreed that young foreigners who take an MBSE course may obtain a work permit upon completion, rather than waiting two years from the date of entering the country, as is normally the rule. It is doubtful whether MBSE courses are of much use to late entrants, whose German is often not adequate to follow lessons. Indeed, there is little to indicate that MBSE courses do much to increase young foreigners' employment opportunities. A recent study by the federal Labour Office indicated that 35 per cent of those completing courses got jobs, and 15 per cent were able to get apprenticeships.[60] Presumably the other half remained unemployed. Moreover, information given to the author by teachers of MBSE courses indicates that jobs obtained upon completion are often of casual and of short duration.

Conclusion

The West German educational system is unable to offer adequate opportunities to foreign youth. They start off with the disadvantages of insecure legal status, language difficulties and the stress of inner-city life. The contradictory 'dual strategy', which aims at both integration in West Germany and preparation for repatriation, makes it impossible for foreign parents and children to develop clear perspectives. Overcrowded schools with poor facilities and inadequately trained teachers cannot give foreign children the support they need. The result is poor school attendance, early drop-outs and underachievement. A large proportion of young foreigners are labelled as failures before they even enter the world of work. The process is continued by poor access to vocational training, great difficulty in obtaining apprenticeships, and extremely high rates of unemployment. The situation of foreign youth in West Germany is very similar to that of black youth in Britain.

This picture is typical for the whole of Western Europe. In France, for instance, the Marange–Lebon Report has evidence of language difficulties, poor academic performance and over-representation of foreign children in non-academic secondary education. About a quarter of foreign children are estimated to be two years or more behind the curricular requirements for their age. In response, the French education authorities have set up preparatory and native language classes; and similar problems to those in West Germany have arisen. The report also mentions high rates of assignment to ESN schools. Foreign youth find it very difficult to get vocational training, and their rate of unemployment is very high. Young foreign women are especially hard hit by problems in finding work.[61]

The OECD study on *Young Foreigners and the World of Work* shows a broadly similar pattern in all five countries examined (West Germany, France, Belgium, Sweden and Switzerland). It concludes that:

> In the host countries as a whole, the various causes which help to handicap young foreigners in the process of integration in working life tend to favour a certain 'reproduction' of the labour force from generation to generation, that is to say to fix second generation migrants in a socio-professional situation akin to that of their parents.[62]

So in a certain sense, the foreign or minority working class is being reproduced. The first generation of labour migrants were recruited and hired for low-status manual jobs. Institutional discrimination, lack of educational opportunities and poor access to vocational training are forcing their children – the second generation – and increasingly, their children's children – the third generation – into the same social position. This trend was predictable at the beginning of the seventies or earlier,[63] and if the states concerned had been serious about offering equality of opportunity, they should have taken appropriate steps at that time. They did not do so, because the second generation was seen as a useful reserve of manual labour.

However, the reproduction of the foreign or minority working class is succeeding only partially. Because a large proportion of young people have no real chance of finding long-term employment, they are not being integrated into the labour process. Institutional discrimination and the failure of schools are so blatant that the ideology of equality of opportunity loses all credibility; minority youth see that they are not individually responsible for failure, but that the system is constructed to make them fail. The result is the emergence throughout Western Europe of growing numbers of young blacks or foreigners who are not only unemployed, but who have never been employed and are never likely to be employed. The institutions designed to socialise them into the wage-labour relation cannot function, because wage labour is not a feasible option for them. This is a major threat to state agencies of social control.[64]

On the surface, the socio-economic position of the second generation may look very similar to that of the original migrants, but this masks a much deeper subjective deprivation. As members of the black community of Southall in London have put it:

> The first generation of Southall's black settlers had a dual consciousness and a double burden. For while striving here to fulfil their duties to their family, they also had responsibilities to their extended family back home. Whilst living in the British present, they also had a vision of the future – a return home. For their children there was no dual consciousness, no 'home' where they belonged. There was nothing with which they could transmute the racism they encountered.[65]

First-generation migrants tend to compare their living and working conditions with the poverty and unemployment that caused them to migrate. They may be at the bottom of the pile in Western European stratification but that is not their sole frame of reference. Their aspirations remain fixed on return to the country of origin, however unrealistically.

But the second and third generations have a new frame of reference. Having grown up in Western Europe and having passed through the same learning processes as other young people, they often share the same aspirations about work, social life and personal development. But racism and discrimination bar the way to fulfilment of these aims. Denied a real chance of achieving the things they have been educated to strive for, members of the second and third generation become alienated, seek refuge in their own ethnic groups, and look for other ways of getting their rights.

Within their own communities, black and foreign youth develop their own forms of work and social interaction, which are often defined as threatening or criminal by the media and the state. Hence the attention paid to statistics on 'foreign criminality' throughout Western Europe.[66] Criminalising minority youth may be effective as a short-term strategy of social control, but it does nothing to change the conditions that cause cultural separatism and protest. The long-term effect must be to give demands for equal rights and opportunities a more political and militant character.

The US ghetto risings of the sixties were led by young blacks born in the industrial cities of the north and of California, rather than by the original migrants from the south. In Britain, black youth is rejecting 'shit work' and taking up the fight against police oppression in their communities. Are the urban risings in the USA and Britain portents of what is to come in the cities of the Continent? Certainly, there are special factors in Britain and the USA: the traditions of colonialism and slavery make racism in these countries especially virulent. The orientation of black youth towards Third World struggles makes militance all the greater.

But the main factor determining struggle is social experience. As children of migrant workers grow up with social and educational deprivation, and then find themselves denied a fair chance on the labour market, their awareness of racism and discrimination grows. If political consciousness and readiness to fight back in other Western European countries have not yet reached the same levels as in Britain, it is because the migratory process is at an earlier stage. Developments are a decade behind, but the direction is the same.

7. Racism and politics

The upsurge of hate

May Day 1982: I stand with a group of Germans and foreigners around the banner of the Initiative against Racism at the trade union rally in Frankfurt's central square. Suddenly we hear shouts of '*Sieg Heil*' and '*Ausländer raus*' (foreigners out). Several hundred young men with football scarves run across the road and smash into the crowd, attacking anyone who looks foreign with sticks, boots and tear gas. The Turkish workers break their flagpoles over their knees, and set about the young thugs, driving them off after a bitter fight. The police, with their riot gear and water cannon, only move in when it is all over. Later we discover that the attackers were Nuremberg Football Club fans in Frankfurt for a match and that they had been led to the trade union rally by neo-Nazis.

24 June 1982: A 26-year-old building worker called Helmut Oxner walks into a Nuremberg discotheque, pulls out a pistol and starts shooting at anyone who looks foreign. After killing three foreigners and wounding three more, he turns the pistol on himself. Oxner was a former member of the youth section of the neo-Nazi NPD (*Nationaldemokratische Partei*), and police found stickers of the NSDAP-AO (Organisation for the Rebuilding of the Nazi Party) in his pockets. Although Oxner had repeatedly been charged with racist offences, police had not taken away his gun permit.[1]

June 1982: In a Frankfurt housing estate occupied by foreigners and by Germans at the bottom of the poverty scale, a middle-aged German feels disturbed by the noisy games of Turkish children. He grabs three-year-old Aladin Cosgun and pushes him into the concrete box where the dustbins are, slamming the door shut. To a German woman who remonstrates with him, the man says,

'They're just filth, they must get out of here.' A few weeks earlier, in a similar incident, a German had actually shot children with an airgun, because he found them too noisy.[2]

October 1982: Gerhard Kromschröder, a reporter on the mass-circulation magazine *Stern*, dyes his moustache black, dresses up in guest-worker style – badly cut suit, white shirt, loud tie and cloth cap – and tries to get a drink in bars and cafés in Frankfurt. Again and again he is refused service and thrown out. Publication of his report leads to a flurry of letters and protests. When an anti-racist group goes to talk to the manager of one of the cafés concerned, they get ejected by the police; but the mayor does promise to take steps to stop this type of discrimination.[3]

October 1982: A major insurance company announces its intention of charging Turkish customers 50 per cent extra on motor insurance policies; Yugoslavs and Greeks are to pay 25 per cent extra.[4]

November 1982: The new chancellor, Helmut Kohl (CDU), states that there are too many foreigners in the Federal Republic, and that policies to stop immigration and encourage repatriation are one of his government's three principal tasks. The CDU distributes leaflets to all households in West Germany outlining this policy.

December 1982: A football match in West Berlin. Teenage fans wear jerkins with SS insignia and shout '*Sieg Heil*' when their team appears. The chant changes to '*Jude, Jude*' (Jew, Jew) when the other side has the ball.[5]

January 1983: The papers are full of articles reminding us of the fiftieth anniversary of Hitler's rise to power. My 12-year-old daughter comes home from school and tells me jokes that are going round her class. 'How do you get eight Turks in a VW? Four on the seats, the rest in the ashtray!' 'What is the difference between the Jews and the Turks? The first lot have already got it behind them!'

February 1983: Millions of Germans watch the live transmission of the traditional Mainz Carnival. The audience in the vast hall includes celebrities and leading politicians in evening dress, adorned with fools' caps, who have paid DM 150 for a ticket. On the stage two German men dressed up in something meant to look like traditional Greek costumes dance a *Sirtaki* and wave strings of garlic around, while singing about how much they stink. The tipsy dignitaries laugh and cheer.

These are just a few examples of racist behaviour that I experienced personally or read about in the newspapers, while writing this book. I could give many more. Reports and anecdotes do not, of course, prove that the majority of Germans support or condone racism, but they are indicative of a climate of hostility towards foreigners. Moreover, such outbursts have become increasingly common in the last few years and, as the widespread anti-Turkish jokes show, they are increasingly socially acceptable. A disturbing aspect of several of the examples is the linking of hostility towards foreigners with anti-Semitism, and the growing influence of neo-Nazi ideas.

This upsurge of racism is not a specifically West German phenomenon: it is apparent in all the countries that experienced mass labour migration and subsequent settlement. The World Council of Churches has presented evidence on 'the escalation of racism' throughout Western Europe.[6] In the case of Britain, the point needs little elaboration, for the extent of prejudice and discrimination has been repeatedly documented.[7] Racist ideas have shaped policies on immigration, on immigrants' rights, and on control of black youth since the late fifties. The growth of far-right organisations like the National Front and the British Movement has been based on campaigns against black people. Widespread popular acceptance of what has been called 'common-sense' racism,[8] has been reflected in and stimulated by sections of the media. Racism is playing a major part in the reshaping of the conservative ideologies embodied in Thatcherism, or 'new Toryism'.[9]

In the case of France, the World Council of Churches notes a growing number of racially motivated attacks on members of minorities, particularly North Africans. Opinion polls report that between 60 and 70 per cent of those interviewed think that there are 'too many' North Africans in France, and up to half the respondents feel there are 'too many' Spaniards and Portuguese.[10] Despite the less restrictive policies of the Socialist government since 1981, institutional discrimination and police harassment remain major problems for foreigners in France. There are still police raids on migrant workers' hostels, or check-points in the Métro, when everyone with a black or brown face has to produce identity papers. Neo-fascist groups have made their main slogans racist, claiming that 'our religion is threatened with extinction, our religion with subjection to Islam'.[11] Even the left is not immune to racism. Prior to the 1981 election, Communist mayors actively supported actions to stop the construction of foreign workers' hostels in their communities.

In Switzerland, there is a long tradition of movements against 'foreign swamping' (*Überfremdung*) which have pressed for the deportation of foreign citizens. In 1970, the 'Schwarzenbach Initiative' sponsored a referendum to limit the number of foreigners to a maximum of 10 per cent of the population in each canton. Forty-six per cent of the electorate (men only at that time) voted for the move, and 54 per cent against it. Switzerland's legislation on immigration and foreign residents' rights is among the most restrictive and discriminatory in Europe, and a recent referendum defeated an attempt to marginally improve the situation. There is widespread hostility towards foreign workers, even though the majority are whites from a neighbouring country.

Even countries like Sweden and the Netherlands, which pride themselves on their tolerance, are experiencing growing tensions. Both have tightened up immigration rules. There are reports from Sweden of discriminatory treatment by police, officials and landlords, of anti-immigrant graffiti on the walls, and of attacks by youth gangs on Chileans and Turks.[12] There have been anti-Turkish riots in various Dutch towns and the militant actions of Moluccan youth in the mid seventies appear to have furthered the growth of racist attitudes. Dutch workers feel threatened by unemployment, and seem willing to blame it on foreign workers. It is reported that 'today the ordinary Dutchman is prepared to voice racial opinions that would have been unthinkable ten years ago'.[13]

Racism is a daily reality to members of the new ethnic minorities throughout Western Europe. It makes nonsense of all ideologies of equal rights or equal opportunities. Hostility and discrimination towards blacks and foreigners is not in itself new. At the end of the sixties, there was already considerable evidence of racism.[14] Yet there have been important shifts. The most obvious is the increasing incidence of racism, whether the yardstick is the number of racially motivated attacks, the size of neo-Nazi organisations, or the emphasis on race in the media and politics. More important, if less obvious, is the changing character of racism. The migratory process has matured from migration of labour to settlement of new ethnic minorities, while the general outlook has moved from expansion and optimism to stagnation and crisis. Racism has taken on a new social significance as a popular explanation for the decline, and as a key element of state strategies of crisis management. Detailed analyses of this new racism have been made for Britain by Martin Barker[15] and the Centre for Contemporary Cultural Studies.[16] Their arguments will not be repeated here, but the development of racism in West Germany will be described to see if there are parallels with Britain.

English-speaking people today use 'racism' principally to refer to ideologies and practices directed against black, brown and yellow people by whites in, for instance, Britain, the USA, South Africa. It may therefore seem strange to use the term with regard to treatment of white Italians by white Swiss, or white Yugoslavs by white Germans. In Germany and France, on the other hand, the term racism (*Rassismus* in German, *racisme* in French) used to be applied mainly to anti-Semitism, although it was also used for colonial situations. In the last two decades, French-speaking people in France, Switzerland and Belgium have taken to using *racisme* to refer to the treatment of foreign residents. The commonest term in West Germany is *Ausländerfeindlichkeit* (hostility towards foreigners), but the expression *Rassismus* is becoming increasingly common. Choice of terminology is not neutral: it implies a political perspective. Continental anti-racists speak of racism to emphasise that the treatment of foreign residents has much in common with past treatment of Jews or subjugated colonial peoples.

No precise definition of racism will be attempted here. There has been a long and often sterile dispute on it among sociologists.[17] The more precise sociological definitions become, the more abstract and ahistorical they tend to be, often blocking our way to an understanding of historical changes in the nature and function of racism. Most definitions of racism tend to be based on the concept of biologically determined superiority of one human population, group or race over another. As Martin Barker has pointed out, some leading proponents of racial discrimination can accept this definition, and use it to show that they are not racists.[18]

The trend is away from the old Nazi ideas of the innate superiority of the white or the 'Germanic' race, towards a new emphasis on the distinctiveness of each nation. Many of the new racists claim to accept that blacks are as good as whites, or Turks as good as Germans, but they regard each ethnic group as innately different, and claim that 'natural' urges to maintain one's own group or nation and to exclude aliens make integration or multi-cultural coexistence impossible. Here is the basis for claims that policies of compulsory deportation are in the interests of the minorities, for they are thus helped to maintain their distinctive ethnic character and culture.

The new racism attributes barriers between people to human nature, and suggests that national separatism is natural and inevitable.[19] But racist attitudes and practices are not coherent, nor are they always based on a clear and conscious ideology. As will be shown for West Germany, racism takes many forms, including unreflected spontaneous hostility and discrimination, organised neo-Nazi campaigns and attempts to provide a 'scientific' basis for racist policies. The danger is that widespread popular racism could be taken up by the ruling class, and given a systematic and legitimate character, as a way of coping with the present crisis. That has happened in Britain,[20] and it appears to be the trend in West Germany. The German ruling class has followed this strategy before; big industrialists financed Hitler's rise to power because they thought Nazism would deal with threats from the left in the crisis of the thirties. The consequences are well known.

Development of racism

Four factors – colonialism, nationalism, the treatment of internal minorities and the experience of migrant labour – have shaped the history and ideologies of racism in West Germany.

The first factor may seem surprising. It has often been argued that a major distinguishing feature of events in Britain is that most migrants were black people from former colonies. Both the political behaviour of blacks in Britain, and attitudes of the white population towards them have been shaped by traditions of racial domination in the colonies. Clearly, this would apply to former colonial subjects in France and the Netherlands, but West Germany, Sweden, Belgian are seen as different, because the migrants are mainly white people from Southern Europe and Turkey. But it must be remembered that ethnocentric attitudes are deeply rooted in Western European culture, even in countries that were not major colonial powers.

At the end of the nineteenth century, Imperial Germany was struggling hard to catch up in the race for colonies. Germany was economically and politically backward, only achieving unity as a nation-state in the mid nineteenth century. Industrialisation came late and rapidly took on an imperialist form, through the merging of industrial and financial capital and their close association with an absolutist state. The developing monopolies desperately needed colonies as outlets for capital and manufactured goods and sources of raw materials and labour. Germany managed to secure only three African colonies (Tanganika, Namibia and parts of the Cameroons) and to get a foothold in China and the South Pacific. Imperial Germany also pursued the age-old Central European dream of expanding south-east into the Balkans. By 1914, Germany was well on the way to turning the Ottoman Empire (Turkey) into a client state. The legacy of this period is attitudes towards non-European people every bit as racist as those in more successful colonial powers. The dream of south-eastward and eastward expansion was later revived by the Nazis. The ideology of Germanic racial superiority over Slavs and Mediterranean peoples provided legitimacy for this imperialism.

German nationalism is indeed hard to separate from expansionist colonialism and racism. Patriotic ideologies took a particularly extreme form as a result of Germany's late emergence as a unified state. Germans came to see rapid industrialisation and strong bureaucratic administration as signs of their superiority – attitudes reinforced by the first world war, and later by Nazi propaganda. Military defeat and insurrection were taken not as signs that there was something wrong with the way society was organised, but as the result of a 'stab in the back' by racial enemies mainly the Jews, Southern Europeans, and alien Communists.

Jews and gypsies have suffered centuries of persecution in Germany. In the nineteenth century, the social upheavals of industrialisation intensified racism. Political parties based primarily on anti-Semitism were able to get candidates elected to parliament. The Nazis could draw on deeply rooted attitudes of anti-Semitism in their rise to power. The crisis of the inter-war period had made many German workers reject capitalism and support left-wing parties. Nazi propaganda aimed to convince workers that the crisis was caused not by the capitalist system as such, but by Jewish capitalists out to destroy the German people. In this way, nationalism and anti-Semitism were linked to apparently socialist demands. German capitalists helped finance Hitler, because they saw National Socialism as a way of mobilising workers for a policy diametrically opposed to their real interests.

Nazi propaganda and race laws defined members of minorities as no longer belonging to the *Volk* (people). Jews and gypsies were deprived of citizenship and denied all civil and human rights. The holocaust was the logical conclusion of this policy: 6 million Jews, 1.5 million gypsies, hundreds of thousands from other minorities (homosexuals, the chronically ill, religious groups) and political opponents were murdered. All Germans over 50 years old today have had some experience of Nazi education through school, Hitler Youth, women's organisations, the army: somewhere. This must have affected attitudes towards present-day minorities. Younger Germans have also been influenced by the views of their parents and teachers. Even today, the surviving gypsies in West Germany have to endure racism and discrimination. Many still have not had citizenship restored to them and are treated as stateless; they have demonstrated at former concentration camps to draw attention to their plight.

Historical experience of migrant labour is particularly relevant to contemporary attitudes of workers and employers towards foreign workers. German employers – like those of other countries – recruited migrants during the period of industrialisation.[21] Between 1870 and 1914 large numbers of Poles were recruited for the mines and factories of the Ruhr, and Italian workers were employed in the estates and factories of southern Germany. These migrants encountered considerable hostility from German workers, who regarded them as competitors for jobs and potential wage-cutters.[22] Later, foreign workers played a major role in the Nazi war economy. Seven and a half million people from occupied countries and prisoners of war were forced to work in Germany, to replace the 11 million men withdrawn for military service. Often their conditions were tantamount to slavery. Many were literally worked to death, others were executed or sent to concentration camps as punishment for disobediance. The few remaining German men in the factories often became overseers. Armed with rifles and pistols, their task was to keep up production, but also to safeguard

198/ Here for good

the racial purity of the German women working alongside the foreigners.[23]

Attitudes towards foreign workers

When West German capital decided to return to the strategy of labour import in the fifties, there was some initial opposition from the trade unions. Between 1956 and 1973, all significant interest groups in West Germany accepted the guest worker system. Many of the laws and regulations made to administer that system still apply, continuing discrimination even of children born to foreign parents within West Germany. The guest worker system was a reflection of widespread racist attitudes; it functioned because a sizeable proportion of the population was willing to accept the legitimacy of labelling foreigners as permanently inferior and denying them civil and political rights.

The first foreign workers – mainly Italians – met with considerable hostility at their places of work, and in the neighbourhoods where they lived. Spaich reports that they were often seen as 'the people who let us down in the war'.[24] Opinion polls carried out in the early sixties found that anything from 50 to 80 per cent of respondents had negative attitudes towards foreign workers and wanted to get rid of them. Their attitudes correlated with class, the highest incidence of anti-foreign worker feeling being among manual workers.[25]

Attempts were soon made to exploit such attitudes for political ends. In May 1964, Chancellor Erhard called on German workers to work longer hours in order to get rid of foreigners. The call was taken up by the employers' organisations and newspapers close to them.[26] A neo-Nazi party established in the mid sixties, the NPD (Nationaldemokratische Partei), concentrated its propaganda on anti-migrant themes and managed to get between 2 and 10 per cent of the votes in *Länder* elections, actually getting into parliament in Hesse, Bavaria and Rheinland-Palatinate.

The shift to the left in West German politics in the late sixties and early seventies (marked by the SPD–FDP coalition in Bonn, and the left-wing student movement), seems to have been matched by a temporary decline in racism. The NPD lost electoral support, and failed to get into the federal parliament. Immigration does not appear to have been a major political issue between 1968 and 1973

– the period of the most rapid growth in the foreign labour force. The prevailing view seems to have been that labour migration was a regrettable necessity for the maintenance of economic growth; the foreign workers themselves were seen as 'not very clean, rather untidy', 'after German girls', 'angry and often aggressive', but on the other hand as 'hard-working' and 'thrifty'.[27]

The crisis and the growth of popular racism

These patronising stereotypes of the useful but somewhat primitive guest workers did not last long, once the boom ground to a halt in the mid seventies. The ban on labour migration in November 1973 labelled foreign workers as a cause of growing unemployment (the other being seen popularly as the 'oil sheikhs'). Many Germans supported the view that foreigners should be sacked and deported to prevent German workers becoming unemployed.[28] Even prominent trade unionists called for such policies. The slogan *Ausländer raus* began to appear on walls. As temporary recession turned into long-term stagnation, and unemployment climbed to one and then 2 million, calls for mass repatriation became widespread. By 1982, opinion polls were reporting that 82 per cent of Germans thought there were 'too many' foreigners in the country.[29]

The causes of increasing racism cannot be reduced to simple fears of unemployment.

The original migrant workers had been mainly young men, housed in out-of-the-way sheds on building sites and factory yards. They had been visible to Germans only at work, or on Sundays when they used the railway stations as meeting places. There had been enough complaints about that, but after all, Germans did not have to spend much time at railway stations. Now, however, foreign families were finding housing in the inner cities. Whole districts were turning into foreign communities, with their own shops, bars, churches, mosques, clubs. The foreign population did not grow dramatically in the late seventies, but it became far more visible to Germans, as competition for housing and social facilities increased.

At the same time, the number of foreigners from Southern Europe edged down while the number from Turkey and other non-European countries grew. There was prejudice and discrimination against Southern Europeans, but at least they were white and Christian, and their languages and culture were not altogether alien. Germans seem to perceive Turks as alien and threatening. Differences in language, culture and appearance are much more marked, and anti-Turkish feeling has deep historical roots, connected with medieval struggles between Christianity and Islam, and Turkish expansion westwards up to the seventeenth century. The defeat of the Turks before Vienna in 1683 is a major historical event in Germany.

Above all, the presence of foreign youth has brought home the reality of settlement to Germans. As more and more foreign children have entered inner-city schools, they have become a focus for conflict and racist agitation. The media and politicians portray foreign youth as a long-term threat to social peace. Many young Germans have tried to keep foreigners out of youth clubs, sports clubs and bars. Fights and disputes often end with segregation; many clubs and bars are now used virtually only by foreign youth, while others are closed to them.

Over and above all this, between 1979 and 1981 about a quarter of a million refugees entered West Germany in search of political asylum. Most came from Third World countries like Afghanistan, Eritrea, Argentina, Iran and Turkey. This represented a considerable increase over previous years, and led to an outcry by sections of the media, led by the mass-circulation *Bild-Zeitung* (the West German equivalent of the *Sun*). The refugees were portrayed as phonies, out to take advantage of social security benefits. The impression was given that West Germany was about to be swamped by millions of Africans and Asians, and the result would be Third-World-style poverty for the whole population.

The neo-Nazis circulated racist leaflets and slogans, and carried out bomb attacks on refugee hostels, killing several people. The CDU and CSU campaigned for tighter rules to keep out 'economic refugees' and attacked the government for its lax immigration policies. Indeed, the SPD–FDP coalition changed the law to curtail entry of refugees in 1980 and again in 1981. The number of asylum-seekers entering West Germany has in the meantime declined substantially, mainly because of the introduction of entry visas for Turks and other Third World citizens. Around 80 per cent of applicants are denied asylum, even in cases where they are likely to be tortured or imprisoned if returned to their home countries.[30] The campaign against refugees did much to stimulate racism against all foreigners, and its impact may be compared with that of the campaign against the East African Asians in Britain in the mid seventies.

This does not imply that all Germans, or even the majority, are racists. The problem is rather that racist explanations of social problems are gaining currency and acceptability, and that very large numbers of people are prepared to accept them uncritically and passively. There is another side to the picture: more and more Germans have become aware of the resurgence of racism, and have realised that it is a serious threat not only to foreigners, but to the labour movement, the left and indeed most sections of society. The growing anti-racist movement will be discussed in chapter 8.

Neo-Nazism

The recent increase in neo-Nazi activity in West Germany is closely linked with racism. Encouraging racism has been the main concern of neo-Nazi groups, and their way of attracting members. The government estimates that far-right and neo-Nazi organisations have about 20,000 members.[31] Membership declined in the seventies and then started increasing in the early eighties. In 1982, there were estimated to be 74 far-right and neo-Nazi organisations. The largest is the DVU (*Deutsche Volksunion* – German People's Union), led by Gerhard Frey, with over 10,000 members. Its newspapers have a circulation of about 100,000. The NPD (*Nationaldemokratische Partei* – National Democratic Party) has been declining since its heyday in the late sixties. Most of its 7,000 members are pensioners. It is not militant enough to attract young people, and its youth organisation is now down to 500 members.

In the 1980 and 1983 federal elections, agitation against foreigners was virtually the NPD's only theme. But voters are reluctant to support openly Nazi parties. The NPD got less than half a per cent of votes cast, compared with 4.3 per cent in 1969. Both the NPD and the DVU have taken to setting up front organisations devoted entirely to racist campaigns. The NPD's *Bürgerinitiative Ausländerstopp* (Citizens' Initiative to Stop Foreigners) has collected thousands of signatures in petitions for compulsory repatriation, and for separate classes for German and foreign children. The DVU has set up a similar *Initiative für Ausländer-begrenzung* (Initiative for Restriction of Foreigners). Such fronts are able to mobilise more popular support than the parties themselves; for instance the Kiel List for Restriction of Foreigners got 3.7 per cent of the poll in the May 1982 municipal elections. In inner-city working-class districts they got up to 9 per cent.

Many of the younger Germans attracted to neo-Nazism by racist propaganda in recent years have joined the 20 or so militant organisations that reject electoral participation, and carry out campaigns of terrorism. Official estimates put membership of such groups at just over 1,000 in 1982,[32] but are unreliable because the organisations are clandestine. The number of criminal offences attributed to the far right grew from 136 in 1974 to 2,047 in 1982.[33]

The trend is towards systematic violence against foreigners, Jews, members of left and anti-racist organisations and – most recently – US soldiers. For instance the *Wehrsportgruppe Hoffmann* (Military Sport Group Hoffmann) gave military training to its 400 members, many of whom have since been involved in crimes of violence. The most notorious of these was the bombing of the Munich October Festival, in which 13 people were killed and 200 wounded. The *Wehrsportgruppe* was banned in 1980, and its members moved into other groups. The *Deutsche Aktionsgruppe* (German Action Group) carried out a campaign of bombings and arson against foreign workers and refugees in 1981, killing two Vietnamese refugees. Other offences committed by Nazi groups include Molotov-cocktail attacks on homes and shops belonging to foreigners, demolishing Jewish cemeteries, beating up anti-racists, and the theft and smuggling of weapons and explosives.

Most recently the so-called 'national revolutionary' groups have emerged. These claim to be anti-capitalist in their aims and to represent the class interests of German workers. Their ideology is based on the Strasser-Röhm wing of the Nazi Party, and their actions and form of organisation are modelled on the SA (Hitler's Storm Troopers) who were recruited largely among workers. Such groups hope to attract working-class youth through their image of violence, toughness, comradeship and leadership. They recruit in football fan clubs, where racist violence is becoming increasingly accepted, and among male working-class youth sub-cultures such as rockers and skinheads. In February 1983, five members of the *Volkssozialistische Bewegung Deutschlands* (German People's

Socialist Movement) were arrested and charged with a series of bomb attacks on US vehicles and buildings.

The far right is also trying to gain a foothold in the ecology movement. The argument of groups like the Young Nationalists (NPD youth section) is that the destruction of the environment is the work of rapacious capitalists, who want growth at any price, and therefore flood the country with foreign workers. Thus, foreigners can be blamed for the pollution of air and water, for the destruction of the forests, and for generally ruining the German homeland. Forced repatriation is therefore a way of safeguarding the environment and stopping over-industrialisation. The aim of such slogans is to gain support among young people who are very much involved in environmentalist politics.[34]

The differences between the extreme right-wing tendencies should not be over-emphasised. All the groups certainly concur on the issue of racism, and in their willingness to use violence against foreigners. Members tend to move from one group to another, and the more violent undercover groups often have close links with large legal organisations like the NPD and DVU. The German Nazis also have strong bonds with similar groups in other countries – the British Movement and Column 88, FANE in France and NAR in Italy. There is frequent interchange of members for carrying out terrorist actions. German Nazis are alleged to have been involved in attacks on synagogues in France and on the Bologna railway station in Italy. Two of the members of the German People's Socialist Movement arrested in February 1983 were found harboured in Britain.[35]

The neo-Nazis are certainly a serious threat for members of the ethnic minorities; but is there a risk of a Nazi resurgence on a large scale? At the moment they are a small lunatic fringe, but then so was Hitler's party in the mid twenties. The overwhelming majority of Germans reject fascism, but there is a growing willingness to give an ear to racist slogans, and to accept discriminatory and authoritarian policies. The most disturbing factor is the increasing attractiveness of neo-Nazis for young working-class Germans, especially the jobless. Of the neo-Nazis convicted of criminal offences in 1982, 45 per cent were aged 14–20, 25 per cent were between 21 and 30.[36] In Berlin, teachers have reported that they are having increasing difficulties in coping with the racist views and fascist slogans of a growing number of students.[37]

A number of surveys have attempted to assess the extent of far-right views among young Germans. All of them found growing willingness to accept Nazi slogans and authoritarian solutions to social problems. For instance, 23 per cent of school students interviewed in Frankfurt thought that social problems could be solved by 'eliminating the lazy, the criminals, and the mentally ill from society'. Fifteen per cent thought that 'a man like Hitler could cope with the problems better than our present politicians'. The percentage of youth supporting such views varies in the different surveys, with a sizeable minority (perhaps 10–20 per cent) willing to go along with them, while a small group (perhaps 2–5 per cent) is actually ready to get involved in violent action.[38]

Making racism respectable

Nazism seemed a viable political strategy to the German ruling class in the crisis of the thirties. Neo-Nazism is quite clearly not a valid option for the ruling class of West Germany in the crisis of the eighties. Yet the growing acceptability of racist slogans encourages a shift of the major parties towards more openly nationalistic policies. Neo-Nazi ideas are taken up, transformed and made respectable by sections of the establishment.

What is known as 'scientific' racism, for example, is being resurrected. Racist science is nothing new in Germany. The Nazis made great efforts to develop a branch of anthropology called *Rassenkunde* (race science), which set out to prove the superiority of the 'nordic' race, and to justify domination and exploitation of other nations. Although totally discredited, this older type of 'scientific' racism persists in a network of academics and journals throughout Western Europe and North America. 'Scientific' racism has had new impetus in recent years: through psychological studies purporting to show the innate superiority of whites over blacks;[39] and the growing significance of 'sociobiological' theories, that set out to show that coherence of ethnic groups and exclusion of strangers are part of 'human nature'.[40]

'Scientific' racism went on the offensive for the first time in contemporary West Germany through the publication of the *Heidelberger Manifest* (Heidelberg Manifesto) in August 1981.[41] This document, signed by 15 professors, warns that the German people is being undermined by the immigration of millions of foreigners, and that German culture, language and national character (*Volkstum*) is being swamped. The manifesto asserts the impossibility of integrating the foreigners, and says that the German people will be destroyed by the 'ethnic catastrophe' of a multi-cultural society. The professors insist that they are neither racist nor right wing. They regard it as in the best interests of foreigners to return to their countries of origin, so that they too can preserve their culture and national values. The manifesto's aim is to 'preserve the German people' through immigration control, forced repatriation and measures to increase the birth rate of German women. Soon after its publication, a League for the Defence of the German People (*Schutzbund für das deutsche Volk*) was set up to implement its aims.

The group behind the Heidelberg Manifesto is not just part of a lunatic fringe, although it does have contacts and influence in neo-Nazi organisations. More significant are links with the right wing of the CDU and the Bavarian CSU. Richard Stücklen, a leading member of the CSU and speaker (*Präsident*) of the federal parliament until March 1983, has stated that the central value of the West German Constitution is the concept of the 'German people'. He called for measures to encourage love for home and country, for the German language, folk music and culture.[42] Another CSU leader, Hans Stützle, has warned that the German people is on the verge of extinction due to its low birth rate, and called for measures to strengthen the German family.

During the campaign for the federal elections in March 1983, the *Frankfurter Allgemeine Zeitung* (West Germany's major, serious, conservative daily, comparable to the *Daily Telegraph*) published a large advertisement for the League for the Defence of the German People. It started: 'The greatest danger which threatens our people today is the development of an alien population in Germany, while the German state people is rapidly shrinking.' After the usual allegations about high birth rates and sponging off social security, the advertisement called on voters to support candidates opposed to foreign settlement in West Germany.[43]

Editorial comment in serious papers like the *Frankfurter Allgemeine Zeitung* and *Die Welt* has become increasingly racist. A leader in the *Frankfurter Allgemeine Zeitung* in February 1982 was entitled 'The full boat' and called for a complete stop to immigration: 'The next million Turks must not come.' In December

1982, a leader with the headline *Fremde und Allzufremde* (aliens and too-much-aliens) clearly named Turks as the target for racism:

> Apparently it is not permissible in this country to become conscious of the fact that there are various degrees of being alien, and that, for natural reasons (or more precisely cultural reasons), coexistence is most difficult with the particularly alien. Matters are reasonably good with the Eastern, Southern and South-Eastern Europeans in the Federal Republic. Even a few Italian Mafiosi can be coped with. That is not surprising, for ever since the period of the historic migrations of peoples, the interchange between Slav, Romanic, Germanic and also Celtic peoples has become a habit. A tacit we-feeling has arisen in one and the same European culture. But excluded from this are the Turk-peoples, and also the Palestinians, North Africans and others from totally alien cultures. They, and only they, are the 'foreigner problem' in the Federal Republic.[44]

This editorial demonstrates how far racist ideologies, evoking older anthropological theories and newer ideas of cultural separateness, are becoming acceptable within the West German establishment. The trend is a shift in ruling-class attitudes towards foreigners. As long as West German industry needed additional labour, employers and politicians, who represented employers' interests, favoured recruitment of migrant labour. They supported measures to integrate foreign workers, in so far as this was necessary for efficient participation in the labour force.

Now that additional labour is no longer required, conservatives are beginning to warn of the dangers to public order and national unity presented by foreign settlement. The German Employers' Federation states that the 'foreigner question' is becoming the 'principal strain on our society'.[45] Employers' leaders assert that integration and naturalisation are unacceptable strategies, for Turks and Yugoslavs could hardly be expected to fight for the German Federal Republic in the event of a war.[46] The influence of right-wing ideas is clearly visible in the Employers Federation's current recommendation on foreigners policy – stop immigration, restrict family reunification, further curb civil and political rights, and increase use of deportation powers.

The political parties and the shift towards repatriation

In the early eighties, racism has come to play an increasing part in West German politics, and all the major parties are involved. Policies of increased institutional discrimination and of enforced repatriation are advocated as solutions to growing economic, social and political difficulties. The turning point in party policies came with the debate on the Kühn Report in 1979. Adoption of Kühn's recommendations would have meant accepting permanent settlement as a fact, and introducing policies to improve the legal and social position of the minorities. Kühn's proposals were vehemently rejected by the CDU and CSU opposition, but the SPD–FDP coalition was also unwilling to implement them. Rejection meant trying to maintain the fiction that foreigners were still temporary guest workers, and therefore keeping them permanently rightless and insecure. Such a policy, in the deepening crisis, could only lead to growing social conflicts; the logical outcome was the shift towards enforced repatriation advocated by the CDU–CSU coalition which came to power in late 1982.

By 1981, growing popular racism and the campaign against refugees had made foreigners a major political issue in West Germany. The language of the CDU was becoming increasingly nationalistic: 'The role of the German Federal Republic as a national unitary state and as part of a divided nation does not permit the commencement of an irreversible development to a multi-ethnic state,' said a CDU resolution in the federal parliament in November 1981.[47] The SPD–FDP cabinet hastened to agree that 'the German Federal Republic is not a country of immigration and ought not to become one'.[48] Three weeks later, the government announced further restrictions on immigration of foreign workers' dependants.

In February 1982 there was a major debate on policy towards foreigners in the federal parliament. Alfred Dregger, leader of the CDU-CSU parliamentary group, took the opportunity to warn of a new alien influx, pointing out that Turkey's Treaty of Association with the European Community would lead to free movement of labour from 1986:

In Turkey, millions of people are waiting for this day. If
this wave breaks over us, then our welfare state, which is in

any case seriously endangered through financial exhaustion, will also break . . . But Turks, with some exceptions, cannot be assimilated, indeed, they can only be integrated with great difficulty. Since Turks are different from Germans in culture and mentality, and want to stay different, it is only natural that they seek the proximity of their fellows in Germany. That means that Turkish quarters, also known as ghettos, are developing in our cities. That could only be prevented by force, not by social security benefits or persuasion . . . We have no reason to let critics at home and abroad accuse us of racism, when we insist that the German Federal Republic must not become a country of immigration. Anyone who disregards this natural and justified feeling of our fellow citizens is preparing the way for the extreme right . . . The question of a reasonable and humane rotation must be reconsidered.[49]

Dregger's speech is worth quoting at length, because it evokes so many themes familiar to British readers from the speeches of Enoch Powell, or the writings of Alfred Sherman:[50] the idea of being overwhelmed or swamped by aliens; the idea of cultural differences, which make integration impossible; the idea of 'natural feelings' of 'ordinary people', who will understandably move to the right if the established parties do nothing. Only the call for repatriation takes a form unlike Britain's. Dregger wants to return to 'rotation' of foreign workers, letting them in only temporarily and without dependants.

The SPD–FDP had no strategy against this. The government merely issued a statement reiterating its aims of maintaining the ban on labour immigration, encouraging voluntary return, and supporting the economic and social integration of foreigners who had already been in West Germany for a long time.[51]

The CDU–CSU remained on the offensive, making deportation a major electoral theme. A CDU leaflet distributed during the state elections in Hesse in the autumn of 1982 bore the title 'Dealing with the Foreigner Problem', and declared that the CDU would reduce the number of foreigners in West Germany by a million in the next five years. The demands of the leaflet can hardly be distinguished from those of neo-Nazi organisations:

Keeping the ban on entry of foreign workers.
No further immigration of family members from outside the
European Community.
Stopping the fraudulent exploitation of the German social
security system.
Better laws against the flood of economic refugees.
Deportation of foreign criminals to their countries of origin.
Strict measures against foreign political extremists.[52]

Racist policies with enforced repatriation as their final consequence have found wide acceptance in the CDU and CSU.
Attitudes within the SPD are more complex. Many members are
strongly opposed to racism, and co-operate with foreigners in
neighbourhood groups and anti-racist organisations. The leadership of the SPD calls for measures to integrate foreigners and
improve their rights, and demands measures to stop neo-Nazi
agitation. But, the policies of the SPD while in power were
discriminatory and restrictive. SPD leaders fear loss of popular
support because of growing racism. Willy Brandt said recently
that 'we cannot cope with any further immigration'.[53] In a
statement on the local elections in Kiel in 1982, Peter Glotz,
general secretary of the SPD, said that his party was in danger of
losing votes to right-wing 'populist' groups, and called for measures
to stop further growth of the foreign population.[54] This change in
SPD thinking can be documented in two statements made by
Holger Börner, the SPD prime minister of Hesse. In 1978, Börner
called for measures to integrate foreigners and improve their
rights:

> We must learn that we are on the way to a multi-cultural
> and multi-racial society . . . We should regard our foreign
> fellow citizens as European citizens. Many of them will stay
> in the Federal Republic forever. For them our country has
> in fact become a country of immigration.[55]

By 1982, Börner had changed his tune:

> The Federal Republic is not a country of immigration, the
> limits of our endurance have been reached . . . The principle
> is that we must give them the opportunity of integration
> within the framework of our legal system. And, of course,
> they have a right to work and housing like German citizens.

> But to achieve this it is necessary to strictly close the frontiers against further immigration, for this problem will otherwise become insoluble . . . I regard further immigration of Turks to the Federal Republic as impossible.[56]

The SPD formed a federal government (together with the smaller FDP) from 1969 to 1982. It came to power at a time of expansion and optimism. Social democratic strategies of co-operation with capital, and redistribution of income through the welfare state worked well in the late sixties and early seventies. Working-class demands could be met without constraints on capital; the fight about relative shares of the cake could be forgotten because the cake was growing fast. The political climate was very like Britain's 'never had it so good' period of the sixties.[57] Prosperity and welfare for all, without class struggle, seemed within reach – although the foreign workers were always the outsiders.

Efforts by the SDP–FDP government to restore confidence and revive growth at the beginning of the eighties got bogged down in growing national debt, soaring unemployment and refusal of co-operation by bankers and industrialists. The coalition collapsed in the autumn of 1982, and was replaced by a CDU–CSU–FDP government. The new coalition wanted a reduction in wage and welfare costs to stimulate industrial investment and a new emphasis on a strong state to guarantee 'law and order'. An offensive against the rights of foreign residents was seen as an integral part of this strategy. In his first statement as chancellor, Helmut Kohl announced that a new policy towards foreigners was one of the three main planks of his programme. Although lip service was still paid to integration, the emphasis was now on stopping immigration, drastically reducing family reunification, keeping out refugees, and encouraging repatriation.[58] Kohl emphasised that repatriation was to be voluntary and 'humane', but the government's aim was to reduce the number of foreign residents by a million before the end of the decade.

At the time of writing, it is not possible to say exactly what measures will be introduced, although the following are probable: a new Foreigners Law restricting immigration and increasing deportation powers; reduction of the maximum age of entry of dependant children (probably to five years); introduction of residence permits for children under 16; deportation in the event of unemployment or inadequate housing; financial incentives for voluntary departure (already introduced for certain categories); and further restrictions on political rights.[59]

The principle underlying the new policy appears to be the division of the foreign population into those who are to be assimilated and those who are to be repatriated. The main European minority groups (except the Yugoslavs) are shielded from the effect of new discriminatory legislation – Italians and Greeks through EEC membership, Spaniards and Portuguese through EEC association. They will be allowed to stay, but they must remain in employment, not claim social security benefits, and must conform to German expectations about housing and lifestyle. Preservation of national cultures will only be permitted in the form of folklore; the establishment of separate communities will not be tolerated.[60] In the long run, the aim is naturalisation, and 'Germanisation'. The West German government speaks of 'integration', but its policies are shifting to assimilation.

The people to be repatriated are all those unable to participate in the labour process – the unemployed, the elderly, the handicapped, the chronically ill – and the overwhelming majority of non-Europeans, above all the Turks. The CDU–CSU regards it as impossible to assimilate, or even integrate these groups, and sees them as a threat to the German nation. The pre-condition for carrying out this policy is the abrogation of the Treaty of Association between Turkey and the EEC, which provides 'for free movement of labour from 1986. The issue is delicate, for Turkey is a NATO partner, and unilateral refusal to implement the treaty would smack of racism and illegality. The West German government is therefore doing everything possible to appease the military junta, in the hope of persuading them to agree to the repeal of the free movement provisions.[61] That is why the Federal Minister of the Interior has promised to extradite the junta's political opponents from West Germany and why Cemal Kemal Altun was hounded to his death in West Berlin on 30 August 1983.

Structural racism

The new racism in Britain, West Germany and other countries is the current historical expression of *structural racism*, which has led to the creation of the new ethnic minorities, and which now determines their position in society. Structural racism has several, closely linked aspects:

The racist and ethnocentrist character of European imperialism created the pre-conditions for labour migration by transforming the modes of production of the colonies, and by causing uneven development within Europe.

The new stage of uneven development, represented by the dramatic expansion of the West European economies after 1945, led to a system of labour recruitment based on institutional discrimination. This system increased the profitability of migrant labour, by imposing a large part of its reproduction costs on the countries of origin. Its social effect was the dissolution and restructuring of communities and families in the areas of origin, which helped to accelerate the breakdown of the previous mode of production.

When the crisis and the restructuring of the labour process made recruitment of further labour superfluous, the West European states unilaterally stopped it, with no regard for the economic and social effects on the countries of origin. At the same time, new methods were evolved to exploit even cheaper labour in the free trade areas of the Third World.

Colonialism and nationalism have made racism a basic component of Western European culture. The resulting patterns of hostility, prejudice and discrimination reinforce the effects of institutional discrimination. At times of crisis, like the present, racism becomes an increasingly important aspect of ruling-class strategies of social and political control. It is a threat to members of minorities, but it is also an attack on the working class as a whole.

8. Consciousness and class formation

Perceptions of migration, racism and class

Members of Western Europe's new ethnic minorities belong predominantly to the working class. That is to say, most black and foreign workers have a typically proletarian relationship to the means of production, being deprived of ownership and forced to sell their labour power. Indeed, on the basis of employment, working conditions and socio-economic status, most blacks and foreigners are not just members of the working class, but generally part of its most exploited and disadvantaged sections. The same applies outside work; the minorities are concentrated in inner-city areas, marked by deprivation in housing, health care, education and other social amenities. Various writers have suggested analytical categories to express this situation: 'a lower stratum of the working class',[1] a 'class fraction created by racial categorisation',[2] 'racially demarcated class fractions'.[3] What is common to them is emphasis on the separation of the minorities from other parts of the working class through racism.

The starting point for an understanding of the minorities within the working class is an analysis of the rapid and drastic changes taking place in the structure of capitalist society. The long-drawn-out economic crisis – itself an expression of the re-structuring of the labour process – is transforming the working class. Particularly affected are the skilled manual sections which used to be the backbone of the labour movement. The nature of work is changing, and hence also its meaning for important social groups.[4] The classic marxist analysis of class, with its objective component of 'class in itself' and its subjective component of 'class for itself', is no longer sufficient to grasp what is happening. This is a theme which cannot be adequately treated here, but it is important for understanding the consciousness of minority youth.

Chapter 6 showed that extremely high proportions of the second generation are out of work, often 50 per cent or more. But, as Sivanandan has pointed out: 'they are not the unemployed, but the never employed'.[5] In marxist terms, it could be said that black and foreign youth is part of a new, internal, industrial reserve army, just as the unemployed and underemployed masses of the Third World and the European periphery formed an external reserve army during the post-war boom. But this concept is not sufficient to describe the growing political consciousness and militance of minority youth. Their struggles are not primarily to secure access to the labour process, but to defend themselves and their communities from racism. Their direct opponent is not the capitalist employer, but the state, represented by school, welfare bureaucracy and police.

Objective class position is not sufficient to explain class consciousness and behaviour. People are not just passive objects of overpowering social forces; they collectively form a perception of the world around them and take action in response. The ideological struggle around shaping and control of consciousness is as important as struggles for economic resources or political power. The theme of the present chapter is the social consciousness of black and foreign workers, and the role this plays in class formation.

The various aspects of structural racism summarised at the end of chapter 7 are the social forces with which migrant workers and their descendants have to contend. Reactions to structural racism are not simply determined by social structure, and can vary widely. Indeed the experience of migration and settlement is a learning process which gives rise to a wide spectrum of forms of consciousness and action, both individual and collective.

To illustrate this point, some typical patterns of consciousness and behaviour are listed here. Reality is, of course, more complex: the social situation is perceived on several (often contradictory) levels at once; the perception is dynamic, changing and evolving in a continuous collective process.

In an initial phase, many migrant workers respond as employers and the state intend. They come as 'target earners' to save a lot in a few years, and are willing to put up with isolation and rightlessness because migration is seen as temporary.

Soon, some migrants find that they cannot save enough quickly, and that they cannot stand isolation in the long run. They bring in dependants or set up new families, and the process of settlement begins, often without a conscious decision.

Others intend from the outset to settle, or soon come to realise that return is not viable. Often their initial view of the immigration country is very positive, and they may seek integration or assimilation as individuals, being willing to give up their national culture, language and values. They sometimes isolate themselves from their compatriots, in the hope of gaining acceptance from the indigenous population.

Another group see themselves primarily as workers, and seek integration and social contacts through trade unions and political struggle. This applies especially to those who were industrial workers before migration.

Others seek to preserve their own language, values and behavioural codes in the new country. Indeed, the religion and norms of the society of origin may be adhered to more closely than before migration, as they offer cohesion, solidarity and security in a threatening environment. In this context, concentration in the inner cities has a positive side, as it allows the building of minority communities, with their own social and cultural institutions.

Members of the groups who have sought integration as individuals, may find their efforts blocked by institutional racism or by the hostility of indigenous people. They too may have to seek refuge in the minority communities, which offer a measure of protection through autonomous structures.

Black and foreign youth who go through the education systems of the immigration country are often willing to accept the aspirations and values presented to them. Yet they find that institutional racism and discriminatory practices prevent them from achieving these vocational and social goals. The result is often alienation and the search for alternative aims and social structures.

Ethnic minority communities are far from homogeneous, both with regard to socio-economic position and class consciousness. As community institutions are developed, a *petite bourgeoisie* grows within the minority: shopkeepers, agents of various kinds, landlords and the like. They are joined by professionals and intellectuals, many of whom have received education and training in Western Europe. This class is relatively small, as most members of the minorities remain manual workers. Their position is ambivalent. On the one hand, their relationship to other sections of the community is sometimes parasitic or exploitative. They are often the immediate representatives of large-scale capital in the minority community, through their role as sub-contractors for big business. State strategies of crisis management are designed to offer privileges to the minority *petite bourgeoisie*, in order to secure their co-operation as agents of social control. On the other hand, some members of this group are acutely aware of racism and discrimination, and provide militant community leadership.

The growth of ethnic minority communities is a crucial factor in the development of class consciousness and class organisation of black and foreign workers.[6] This may seem paradoxical; race or ethnic group consciousness is often seen as a form of separatism that blocks awareness of belonging to the working class as a whole. But as Stuart Hall has pointed out for Britain: 'The class relations which inscribe the black fractions of the working class function as race relations. The two are inseparable. Race is the modality in which class relations are experienced.'[7]

Similarly, foreign workers in other countries experience their class position as the specific result of institutional discrimination and racism, rather than as the result of the relationship between labour and capital in general. Mobilisation against exploitation and racism finds its first expression in organisations based on common national or ethnic origin, arising within ethnic minority communities. This struggle is the pre-condition for linking with other sections of the working class in an anti-racist movement to confront capital and the state as a class movement. Then, as Sivanandan has put it, black or foreign workers have to 'fight simultaneously as a people and as a class', and the struggle against racism becomes a struggle for the class.[8]

The responses to migration, racism and class position mentioned here are not simply phases that follow each other in some logical, linear progression. They are aspects of a complex and contradictory process of class formation, marked by struggles within ethnic minority communities, between minorities and other sections of the working class, between the working class (or fractions of it) and capital, and between the working class (or fractions of it) and the state. Much has been written about this process in Britain.[9] Can similar patterns of class formation and development of political consciousness be observed among the new ethnic minorities in other Western European countries? The rest of this chapter will try to provide some evidence on the issue for West Germany.

Culture of emigration and class consciousness

Surprisingly little research has been done on the development of consciousness among migrants and their descendants in West Germany. Most empirical studies have done little more than ask foreign workers if they intended to return to their country of origin, and if they were 'satisfied' with conditions in West Germany.[10] In view of their lack of political rights and the threat of deportation, foreigners have every reason to be cautious about giving information. So the evidence available is impressionistic and unrepresentative. It consists of observations on the development of cultural, social and political organisations, reports on industrial and political struggles, and interpretations of such events by foreigners involved in them.

At present, much of the information on the development of consciousness is to be found in literary or artistic form, rather than in political statements or sociological analyses. The epic poems of Aras Ören, the short stories of Franco Biondi and Rafik Sami, the novels of Aysel Özakin, the songs of Fuat Saka and the drawings of Dragutin Trumbetas, to give just a few examples, tell us more about the experience of migration, settlement and struggle against racism than do the studies of a host of German sociologists. The writers, artists and musicians who are emerging from the foreign working class draw heavily on the cultural forms and traditions of the countries of origin, but they are just as strongly affected by migration and proletarisation in the factories of an advanced capitalist country.

The nascent cultural expression of the foreign minorities in West Germany cannot be reduced to a simple transplantation of Greek, Italian, Spanish or Turkish culture. It can best be described as a culture of emigration, linking diverse and contradictory experiences: of poverty, exploitation and class struggle in the country of origin; of isolation and cultural alienation in the migratory process; and of exploitation, racism and class struggle in West Germany. As the migratory process matures, the focus shifts to the effort to construct cultural expressions of the situation of minority communities, as part of the battle against racism.

One relatively new aspect of this is the attempt to surmount barriers of language between the various nationalities. Several publishing houses have been set up specifically to publish works by foreigners either in dual language editions, or in German. Foreign workers are learning not only German, but also each others' languages, while many Germans are learning Turkish, Italian, and so on. Sometimes their motives are professional (for teachers, social workers, doctors), but there is also a widespread desire to communicate for cultural, social and political purposes.

The shift from temporary labour migration to settlement lies only about a decade back. But awareness of this transition came much later – probably a large proportion of foreigners in West Germany still nourish themselves with the hope of return, however unrealistic this has become. A recent paper by a Turkish anti-racist group identifies this as a main cause of what they call the 'relative passivity of the Turkish people in the German Federal Republic':

> To put it metaphorically, many workers are in the situation where their feet stand in the German Federal Republic, but their heads are at home. As it became clear that the stay in Germany was going to be of long duration, and the foreigners therefore brought their families over, this situation did not change much, because the wish to return home still exists. This is the cause of the far greater interest in political and social events in the country of origin than in Germany. But the fact that this situation persists for many years is due to the attitude of the German population and the German state towards the foreigners. The experience of relative segregation is linked with the constant perception that foreigners are excluded from the human, political and social life of the German Federal Republic.[11]

In the early years of migration, most political activity was concerned with problems of the country of origin. One reason was that many migrants were political and trade union militants, whose emigration was caused as much by political persecution as by economic need. But the distinction between the politics of the countries of origin and those of West Germany is an arbitrary one, since the ruling classes are closely linked. West German economic involvement in Southern Europe and Turkey has been heavy throughout the period. Military and political co-operation through NATO and the European Community has grown in importance. The West German state has always done its best to suppress activities of foreign militants, even if these were apparently unconnected with West German internal affairs. It is no coincidence that the Foreigners Law of 1965 provided for prohibition of political activity by foreigners if it was regarded as likely to harm German foreign policy aims.

Foreign militants have thus influenced West German politics, even when mainly concerned with their country of origin, and because of restrictions on such activity, they have been forced to take up the struggle for political rights in Germany. Moreover, foreigners have come to play an increasingly important role in the West German labour movement; this was inevitable in view of their concentration in the type of work that has been the traditional basis of the trade unions. The number of German workers to be seen at DGB May Day rallies has shrunk from year to year, while the number of foreigners has grown. Spanish was the most frequently heard language on such marches until the death of Franco; today it is Turkish. At the Frankfurt May Day rally of 1982 there were about four foreigners for every German. The leadership, who made the speeches, are Germans, with a token foreign speaker for each nationality.

Foreign workers' militance and experience of class struggle has had a strong influence on West German politics, particularly through its impact on the student and youth movements of the late sixties and early seventies. The Italian revolutionary group, Lotta Continua, and the Spanish *comisiones obreras* (workers' commissions) were models for young Germans trying to blow life into the moribund bureaucracies of the vast union machines, although admittedly the long-term success of such efforts has been small. Foreign workers have played a major part in most industrial disputes since the mid sixties. They have often played a vanguard role, introducing new methods, like factory occupations, work-ins and blockades.

Foreigners in West Germany were workers long before they became settlers. Involvement in workers' struggles therefore predates community formation. Family immigration and the move of foreign workers out of factory-site hostels were developments of the seventies. As elsewhere, inner-city concentration was a result of racism, but it was also a pre-condition for community development. Where people of one nationality are clustered together they can set up and support the services and institutions they need. Several Turkish newspapers now have editorial staff and printing works in West German cities. There is also a booming trade in video and audio cassettes. In the inner-city areas, foreign lawyers, teachers, doctors and other professional people are to be found. But all in all, the foreign *petite bourgeoisie* seems smaller and less influential than comparable groups in Britain. Moreover, the state has only just begun to consider use of *petit-bourgeois* community leaders for social control of the foreign population. Emphasis is still on direct control through police, schools and bureaucracy, so that programmes to develop foreign business or cultural institutions hardly exist as yet.

Within the foreign communities, a struggle for political and ideological control is taking place. The states of the countries of origin fear the radicalisation of their citizens through the experience of work and life in West Germany, and through the influence of trade union and political militants. They try to prevent this by setting up loyalist political associations and cultural circles, and by repression against workers who step out of line. One method is withdrawal of the passports of militants, who are then subject to deportation by the West German authorities unless they can get political asylum (80 per cent of applications are turned down). The consulates also finance foreign language newspapers, and attempt to influence the content of radio and television broadcasts by West German stations for foreign workers.

The most drastic current struggle for control of a minority community concerns Turkish workers. In the period of political violence prior to the military coup of 1980, the fascist MHP sent large numbers of thugs to West Germany, who set up 'Idealist Associations' and 'Grey Wolf' groups, to terrorise trade unionists and other political opponents. The 'Grey Wolves' have carried out a large number of acts of violence, including several murders, in West Germany. Since 1980, there has been a steady influx of left-wing militants forced to leave Turkey for fear of execution, imprisonment or torture by the military regime. The West German state has done its best to keep them out, deporting even those certain to be persecuted in Turkey.

Many Turkish workers seem willing to embrace reactionary ideologies. The following quotation from a Turkish anti-racist group tries to explain why, and also says a lot about the way Turkish workers experience West German society:

> As the Turkish workers were recruited and later, as their families came, they discovered at first that they were welcome as workers but despised as human beings. Where they sought a dwelling, which they often only found with great difficulty, they had the experience that Germans moved out, because they did not want to live under the same roof as Turks. Where they were provided with dwellings by the state or their employers, these were often dwellings in which Germans no longer wanted to live because there was a lack of sanitary facilities, etc. The different culture of the Turks, their different socialisation, was unilaterally rejected by the majority of the German population as backward or even uncivilised. Even members of the German left put emphasis on issues like the severe repression of Turkish women, without knowing its causes through their own experience, while ignoring for instance the significance of mutual neighbourly help. This meant that foreign citizens were not treated humanely by the Germans, and were forced into a ghetto situation. At the same time, such treatment created the desire among Turkish citizens of at least maintaining a degree of national and cultural identity. The process of withdrawal from a society in which foreigners were only welcome as workers began. Turkish associations and tea-rooms were set up, in which it was possible to find some part of that emotional security which had been lost through emigration to an alien and hostile country. But exclusion from German society also created the conditions for the spread of mistaken nationalist feelings and even fascist ideas among foreigners. The idea that all Germans were bad arose for many people from the shattering experiences of daily life in Germany. Today German racist nationalism is therefore matched by nationalism on the part of the foreigners. Nationalism is in

> principle a mistaken and harmful idea, but it is necessary to
> differentiate between the nationalism of the oppressor and
> the nationalism of the oppressed which arises in response.
> The nationalism of the oppressed is wrong and harmful and
> must therefore be overcome through joint struggle; the
> nationalism of the oppressor is a crime.[12]

Many foreigners perceive West German society as a 'hostile monolithic block'.[13] Even members of the left, who regard themselves as internationalists, are often seen as patronising and domineering. The result is that many foreigners, especially Turks, adopt reactionary political and religious ideas and leadership. This would appear to be a rather different trend to that in Britain, where traditions of anti-colonialist struggle have given black movements a generally anti-imperialist and anti-capitalist direction. The Turkish far right is at present able to mobilise large numbers of Turkish workers in West Germany around racist ideas of ethnic superiority and Pan-Turkish expansionism. Clearly, such ideas find resonance because they help to transmute experiences of racism and exploitation. But the consequence is a policy of cultural separatism which plays into the hands of the German right in their rejection of settlement and their call for repatriation.

Within the Turkish communities in West Germany, the struggle is between such far-right tendencies, with their emphasis on Islam and Turkish nationalism, and the left, with its orientation towards trade unionism and anti-capitalist struggle. But the left too is shifting towards assertion of the need for the development of autonomous organisations and cultural institutions in the struggle against racism and for civil and political rights. Turkish workers and youth have found that their interests are not adequately represented through German political and union organisations, and that they must organise around their own demands to obtain support within the labour movement as a whole. The focus of this struggle is the local community, where direct struggles against racism and exploitation can draw in people of varying ideological persuasions.

The anti-racist movement and the left

In a country where racism is laid down by law and administered by the police and the civil service, the anti-racist struggle is bound to confront the state. Early workplace struggles of foreign workers soon widened to embrace resistance to deportation of militants and police intimidation of picket lines. By the seventies foreign workers were willing to go on the streets to demonstrate against discriminatory social security legislation (For example, the changes in child allowances in 1975) or to demand better schooling for their children. It became increasingly obvious to the settlers that disenfranchisement and lack of political rights was preventing them from achieving just treatment in economic and social matters. By the end of the seventies the demand for voting rights (at least in local elections to start with) and for a new Foreigners Law, granting full civil and political rights, was being advocated by minority organisations. Their actions included leafleting, public meetings, demonstrations and silent pickets of polling booths. But increased racism, neo-Nazi attacks and moves towards even more restrictive laws at the beginning of the eighties have pushed minority organisations back on the defensive. At the time of writing, the struggle is focused on stopping deportations, mobilising public opinion against racist laws, and campaigning against racist ideologies.

The conditions for this struggle are extremely difficult, as demonstrated by the March 1983 electoral victory of the CDU–CSU, on an explicitly anti-foreigner and anti-working class programme. The election also showed the significance of disenfranchisement of the foreign working class; if over 3 million foreign adults had had the vote, the result might have been different. Certainly the CDU–CSU would have had difficulty in campaigning on an openly racist policy.

What has been the part of the West German left in all these struggles? After a long period of insignificance in the aftermath of fascism and the cold war, the left began to re-emerge as a political force in the late sixties. Its most visible expression was the student movement, which had a considerable impact on the whole education system. In the seventies, the left became fragmented, isolated and confused, as various tendencies struggled to find a new ideological, political and social basis. It proved extremely difficult to get a foothold in the highly bureaucratic unions; they were firmly in the grip of right-wing reformist social democrats. The left won its first real breakthrough in the late seventies in the movement against nuclear power and for the defence of the environment. The success of the new Green Party was in securing representation in the federal parliament in March 1983 was a milestone. The Greens are not just an environmentalist party: they also link left-orientated groupings, such as the peace movement, the civil liberties movement, anti-imperialist groups, left-wing trade unionists, and the old intellectual new left.

The left's relation to foreign minorities has been marked by hesitance and confusion, although from the outset there has been an awareness of the problem of the disenfranchisement of the foreign working class, and of the division of the working class through racism. The initial reaction was an abstract call for 'international solidarity' and 'class unity', without any serious investigation of the situation and consciousness of foreign workers. The underlying idea of the student activists of the early seventies was that foreign workers were the sort of picture-book proletarians, with cloth caps and class consciousness, that German workers supposedly used to be in the heroic days of the pre-1933 German Communist Party. The maoist and trotskyite splinter parties were impressed by the militance and the creative forms of struggle of Italian, Spanish, Portuguese and Turkish workers, and tried to recruit them as members. Some young German intellectuals even went to work on the production lines of Opel and BMW where they were treated indulgently for what they were: well-intentioned visiting sociologists, who could go back to a safe and well-cushioned existence if things got tough.

The few foreign workers who did join left-wing groups often discovered that 'they were welcome, as long as they strengthened the ranks of the left, and took part in the political work of the German group as if they were Germans themselves'.[14] Such foreigners found that their role was proletarian fig-leaf for student-based organisations, which were willing to assimilate them on an individual basis, but not to relate to foreign workers as a collective force with its own interests, culture and organisations. At the same time, many left groups looked down on the masses of foreigners who were not active trade unionists and left militants. They were unable to communicate with them and regarded them as backward and reactionary, failing to understand the reassertion of national identity and culture as a mechanism for protection against the racism of German society.

Left-wing students and people on the 'alternative scene' tend to live in the same inner-city areas as foreigners, and problems often arise in daily social interaction. Young Germans do admire the warmth and communality of social relations among Turks and Southern Europeans. But there is a dislike of certain forms of social behaviour, particularly the repressive role of some foreign men towards women and children. Members of the women's movement reject political co-operation with minority organisations for this reason. Many progressive Germans regard the growth of Koran schools and conservative parents' associations as a sign that foreigners are reactionary, and that a joint struggle is impossible.

However, some sections of the left are moving away from patronising attitudes towards foreigners and attempting to use them to resurrect long-dead bolshevik parties. More and more members of the West German left are trying to gain a deeper understanding of foreigners by learning their languages, making neighbourhood contacts through cultural organisations and parents' associations, and by visiting the countries of origin. And the left has become increasingly aware of the function of racism in mobilising support for neo-fascist and right-wing politics. If the state can enforce assimilation of 'desirable' foreigners and repatriation of 'undesirable' ones, this will strengthen pressure for curbs on the unions, an attack on women's rights, and further restriction of civil liberties. If the neo-Nazis can get away with murder and arson against foreigners, then their next targets will be the German left.

So there is a growing consciousness of the need to fight racism – not out of humanitarian sympathy for the oppressed, but as a vital interest of all trade unionists and progressive people. The result is a spate of anti-racist action groups throughout the German Federal Republic. These groups embrace various sections of the left, progressive Christians and trade unionists. Foreign members may be representatives of political groups (usually of the left), members of parents' associations or cultural groups, or people not otherwise organised. The strength of the movement is its diversity, making it possible to mobilise a broad spectrum of public opinion around demands for civil rights. But this diversity is also a weakness; it makes co-ordination difficult, and hinders the development of clear political demands and strategies. The Green Party, which is playing an increasingly active part in the struggle against racism and for minority rights, could have an important role in helping to co-ordinate the nascent movement.

The emergence of an anti-racist movement is significant for foreign militants. The German population ceases to appear as a 'hostile monolithic block', and it is possible to find allies among them. That helps foreign trade unionists and socialists to combat nationalism and fascism among their compatriots, for it can be shown that the opponents are not 'the Germans' but the state and capital. So a unified fight against racism is the pre-condition for achieving class unity in the struggle against the anti-working-class policies of the CDU–CSU state. The campaign against racism and discrimination is not a sectarian battle in the interests of the ethnic minority alone, but a necessary pre-condition for overcoming the split in the working class. Moreover, this struggle inevitably transcends the frontiers of the nation-state. In recent years, both German and foreign socialists have become increasingly aware of the imperialist links between the ruling classes of West Germany and of the countries of origin. The struggle against racism in West Germany, and for the rights of foreign workers, is coming to be seen as part of a broader anti-imperialist struggle.

It would be wrong to give the impression that the anti-racist movement is strong enough to take the offensive at present. The contrary is the case: the military coup of 1980 was a defeat for the Turkish left, just as the election of a government with racist and anti-working-class policies in 1983 was a defeat for the West German left. But the emergence of an anti-racist movement linking the West German left with progressive minority organisations is a step forward. There is still a very long way to go before the split within the working class can be overcome.

To sum up, there are clearly some major differences between West Germany and Britain with regard to patterns of migration, the role of the state, and the political and cultural backgrounds of the minorities. These affect the way minority and class consciousness develop, and are translated into political action. But there are also significant parallels, and these are growing in importance, as minority communities are established and become the site of struggles against racism. Important questions must remain open at this stage.

In Britain, black youth moved into the vanguard of the struggle in the mid seventies, developing new and more militant forms of anti-racist struggle. In the late seventies the black women's movement, co-ordinated by groups like the Organisation of Women of Asian and African Descent (OWAAD), took on a leading role in industrial and community struggles. Such developments are only just beginning to become evident in West Germany. Foreign women did play a leading role in the strike movement of 1973, and in some subsequent industrial disputes. Foreign youth are beginning to fight back against racist violence on the streets. These trends are not yet as pronounced as in Britain, but in view of the lesser maturity of the migratory process in West Germany, that is hardly surprising. There is every reason to expect an upsurge in the struggle against racism and for equal rights in the years ahead.

Perspectives

At the beginning of the seventies, it was already apparent that the crucial impact of labour migration on society was its role in the restructuring of the working class.[15] Since then, labour migration has been drastically restricted, and many of the former migrants have become settlers. This development was predictable; nonetheless, it was unexpectedly sudden and rapid. Settlement is taking place through the establishment and development of ethnic minority communities, in most major Western European cities, under extremely unfavourable conditions of profound economic, social and political crisis. The strategies of capital and the state are designed to impose the costs of transforming the labour process on the working class, through reduction of real wages and cuts in social benefits and services. The strains and insecurity felt by workers in a situation of falling living standards and increasing competition for jobs, housing and social amenities have nurtured the growth of racism and the rebirth of fascism. The states which brought in migrant labour at the request of capital have had no long-term policies for supporting the establishment of the new minority communities. On the contrary, they have stumbled from one ad hoc measure to another, and have resorted to institutional racism and forced repatriation when things got tough. Racism is an important element of current conservative strategies of crisis management.

At the beginning of the eighties, the contours of class formation are becoming clearer. It is now possible to identify the processes that are transforming class consciousness, and to name the subjects of these processes. The major battles of the ethnic minorities can be observed: against exploitation of black and foreign labour in industry and the services, against the discriminatory education system, against the institutional racism and compulsory repatriation policies of the state, against neo-Nazi violence on the streets, and against the prevailing culture of racism. The subjects of the process are black and foreign workers, black and foreign youth determined to maintain their culture and defend their communities, and black and foreign women fighting against triple oppression as women, as minorities and as workers. It is also becoming clear that the ethnic minorities can find allies in these struggles, within the left and the labour movement. Awareness is growing that the struggle against racism and for civil rights is crucial to unite the working class against the current offensive of capital and the state.

What is the long-term perspective of the struggle, beyond the immediate priorities of preventing deportation, securing civil rights and beating back fascism? Does success mean that future generations of Turks in West Germany, Italians in Switzerland, Portuguese in France or blacks in Britain will be socially and culturally indistinguishable from the rest of the population? Does equality of rights and opportunities necessarily imply future assimilation? This is certainly not the wish of most members of the ethnic minorities themselves. They are often highly critical of Western European society, of the erosion of popular culture, the disintegration of the family, the coldness of social relationships, the weakness of moral and ethical values. There is a widespread desire to maintain the culture, language and national identity of the country of origin. It is essential for the left and the anti-racist movement to understand that offering equal rights at the price of loss of identity is hardly better than a policy of repatriation.

The issue is the achievement of equal rights and opportunities without pressure to assimilate. This demand has been put forcefully by the black movement in Britain, and it is being voiced in other countries too:

Self-determination means that it is up to foreigners to decide for themselves if they want to stay in the German

Federal Republic, how to shape their cultural life, in what organisational form they want to carry out political activity. This necessarily implies as a pre-condition the right to take part in the political process of the German Federal Republic on an equal basis.[16]

It is on the basis of this demand for self-determination that the coming struggles will be fought.

The citizens of Western Europe no longer have the choice of whether they wish to live in multi-ethnic and multi-cultural societies. They already do. The issue yet to be decided is whether the ethnic minorities are going to be pushed to the margins of society by racism and discrimination, or whether they can succeed in their struggle for equality without loss of identity. Marginalisation and oppression of minorities has a long and unsavoury tradition in Europe. Minorities have become scapegoats and objects for persecution during crises; oppression of minorities has paved the way for the destruction of democracy and the labour movement. The alternative – equality and self-determination of the new ethnic minorities – could enrich our cultures and give our social life a new quality. That choice is still open.

Notes

1. Introduction

1. Jonathan Swift, 'A modest proposal for preventing the children of poor people in Ireland, from being a burden to their parents or country; and for making them beneficial to the public' (1729), in Herbert Davies (ed.), *Irish Tracts 1728–1733*, Oxford: Blackwell 1955.
2. United Nations Economic Commission for Europe, *Labour Supply and Migration in Europe: Demographic Dimensions 1950–1975 and Prospects*, New York: United Nations 1979, p. 272.
3. See Michael J. Piore, *Birds of Passage: Migrant Labour and Industrial Societies*, Cambridge University Press 1979.
4. See Heather Booth, 'On the role of demography in the study of post-war migration to Western Europe', *European Demographic Information Bulletin*, vol. 13 no. 4, 1982.
5. Stephen Castles and Godula Kosack, *Immigrant Workers and Class Structure in Western Europe*, London: Oxford University Press 1973.

2. The rise and fall of the guest worker system

1. Samir Amin, *Accumulation on a World Scale*, New York and London: Monthly Review Press 1974, pp. 37–8, emphasis in original.
2. ibid. p. 38.
3. Marx used the term 'primitive accumulation' for 'the historical process of divorcing the producer from the means of production'. The dissolution of pre-capitalist modes of production involves 'two transformations, whereby the social means of subsistence and production are turned into capital, and the immediate producers are turned into wage-labourers'. Primitive accumulation is the pre-condition for the capital relation, but continues in various forms throughout the history of capitalism. See *Capital*, vol. 1, pp. 873–6.
4. Amin, p. 27.
5. Stephen Castles and Godula Kosack, *Immigrant Workers and Class Structure in Western Europe*, London: Oxford University Press 1973, p. 428.

6. Amin, p. 40.
7. Marx, pp. 896–904.
8. Amin, p. 41.
9. Castles and Kosack, pp. 15–25.
10. Amin, p. 42.
11. The theory of the 'long waves' of capitalist development is helpful to understand the dynamism of capitalism from 1945 to the early seventies, and the current phase of stagnation. It is not possible to explain the theory here, and readers are referred to Ernest Mandel, *Late Capitalism*, Verso/NLB 1975. According to Mandel, the present phase of stagnation is the eighth long wave since the industrial revolution. The waves are caused by long-term trends in capital accumulation, connected with replacements of fixed capital in the wake of fundamental changes in production technology, as well as with changes in the conditions for producing and realising surplus value.
12. Andrew Glyn and John Harrison, *The British Economic Disaster*, London: Pluto Press 1980, p. 5.
13. ibid. pp. 5–7.
14. See Mandel.
15. Glyn and Harrison, pp. 7–9.
16. C. P. Kindleberger, *Europe's Postwar Growth: The Role of Labour Supply*, Cambridge, Mass.: Harvard University Press 1967, p. 3.
17. OECD, *Migration, Growth and Development*, Paris: OECD 1978, p. 7.
18. Marx, p. 784.
19. ibid. p. 786.
20. ibid. p. 790. See also Stephen Castles and Godula Kosack, 'The function of labour immigration in Western European capitalism', *New Left Review*, no. 73, July 1972, pp. 3–7.
21. Marx, pp. 794–8.
22. ibid. p. 796.
23. United Nations Economic Commission for Europe, *Labour Supply and Migration in Europe: Demographic Dimensions 1950–1975 and Prospects*, New York: United Nations 1979, chapter 1. This work gives a detailed quantitative analysis of labour supply in Europe.
24. United Nations Economic Commission for Europe, *Economic Survey of Europe 1961, Part 2: Some Factors in Economic Growth in Europe in the 1950s*, Geneva: United Nations 1964.
25. See Castles and Kosack, *Immigrant Workers and Class Structure*, pp. 396–408 for more detail on this argument.
26. ibid., pp. 244–8.
27. Stephen Castles and Godula Kosack, 'How the trade unions try to control and integrate immigrant workers in the German Federal

Republic', in *Race*, vol. 15 no. 4, April 1974; and Eckart Hildebrandt and Werner Olle, *Ihr Kampf ist unser Kampf*, Offenbach: Verlag 2000 1975.

28. Studienkommission, *Das Problem der ausländischen Arbeitskräfte*, Bern: Bundesamt für Industrie, Gewerbe und Arbeit 1964. See also Castles and Kosack, *Immigrant Workers and Class Structure*, pp. 422–3.

29. Compare John Grahl, 'Restructuring in West European industry', in *Capital and Class*, no. 19, Spring 1983.

30. F. Fröbel, J. Heinrichs and O. Kreye, *The New International Division of Labour*, Cambridge University Press 1980.

31. U. Hiemenz and K. W. Schatz, *Trade in Place of Migration*, Geneva: International Labour Organisation 1979.

32. OECD, p. 8.

33. ibid. p. 25.

34. The arguments for and against this claim are summarised in Castles and Kosack, *Immigrant Workers and Class Structure*, pp. 408–20. See also OECD.

35. International Labour Organisation, *Record of the Second European Regional Conference*, Geneva: International Labour Organisation 1974, p. 19.

36. ibid. p. 22.

37. Hiemenz and Schatz.

38. Centre for Contemporary Cultural Studies, *The Empire Strikes Back*, London: Hutchinson 1982, p. 19.

3. International patterns of migration and settlement

1. In 1981 there were 176,000 foreign workers in Austria and 52,000 in Luxemburg. *OECD Continuous Reporting System on Migration (SOPEMI), 1982*, Paris: OECD 1983. A very high proportion of workers in Luxemburg (especially in the steel industry) are foreigners, mainly Italians.

2. J.A. Jackson, *The Irish in Britain*, London: Routledge & Kegan Paul 1963, p. 14.

3. Bob Hepple, *Race, Jobs and the Law in Britain*, London: Penguin 1968, p. 49.

4. The New Commonwealth comprises those countries of the British Commonwealth whose populations are mainly of non-UK origin. It therefore includes all Commonwealth countries except Australia, Canada and New Zealand. Pakistan left the Commonwealth in 1973, after which it became necessary to refer to the New Commonwealth and Pakistan (NCWP) in order to continue to include people from Pakistan in minority populations.

5. Ceri Peach, *West Indian Migration to Britain*, London: Oxford University Press 1968.
6. Mark Duffield, 'Rationalisation and the politics of segregation: Indian workers in Britain's foundry industry, 1945–1962', in R. Loveridge (ed.), *The Manufacture of Stigma*, London: Wiley (forthcoming).
7. Mark Duffield, 'Racism and counter-revolution in the era of imperialism: a critique of the political economy of migration', unpublished paper, 1981; Research Unit on Ethnic Relations, University of Aston, Birmingham.
8. E.J.B. Rose and others, *Colour and Citizenship*, London: Oxford University Press 1969.
9. Data by birthplace are inaccurate because they include many white British people born abroad, especially in the Commonwealth. In addition, birthplace data cannot be compared with the nationality data available for other countries in Western Europe.
10. Details of the statistics on the population of New Commonwealth and Pakistani ethnic origin are given in Heather Booth and Dave Drew, 'Britain's black population', in Runnymede Trust and Radical Statistics Race Group, *Britain's Black Population*, London: Heinemann Educational Books 1980; and for 1981 data in Heather Booth, *The Demography of the Black Population of Great Britain*, working paper, SSRC Research Unit on Ethnic Relations, University of Aston, Birmingham, forthcoming.
11. Under the 1971 Immigration Act, a patrial is a person who has the right to live in the UK. This includes: those born in the UK; Commonwealth citizens settled before 1973; UK citizens by registration or naturalisation; and Commonwealth citizens with a UK-born parent or grandparent. Patrials thus have close ties with the UK by either birth or heritage. The 1981 Nationality Act changes this definition slightly.
12. Wilfried Dumon, *Het Profiel van de Vreemdelingen in Belgie*, Leuven: Davidsfonds 1982.
13. *Hommes et Migration Documents*, no. 864, 15 May 1974.
14. *OECD SOPEMI 1982*, p. 7.
15. Dumon, p. 32.
16. *OECD SOPEMI 1982*, p. 34.
17. The United Nations Economic Commission for Europe classifies Turkey as belonging to Asia rather than Europe. See UNECE, *Labour Supply and Migration in Europe: Demographic Dimensions 1950–1975 and Prospects*, New York: United Nations 1979. The present book follows this practice, for there is no doubt that Turkey is a Third World country in socio-economic terms, rather than part of the European periphery.

18. *OECD SOPEMI 1982*, p. 85.
19. ibid. p. 34.
20. Office National d'Immigration, *Statistiques d'Immigration*, Paris: annual, mimeo.
21. J. Wisnewski, 'L'immigration, une problème de societé', in *Hommes et Migrations Documents*, no. 961–2, January 1979.
22. Office National d'Immigration, *Statistiques d'Immigration*, Paris: 1968, mimeo.
23. Ministère de l'Intérieur, Paris: 1970, mimeo.
24. CEDETIM, *Les Immigrés*, Paris: Lutter/Stock 1975, p. 165.
25. C. Calvez, *Le problème des travailleurs étrangers, rapport présenté au nom du Conseil Economique et Social*, Paris: 1969, mimeo; and Michel Massenet, 'Action social et politique d'immigration', in *Hommes et Migrations Documents*, no. 761, 15 February 1969.
26. Raoul Weexsteen, 'Algeriens – rompre le dernier lien colonial', in *Le Monde Diplomatique*, July 1974, reprinted in *Hommes et Migrations Documents*, no. 869, 1 October 1974.
27. Paul Dijoud, 'Une politique globale de l'immigration – les 25 mesures nouvelles', in *Hommes et Migrations Documents*, no. 872, 15 November 1974.
28. ibid.
29. Michèle Bonnechère, 'Le statut juridique de l'immigration africaine', *Hommes et Migrations Documents*, no. 971, 1 June 1979.
30. 'Immigration changes in France', in *Race and Immigration*, no. 147, September 1982.
31. *OECD SOPEMI 1982*, p. 58.
32. 'Immigration changes in France'.
33. *Searchlight*, no. 94, April 1983.
34. 'Immigration changes in France'.
35. *OECD SOPEMI 1982*, p. 87.
36. ibid. p. 37.
37. Rinus Penninx, 'The contours of a general minorities policy', in *Planning and Development in the Netherlands*, vol. 13 no. 1, 1981.
38. Rinus Penninx, 'Towards an overall ethnic minorities policy', in Netherlands Scientific Council for Government Policy, *Ethnic Minorities*, The Hague: 1979, p. 9.
39. Rinus Penninx, *Migration, Minorities and Policy in the Netherlands (Report for OECD SOPEMI 1981)*, Rijswijk: Ministry of Cultural Affairs, Recreation and Social Welfare 1981, pp. 22–3.
40. Penninx, 'Towards an overall ethnic minorities policy'.
41. ibid. pp. 92–3.
42. Penninx, *Migration, Minorities and Policy in the Netherlands*, table 12.
43. Penninx, 'Towards an overall ethnic minorities policy', p. 115.

44. Christopher Bagley, *The Dutch Plural Society*, London: Oxford University Press 1973.
45. Netherlands Scientific Council for Government Policy, *Ethnic Minorities*.
46. Penninx, 'The contours of a general minorities policy'.
47. ibid. p. 18.
48. Penninx, *Migration, Minorities and Policy in the Netherlands*, p. 36.
49. ibid. p. 28.
50. *Immigrants in Sweden*, Stockholm: Swedish Institute 1979.
51. *OECD SOPEMI 1982*.
52. *Immigrants in Sweden*; Jonas Widgren, *Report to OECD (SOPEMI) on Immigration to Sweden in 1978 and the First Half of 1979*, Stockholm: Swedish Commission on Immigration Research 1979.
53. *OECD SOPEMI 1982*, p. 44.
54. *Invandrarna och Fackförening*^{...} *relsen – LO's Invandrarpolitiska Handlingprogram för Samhälle och Arbetsliv*, Stockholm: LO 1979.
55. Widgren, *Report to OECD*, p. 29; *OECD SOPEMI 1982*, p. 45.
56. *Immigrants in Sweden*, emphasis in original.
57. *Die Volkswirtschaft*, no. 10, October 1981.
58. *Die Volkswirtschaft*, no. 3, March 1982; *OECD SOPEMI 1982*, pp. 46–7.
59. H.-M. Hagmann, *Les travailleurs étrangers – chance et tourment de la Suisse*, Lausanne: Payot 1966.
60. *OECD SOPEMI 1981*.
61. *Die Volkswirtschaft*, no. 3, March 1982, p. 143.
62. *OECD SOPEMI 1982*, pp. 103–4.
63. For an analysis of voters' motives, see *Basler Zeitung*, 5 August 1982.
64. Heinz Kühn, *Stand und Weiterentwicklung der Integration der ausländischen Arbeitnehmer und ihrer Familien in der Bundesrepublik Deutschland – Memorandum des Beauftragten der Bundesregierung*, Bonn: 1979, p. 10.
65. Figures from Bundesminister für Arbeit und Sozialordnung, Bonn: 1982.
66. *Wirtschaft und Statistik*, no. 1, 1983.
67. ibid.; Victor Pfaff, 'Asylrecht in der BRD', in *Links*, vol. 14 no. 148/9, July/August 1982.
68. Hugo Reister, *Ausländerbeschäftigung und Ausländerpolitik in der Bundesrepublik Deutschland*, Berlin: Fachhochschule für Verwaltung und Rechtspflege 1983, pp. 33–4.
69. Kurt Dohse, *Ausländische Arbeiter und bürgerliche Staat*, Königstein: Hain, 1981.
70. Kanein, *Ausländergesetz*, Munich: 1966, quoted from Hans Heinz Heldmann, *Ausländerrecht – Disziplinärordnung für die Minderheit*, Darmstadt and Neuwied: Luchterhand 1974, pp. 15–16.

236 / Notes to pages 77–108

71. *Allgemeine Verwaltungsvorschrift zur Ausführung des Ausländergesetzes*, paragraph 6.
72. See Reister, pp. 39–44.
73. ibid. pp. 48–50.
74. ibid. p. 52.
75. Wolfgang Bodenbender, *Die politschen und gesellschaftlichen Rahmenbedingungen der Ausländerpolitik*, Bonn: Bundesministerium für Arbeit und Sozialordnung 1982.
76. Bund-Länder-Kommission, *Zur Fortentwicklung einer umfassenden Konzeption der Ausländerbeshäftignungspolitik*, Bonn: Bundesministerium für Arbeit und Sozialordnung 1977.
77. Kühn, p. 15.
78. *Beschlüsse der Bundesregierung*, 19 March 1980.
79. Reister, p. 53.
80. *Frankfurter Rundschau*, 9 August 1983.
81. *Beschlüsse der Bundesregierung*, 2 December 1981.
82. *OECD SOPEMI 1982*, p. 40.
83. Herbert Spaich, *Fremde in Deutschland*, Weinheim and Basel: Beltz 1981, pp. 239–40.
84. *Bundestagsdrucksache*, no. 9/1629, May 1982.
85. Bodenbender.
86. Heldmann, *Ausländerrecht*, gives many examples.
87. UNECE, *Labour Supply and Migration in Europe*, annexe II–3.
88. Mark Duffield, Research Unit on Ethnic Relations, Birmingham forthcoming.
89. Harry Joshua and Tina Wallace with Heather Booth, *To Ride the Storm: 'The Bristol Riot' and the State*, London: Heinemann 1983.

4. The formation of ethnic minorities

1. Quoted from Henri Taifel, 'The social psychology of minorities', in Charles Husband (ed.), *'Race' in Britain*, London: Hutchinson 1982, p. 217.
2. Stephen Castles and Godula Kosack, *Immigrant Workers and Class Structure in Western Europe*, London: Oxford University Press 1973, chapter 11.
3. See Annie Phizacklea (ed.), *One Way Ticket? Migration and Female Labour*, London: Routledge & Kegan Paul 1983.
4. This is confirmed by migration data. See Heather Booth, *Guestworkers or Immigrants? A Demographic Analysis of the Status of Migrants in West Germany*, Birmingham: SSRC Research Unit on Ethnic Relations, University of Aston, forthcoming.
5. Wilfried Schlaffke and Rüdiger von Voss (eds), *Vom Gastarbeiter zum Mitarbeiter*, Cologne: Infomedia 1982.

6. *Bundestagsdrucksache* 9/1629, 1982. (Official record of German federal parliamentary proceedings.)

7. The population of Irish origin now has fewer females per 1,000 males than the average for Great Britain (1,054). Whether it is less or more demographically balanced depends on the age distribution.

8. W. Brass, 'The future population of New Commonwealth immigrant descent: numbers and demographic implications', in D.A. Coleman (ed.), *Demography of Immigrants and Minority Groups in the United Kingdom*, London: Academic Press 1982, pp. 105–18; OPCS Immigrant Statistics Unit, 'Population of New Commonwealth and Pakistani ethnic origin: new projections', *Population Trends*, no. 16, 1979.

9. Rinus Penninx, *Migration, Minorities and Policy in the Netherlands* (*Report for OECD SOPEMI 1982*), Rijswijk: Ministry of Cultural Affairs, Recreation and Social Welfare 1982, p. 16.

10. *Wirtschaft und Statistik*, no. 1, 1983.

11. Bernd Hausmann, 'Nicht die Konzentration, sondern das Getto verhindern', in *Frankfurter Rundschau*, 25 August 1981.

12. For a detailed description of housing during the period of mass labour migration, see Castles and Kosack, *Immigrant Workers*, pp. 240–317.

13. Bundesanstalt für Arbeit, *Repräsentativuntersuchung '72 Beschäftigung ausländischer Arbeitnehmer*, Nuremberg: Bundesanstalt für Arbeit 1973, p. 109.

14. The process of inner-city concentration is well described in Forschungsverbund, 'Probleme der Ausländerbeschäftigung', *Integrierter Endbericht*, 1979, pp. 65–80.

15. ibid. p. 66.

16. See also Bernd Hausmann, 'Nicht die Konzentration, sondern das Getto verhindern'.

17. See Campaign against Racism and Fascism and Southall Rights, *Southall: The Birth of a Black Community*, London: Institute of Race Relations and Southall Rights 1981.

18. Bundesanstalt für Arbeit, *Ausländische Arbeitnehmer 1972/73*, Nuremberg: Bundesanstalt für Arbeit 1974.

19. Forschungsverbund, 'Probleme der Ausländerbeschäftigung', p. 102.

20. ibid. p. 95.

21. ibid. p. 102.

22. Godula Kosack, 'Migrant women: the move to Western Europe – a step towards emancipation?' in *Race and Class*, vol. 17 no. 4, Spring 1976.

23. Forschungsverbund, 'Probleme der Ausländerbeschäftigung', pp. 231–2.

24. Wolfgang Bodenbender, *Die politischen und gesellschaftlichen Rahmenbedingungen der Ausländerpolitik*, Bonn: Bundesministerium für Arbeit und Sozialordnung 1982.
25. Penninx, *Migration, Minorities and Policy in the Netherlands*, pp. 22–3.
26. Compare Michael J. Piore, *Birds of Passage: Migrant Labour and Industrial Societies*, Cambridge University Press 1979, pp. 50ff.
27. Forschungsverbund, 'Probleme der Ausländerbeschäftigung', p. 232.
28. Bundesminister für Arbeit und Sozialordnung (ed.), *Situation der ausländischen Arbeitnehmer und ihrer Familienangehörigen in der Bundesrepublik Deutschland, Repräsentativuntersuchung 1980*, Bonn: Forschungsinstitut der Friedrich-Ebert-Stiftung 1981, pp. 177–8.
29. *Wirtschaft und Statistik*, no. 1, 1983.

5. Migrants and minorities in the labour force

1. Marios Nikolinakos, *Politische Ökonomie der Gastarbeiterfrage*, Reinbeck bei Hamburg: Rowolt 1973, pp. 37ff.
2. Julian Henriques, Peter Long and Shanti Patel, 'Employment', in Runnymede Trust and Radical Statistics Race Group (eds), *Britain's Black Population*, London: Heinemann 1980, p. 59.
3. David J. Smith, *The Facts of Racial Disadvantage: A National Survey*, London: PEP 1976, pp. 73–4.
4. Stephen Castles and Godula Kosack, *Immigrant Workers and Class Structure in Western Europe*, London: Oxford University Press 1973, p. 71.
5. Henriques, Long and Patel, p. 61.
6. Annie Phizacklea and Robert Miles, *Labour and Racism*, London: Routledge & Kegan Paul 1980, p. 19.
7. Bundesminister für Arbeit und Sozialordnung (ed.), *Situation der ausländischen Arbeitnehmer und ihrer Familienangehörigen in der Bundesrepublik Deutschland, Repräsentativuntersuchung 1980*, Bonn: Forschungsinstitut der Friedrich-Ebert-Stiftung, 1981.
8. Castles and Kosack, p. 82.
9. Phizacklea and Miles, p. 18.
10. Henriques, Long and Patel, p. 59.
11. Frank Reeves and Robin Ward, 'West Indian business in Britain', in Robin Ward and Richard Jenkins (eds), *Ethnic Communities in Business: Strategies for Ethnic Survival*, Cambridge University Press 1984.
12. Howard Aldrich, Trevor P. Jones and David McEvoy, 'Ethnic advantage and minority business development', in Robin Ward and Richard Jenkins (eds).
13. Phizacklea and Miles, p. 19.

14. Ann Barber, *Labour Force Information from the National Dwelling and Housing Survey*, London: Department of Employment Research Paper, no. 17, May 1981.

15. Forschungsverbund, 'Probleme der Ausländerbeschäftigung', *Integrierter Endbericht*, 1979, pp. 21–35.

16. ibid. pp. 36–9.

17. Bundesminister für Arbeit und Sozialordnung (ed.), p. 143.

18. Knuth Dohse, 'Ausländerpolitik und betriebliche Ausländerdiskriminierung', in *Leviathan*, nos. 3–4, 1981, p. 515.

19. Forschungsverbund, 'Probleme der Ausländerbeschäftigung', pp. 38–42.

20. Bundesminister für Arbeit und Sozialordnung (ed.), p. 146.

21. David J. Smith.

22. Henriques, Long and Patel, p. 63. See also Phizacklea and Miles, p. 19; Castles and Kosack, p. 78.

23. Nikolinakos, pp. 45–63; Castles and Kosack, chapter 9.

24. See U. Hiemenz and K.W. Schatz, *Trade in Place of Migration*, Geneva: International Labour Organisation 1979, pp. 35–66 and 87–9, for a detailed analysis.

25. *Hommes et Migrations Documents*, no. 969, 1 May 1979.

26. Raymond Pierre, *L'immigration dans la Zone de Fos (1973–74)*, 1977, mimeo.

27. *Hommes et Migration Documents*, no. 969, 1 May 1979.

28. *OECD SOPEMI 1982*, Paris: OECD 1983, p. 59.

29. *Der Arbeitgeber*, 20 March 1966.

30. *Amtliche Nachrichten der Bundesanstalt für Arbeit*, no. 3, 1982.

31. See Michael J. Piore, *Birds of Passage: Migrant Labour and Industrial Societies*, Cambridge University Press 1979, pp. 35–49.

32. Henriques, Long and Patel, pp. 64–8.

33. *OECD SOPEMI 1982*.

34. Bundesminister für Arbeit und Sozialordnung (ed.), pp. 151, 159.

35. Dohse; Forschungsverbund, 'Probleme der Ausländerbeschäftigung', pp. 46–9.

36. *Amtliche Nachrichten der Bundesanstalt für Arbeit*, no. 3, 1982.

37. Dohse, p. 511.

38. Phizacklea and Miles, chapter 3.

39. David J. Smith; Henriques, Long and Patel, p. 66.

40. Phizacklea and Miles, chapter 5.

41. Castles and Kosack, chapter 4.

42. ibid. pp. 129–32; Castles and Kosack, 'How the trade unions try to control and integrate immigrant workers in the German Federal Republic', in *Race*, vol. 15 no. 4, April 1974; Manfred Budzinski, *Gewerkschaftliche und betriebliche Erfahrungen ausländischer Arbeiter*, Frankfurt: Campus 1979, pp. 55–62; Peter Kühne, 'Die

ausländische Arbeiter in der Bundesrepublik Deutschland – eine Herausforderung für die deutschen Gewerkschaften', in *WSI Mitteilungen*, no. 7, 1982.

43. Karl-Heinz Goebels, 'Der Deutsche Gewerkschaftsbund und die ausländischen Arbeitnehmer', in *Gewerkschaftliche Monatschefte*, no. 7, 1982.
44. Budzinski, p. 65.
45. Quoted according to Budzinski, p. 66.
46. Kühne.
47. ibid.
48. Goebels.
49. Kühne; Budzinski, p. 74.
50. Kühne.
51. Goebels.
52. Kühne.
53. Bundesminister für Arbeit und Sozialordnung (ed.), pp. 213–22.
54. ibid. pp. 190–212.
55. Castles and Kosack, *Immigrant Workers*, pp. 152–73.
56. Castles and Kosack, 'How the trade unions'; Eckart Hildebrandt and Werner Olle, *Ihr Kampf ist unser Kampf*, Offenbach: Verlag 2000 1975.
57. Hildebrandt and Olle, pp. 36–45.
58. Dohse; Budzinski, p. 61; Kühne.
59. *Express*, 19 May 1982.

6. Ethnic minority youth

1. Quoted according to Kirsten Baukhage, 'Ausländische Schüler im deutschen Bildungssystem', in *DPA Hintergrund*, no. HG 3066, 14 April 1983.
2. The Marange–Lebon Report, *Hommes et Migrations Documents*, no. 1034, 15 June 1982.
3. Mike Grimsley, Shan Nicholas and Colin Thunhurst, 'Education', in *Britain's Black Population*, London: Heinemann 1980, pp. 92–3.
4. All figures from OECD, *Young Foreigners and the World of Work*, Paris: OECD 1981, table 1–2.
5. ibid.
6. Hessische Kultusminister (ed.), 'Zu · Lage der ausländischen Kinder und Jugendlichen in Hessen', in *Bildungspolitische Informationen*, no. 2, 1981, p. 37.
7. See Gabriele Mertens and Ünal Akpinar, *Türkische Migrantenfamilien*, Bonn: Verband der Initiativen in der Ausländerarbeit 1977.

8. See Ünal Akpinar, Andrés López-Blasco and Jan Vink, *Pädagogische Arbeit mit ausländischen Kindern und Jugendlichen*, Munich: Juventa Verlag 1977, chapter 1.

9. See John Berger and Jean Mohr, *A Seventh Man*, Harmondsworth: Penguin 1975, for an attempt to express the experience of migration.

10. See Lothar C. Tischler, *Ausländerreport Hessen '82*, Wiesbaden: HLT Gesellschaft für Forschung, Planung, Entwicklung 1982, p. 58.

11. See Errol Lawrence, 'Just plain common sense: the "roots" of racism', in Centre for Contemporary Cultural Studies (ed.), *The Empire Strikes Back*, London: Hutchinson 1982, pp. 74–80; Hazel V. Carby, 'Schooling in Babylon', in ibid. pp. 190–1.

12. Hazel Carby, pp. 184–5.

13. ibid. pp. 189–95.

14. *Beschluss des Kultusministerkonferenz, Neufassung der Vereinbarung 'Unterricht für Kinder ausländischer Arbeitnehmer'*, 8 April 1976.

15. *Bundestagsdrucksache 9/1629*, 1982.

16. Akpinar, López-Blasco and Vink, pp. 38–9.

17. *Frankfurter Rundschau*, 29 March 1982.

18. Grimsley, Nicholas and Thunhurst, p. 102.

19. Bernard Coard, *How the West Indian Child Is Made Educationally Sub-normal in the British School System*, London: New Beacon Books 1971.

20. Hessische Kultusminister (ed.), 'Zur Lage der ausländischen Kinder'. Much of the data presented in this chapter relates to the *Land* Hesse, because the federal structure of the education system often makes it difficult to give information for the whole of West Germany. Hesse has a total population of 5.6 million, of which half a million are foreigners. Social and economic structure is typical for West Germany, and educational data may be regarded as fairly representative.

21. Tischler, p. 81.

22. Hessische Kultusminister, *Erlass 'Unterricht für Kinder ausländischer Eltern'*, Wiesbaden 1978.

23. Baukhage, p. 12.

24. Hessische Kultusminister (ed.), 'Zur Lage der ausländischen Kinder'.

25. Hans Maier, 'Bildungspolitische Integration "Modell Bayern"', in *Das Parlament*, 29 August–5 September 1981.

26. Hessische Kultusminister, *Ausländische Schüler – Schuljahr 1981–82*, Wiesbaden: 1982.

27. Maier.

28. Hessische Kultusminister (ed.), 'Zur Lage der ausländischen Kinder'.

29. R. Spaeter-Bergamo, 'Kinder zweiter Klasse – Lehrer zweiter Klasse', in *Hessische Lehrerzeitung*, October 1974.

30. *Hessische Lehrerzeitung*, January–February 1975.

31. Tischler, p. 95.
32. Verity Saifullah Khan, 'The "mother-tongue" of linguistic minorities in multicultural England', in *Journal of Multilingual and Multicultural Development*, vol. 1 no. 1, 1980.
33. Baukhage, p. 3.
34. Tischler p. 81.
35. Hessische Kultusminister (ed.), 'Zur Lage der ausländischen Kinder', p. 13.
36. See, for instance, 'Ausländer im deutschen Schul(un)wesen', in *Informationsdienst Arbeitsfeld Schule*, no. 41, June 1980.
37. U. Boos-Nünning and M. Hohmann, 'Probleme des Unterrichts in der Grund- und Hauptschule aus der Sicht der Lehrer in Vorbereitungs- und Regelklassen', in M. Hohmann (ed.), *Unterricht mit ausländischen Kindern*, Düsseldorf: Schwan 1976.
38. See Sabine Schommer, 'Exemplarisches zur Grundschule', in *Informationsdienst Arbeitsfeld Schule*, no. 41, June 1980.
39. See Erika Fekete, *Eine Chance für Fatma*, Reinbek bei Hamburg: Rowolt 1982.
40. *Bundestagsdrucksache*, no. 9/1629, 1982.
41. Tischler p. 85.
42. ibid. p. 101.
43. ibid. p. 106.
44. *Bundestagsdrucksache*, no. 9/1629, 1982.
45. Akpinar, López-Blasco and Vink, p. 45.
46. Carby, p. 184.
47. Tischler, pp. 133–5.
48. *Bundestagsdrucksache*, no. 9/1629, 1982.
49. Hessische Kultusminister, *Ausländische Schüler – Schuljahr* 1981–2.
50. Knuth Dohse, 'Ausländerpolitik und betriebliche Ausländerdiskriminierung', in *Leviathan*, nos. 3–4, 1981, p. 523.
51. Tischler, pp. 133–5.
52. Winfried Schlaffke and Rüdiger von Voss (eds), *Vom Gastarbeiter zum Mitarbeiter*, Cologne: Infomedia, 1982, p. 61.
53. Dohse, p. 502.
54. Tischler, p. 147.
55. Dohse, p. 503.
56. Tischler, p. 157.
57. All estimates quoted by Dohse, p. 502.
58. Tischler, p. 158.
59. See Carby, pp. 200–205.
60. *Bundestagsdrucksache*, no. 9/1629, 1982.
61. *Hommes et Migrations Documents*, no. 1034, June 1982.
62. OECD, *Young Foreigners and the World of Work*, p. 98.
63. See Stephen Castles and Godula Kosack, *Immigrant Workers and*

Class Structure in Western Europe, London: Oxford University Press 1973, pp. 238–9.
64. Carby, p. 200.
65. Campaign against Racism and Fascism and Southall Rights, *Southall: The Birth of a Black Community*, London: Institute of Race Relations 1981, p. 45.
66. See Autorengruppe Ausländerforschung, *Zwischen Getto und Knast*, Reinbek bei Hamburg: Rowolt 1981, and Paul Gilroy, 'Police and thieves', in Centre for Contemporary Cultural Studies (ed.), *The Empire Strikes Back*, London: Hutchinson 1982.

7. Racism and politics

1. *Frankfurter Rundschau*, 26 February 1983.
2. *Frankfurter Rundschau*, 26 June 1982 and 9 September 1982.
3. *Stern*, 10 October 1982.
4. *Frankfurter Rundschau*, 28 October 1982.
5. *Tageszeitung*, 13 December 1982.
6. World Council of Churches Migration Secretariat (ed.), *Migrant Workers and Racism in Europe*, Geneva: World Council of Churches 1980.
7. E.J.B. Rose and others, *Colour and Citizenship*, London: Oxford University Press 1969; Annie Phizacklea and Robert Miles, *Labour and Racism*, London: Routledge & Kegan Paul 1980; Harry Joshua and Tina Wallace, with the assistance of Heather Booth, *To Ride the Storm: 'The Bristol Riot' and the State*, London: Heinemann Educational Books 1983, are among the many studies giving evidence on racism in Britain. The monthly *Searchlight* provides regular monitoring.
8. Errol Lawrence, 'Just plain common sense: the "roots" of racism', in Centre for Contemporary Cultural Studies (ed.), *The Empire Strikes Back*, London: Hutchinson 1982.
9. See Martin Barker, *The New Racism*, London: Junction Books 1981.
10. World Council of Churches Migration Secretariat.
11. *The Guardian*, 15 March 1978.
12. World Council of Churches Migration Secretariat.
13. *International Herald Tribune*, December 1979.
14. See Stephen Castles and Godula Kosack, *Immigrant Workers and Class Structure in Western Europe*, London: Oxford University Press 1973, chapter 10.
15. Barker, *The New Racism*.
16. Centre for Contemporary Cultural Studies, *The Empire Strikes Back*.
17. See, for instance, Robert Miles, *Racism and Migrant Labour*, London: Routledge & Kegan Paul 1982, chapter 4.

18. Barker, pp. 2–3.
19. ibid.
20. ibid.; Centre for Contemporary Cultural Studies.
21. Castles and Kosack, pp. 16–25.
22. Herbert Spaich, *Fremde in Deutschland*, Weinheim and Basel: Beltz Verlag 1981, pp. 139–68.
23. ibid. pp. 169–208.
24. ibid. pp. 7–8.
25. Castles and Kosack, pp. 433–6.
26. ibid. pp. 167–70.
27. Spaich, p. 218.
28. ibid. p. 220.
29. *Time*, 30 August 82.
30. See Victor Pfaff, 'Asylrecht in der BRD', in *Links*, vol. 14 no. 148/9, July/August 1982; Terre des Hommes (ed.), *Zur Situation der Ausländer in der Bundesrepublik Deutschland*, Darmstadt: Terre des Hommes 1982.
31. Der Bundesminister des Innern (ed.), *Betrifft: Verfassungsschutz '82*, Bonn: Bundesminister des Innern 1983, p. 113. This is the annual report of the West German political police, similar to the Special Branch in Britain.
32. ibid.
33. ibid. p. 153.
34. Ralph Busch, in Klaus Staeck and Inge Karst (eds), *Macht Ali deutsches Volk kaputt?*, Göttingen: Steidl Verlag 1982, pp. 100–111.
35. *Searchlight*, no. 93, March 1983.
36. Der Bundesminister des Innern (ed.), p. 155.
37. GEW Berlin (ed.), *Wider das Vergessen – antifaschistiche Erziehung in der Schule*, Frankfurt: Fischer 1981.
38. ibid. p. 92.
39. See Michael Billig, *Psychology, Racism and Fascism*, Birmingham: A.F. and R. Publications 1979; and Michael Billig, *Die rassistische Internationale*, Frankfurt: Verlag Neue Kritik 1981.
40. Barker.
41. The original version of the Heidelberg Manifesto, which drips with explicit racism, was leaked to the press in August 1981. Its authors published a new version in January 1982. Although the language is milder, there is no change in the ideology and aims. Both versions are reproduced in Staeck and Karst (eds).
42. *Frankfurter Rundschau*, 9 September 1982.
43. *Frankfurter Allgemeine Zeitung*, 15 February 1983.
44. ibid. 2 December 1982.
45. *Der Arbeitgeber*, no. 24, 1981.
46. ibid. no. 3, 1980.

47. Quoted from Initiativausschuss Ausländischer Mitbürger in Hessen, *Argumente gegen die Ausländerfeindlichkeit*, Hofheim: mimeo 1982.
48. Cabinet decision of 11 November 1981.
49. Quoted from Staeck and Karst (eds), pp. 178–81.
50. Barker, especially chapters 2 and 3.
51. Cabinet decision of 3 February 1982.
52. Quoted from Staeck and Karst (eds), p. 145.
53. ibid. p. 49.
54. *Frankfurter Rundschau*, 24 May 1982.
55. Speech to the Synod of the Evangelical Church of Hesse, 4 March 1978; see also Spaich, pp. 234, 239.
56. Radio interview, 13 March 1982, quoted from *Links*, June 1982.
57. Barker, pp. 33–6.
58. Kohl's statement is reprinted in Staeck and Karst (eds), pp. 192–3.
59. Der Bundesminister des Innern (ed.), *Bericht der Kommission 'Ausländerpolitik'*, Bonn: Bundesminister des Innern 1983.
60. See Dregger, in Staeck and Karst (eds), p. 181.
61. For evidence of collusion between the West German government and the Turkish junta in the persecution of political opponents see *Frankfurter Rundschau*, 31 August 1983 and 1 September 1983, and *Tageszeitung*, 31 August 1983 and 1 September 1983.

8. Consciousness and class formation

1. Stephen Castles and Godula Kosack, *Immigrant Workers and Class Structure in Western Europe*, London: Oxford University Press 1973, chapter 11.
2. Annie Phizacklea and Robert Miles, *Labour and Racism*, London: Routledge & Kegan Paul 1980, chapter 1.
3. Paul Gilroy, 'Steppin' out of Babylon – race, class and autonomy', in Centre for Contemporary Cultural Studies (ed.), *The Empire Strikes Back*, London: Hutchinson 1982, p. 284.
4. See, for instance, André Gorz, *Farewell to the Working Class*, London: Pluto Press 1982.
5. A. Sivanandan, 'From resistance to rebellion', in A. Sivanandan, *A Different Hunger*, London: Pluto Press 1982, p. 49.
6. See Gilroy, pp. 286–9.
7. Stuart Hall and others, *Policing the Crisis*, London: Macmillan 1978, p. 394, quoted here from Gilroy, p. 276.
8. Sivanandan, pp. 34–5.
9. See, for instance, Robert Moore, *Racism and Black Resistance in Britain*, London: Pluto Press 1975; Robert Miles and Annie Phizacklea (eds), *Racism and Political Action in Britain*, London: Routledge & Kegan Paul 1979; Sivanandan; Gilroy.

10. See Bundesminister für Arbeit und Sozialordnung (ed.), *Situation der ausländischen Arbeitnehmer und ihrer Familienangehörigen in der Bundesrepublik Deutschland, Repräsentativuntersuchung 1980*, Bonn: Forschungsinstitut der Friedrich-Ebert-Stiftung 1981; Forschungsverbund, 'Probleme der Ausländerbeschäftigung', *Integrierter Endbericht*, 1979.
11. Türkei-Info-Redaktion, *Thesen zum Kampf gegen die Ausländerfeindlichkeit*, mimeo, 1982.
12. ibid.
13. ibid.
14. ibid.
15. Castles and Kosack, chapter 11.
16. Türkei-Info-Redaktion.

Bibliography

The sources used for this book are given in detail in the notes to each chapter. This bibliography gives a selection of the main works referred to.

Akpinar, Ünal, Andrés López-Blasco and Jan Vink, *Pädagogische Arbeit mit ausländischen Kindern und Jugendlichen*, Munich: Juventa Verlag 1977.

Amin, Samir, *Accumulation on a World Scale*, New York and London: Monthly Review Press 1974.

Amtliche Nachrichten der Bundesanstalt für Arbeit, monthly bulletin of the German Federal Labour Office, Nuremberg.

Der Arbeitgeber, monthly journal of the German Employers' Federation, Cologne.

'Ausländer im deutschen Schul(un)wesen', in *Informationsdienst Arbeitsfeld Schule*, no. 41, June 1980.

Autorengruppe Ausländerforschung, *Zwischen Getto und Knast*, Reinbek bei Hamburg: Rowolt 1981.

Barber, Ann, *Labour Force Information from the National Dwelling and Housing Survey*, London: Department of Employment Research Paper, no. 17, May 1981.

Barker, Martin, *The New Racism*, London: Junction Books 1981.

Baukhage, Kirsten, 'Ausländische Schüler im deutschen Bildungssystem', in *DPA Hintergrund*, no. HG 3066, 14 April 1983.

Billig, Michael, *Psychology, Racism and Fascism*, Birmingham: A.F. and R. Publications 1979.

——*Die rassistische Internationale*, Frankfurt: Verlag Neue Kritik 1981.

Bodenbender, Wolfgang, *Die poltiischen und gesellschaftlichen Rahmenbedingungen der Ausländerpolitik*, Bonn: Bundesministerium für Arbeit und Sozialordnung 1982.

Booth, Heather, 'On the role of demography in the study of post-war migration to Western Europe', *European Demographic Information Bulletin*, vol. 13 no. 4, 1982.

——*The Demography of the Black Population of Great Britain*, working paper, SSRC Research Unit on Ethnic Relations, University of Aston, Birmingham, forthcoming.

——*Guestworkers or Immigrants? A Demographic Analysis of the Status of Migrants in West Germany*, Birmingham: SSRC Research Unit of Ethnic Relations, University of Aston, Birmingham, forthcoming.

Budzinski, Manfred, *Gewerkschaftliche und betriebliche Erfahrungen ausländischer Arbeiter*, Frankfurt: Campus 1979.

Der Bundesminister des Innern (ed.), *Bericht der Kommission 'Ausländerpolitik'*, Bonn: Bundesminister des Innern 1983.

——(ed.), *Betrifft: Verfassungsschutz '82*, Bonn: Bundesminister des Innern 1983.

Bundesminister für Arbeit und Sozialordnung (ed.), *Situation der ausländischen Arbeitnehmer und ihrer Familienangehörigen in der Bundesrepublik Deutschland, Repräsentativuntersuchung 1980*, Bonn: Forschungsinstitut der Friedrich-Ebert-Stiftung 1981.

Bundestagsdrucksache, official document of the German Federal Parliament.

Bund-Länder-Kommission, *Zur Fortentwicklung einer umfassenden Konzeption der Ausländerbeschäftigungspolitik*, Bonn: Bundesministerium für Arbeit und Sozialordnung 1977.

Campaign against Racism and Fascism and Southall Rights, *Southall: The Birth of a Black Community*, London: Institute of Race Relations and Southall Rights 1981.

Castles, Stephen and Godula Kosack, *Immigrant Workers and Class Structure in Western Europe*, London: Oxford University Press 1973.

——'The function of labour immigration in Western European capitalism', in *New Left Review*, no. 73, July 1972.

——'How the trade unions try to control and integrate immigrant workers in the German Federal Republic', in *Race*, vol. 15 no. 4, 1974.

CEDETIM, *Les Immigrés*, Paris: Lutter/Stock 1975.

Centre for Contemporary Cultural Studies, *The Empire Strikes Back*, London: Hutchinson 1982.

Coard, Bernard, *How the West Indian Child Is Made Educationally Subnormal in the British School System*, London: New Beacon Books 1971.

Dohse, Knuth, *Ausländische Arbeiter und bürgerliche Staat*, Königstein: Hain 1981.

——'Ausländerpolitik und betriebliche Ausländerdiskriminierung', in *Leviathan*, no. 3–4, 1981.

Duffield, Mark, 'Racism and counter-revolution in the era of imperialism: a critique of the political economy of migration' (unpublished paper, 1981: Research Unit on Ethnic Relations, University of Aston, Birmingham).

——'Rationalisation and the politics of segregation: Indian workers in Britain's foundry industry, 1945–1962', in R. Loveridge (ed.), *The Manufacture of Stigma*, London: Wiley, forthcoming.

Dumon, Wilfried, *Het Profiel van de Vreemdelingen in Belgie*, Leuven: Davidsfonds 1982.

Forschungsverbund, 'Probleme der Ausländerbeschäftigung', *Integrierter Endbericht*, 1979.

Frankfurter Rundschau, Frankfurt daily newspaper.

Fröbel, F., J. Heinrichs and O. Kreye, *The New International Division of Labour*, Cambridge University Press, 1980.

GEW Berlin (ed.), *Wider das Vergessen – antifaschistische Erziehung in der Schule*, Frankfurt: Fischer 1981.

Glyn, Andrew and John Harrison, *The British Economic Disaster*, London: Pluto Press 1980.

Goebels, Karl-Heinz, 'Der Deutsche Gewerkschaftsbund und die ausländischen Arbeitnehmer', in *Gewerkschaftliche Monatshefte*, no. 7, 1982.

Grahl, John, 'Restructuring in West European industry', in *Capital and Class*, no. 19, Spring 1983.

Heldmann, Heinz Hans, *Ausländerrecht – Disziplinärordnung für die Minderheit*, Darmstadt and Neuwied: Luchterhand 1974.

Hessische Kultusminister, *Ausländische Schüler, Schuljahr 1981–82*, Wiesbaden: 1981.

Hessische Kultusminister (ed.), 'Zur Lage der ausländischen Kinder und Jugendlichen in Hessen', in *Bildungspolitische Informationen*, no. 2, 1981.

Hiemenz, U. and K. W. Schatz, *Trade in Place of Migration*, Geneva: International Labour Organisation 1979.

Hildebrandt, Eckart and Werner Olle, *Ihr Kampf ist unser Kampf*, Offenbach: Verlag 2000 1975.

Hohman, M. (ed.), *Unterricht mit ausländischen Kindern*, Düsseldorf: Schwan 1976.

Hommes et Migrations Documents. This documentation service has been appearing regularly for many years and is an invaluable source of information on migrants and minorities in France, Paris.

Husband, Charles (ed.), *'Race' in Britain*, London: Hutchinson 1982.

Joshua, Harry and Tina Wallace with Heather Booth, *To Ride the Storm: 'The Bristol Riot' and the State*, London: Heinemann 1983.

Khan, Verity Saifullah, 'The "mother-tongue" of linguistic minorities in multicultural England', in *Journal of Multilingual and Multicultural Development*, vol. 1 no. 1, 1980.

Kindleberger, C.P., *Europe's Postwar Growth: The Role of Labour Supply*, Cambridge, Mass.: Harvard University Press 1967.

Kosack, Godula, 'Migrant women: the move to Western Europe – a step towards emancipation?' in *Race and Class*, vol. 17 no. 4, Spring 1976.

Kühn, Heinz, *Stand und Weiterentwicklung der Integration der ausländischen Arbeitnehmer und ihrer Familien in der Bundesrepublik Deutschland – Memorandum des Beauftragten der Bundesregierung*, Bonn 1979.

Kühne, Peter, 'Die ausländische Arbeiter in der Bundesrepublik Deutschland – eine Herausforderung für die deutschen Gewerkschaften', in *WSI Mitteilungen*, no. 7, 1982.

Mandel, Ernest, *Late Capitalism,* Verso/NLB 1975.

Marx, Karl, *Capital*, vol. 1, Harmondsworth: Penguin 1976.

Mertens, Gabriele and Ünal Akpinar, *Türkische Migrantenfamilien*, Bonn: Verband der Initiativen in der Ausländerarbeit 1977.

Miles, Robert and Annie Phizacklea, 'The TUC and black workers 1974–1976', *British Journal of Industrial Relations*, vol. XVI no. 2, pp. 195–207.

Miles, Robert and Annie Phizacklea (eds), *Racism and Political Action in Britain*, London: Routledge & Kegan Paul 1979.

Miles, Robert, *Racism and Migrant Labour*, London: Routledge & Kegan Paul 1982.

Moore, Robert, *Racism and Black Resistance in Britain*, London: Pluto Press 1975.

Nikolinakos, Marios, *Politische Ökonomie der Gastarbeiterfrage*, Reinbek bei Hamburg: Rowolt 1973.

OECD, *Migration, Growth and Development*, Paris: OECD 1978.

——*Young Foreigners and the World of Work*, Paris: OECD 1981.

OECD SOPEMI, Organisation for Economic Co-operation and Development, *Continuous Reporting System on Migration*, an annual report on migration to Western Europe prepared by the OECD Directorate for Social Affairs, Manpower and Education, Paris.

Penninx, Rinus, 'Towards an overall ethnic minorities policy', in Netherlands Scientific Council for Government Policy, *Ethnic Minorities*, The Hague: 1979.

——'The contours of a general minorities policy', in *Planning and Development in the Netherlands,* vol. 13 no. 1, 1981.

———*Migration, Minorities and Policy in the Netherlands (Report for OECD SOPEMI 1981)*, Rijswijk: Ministry of Cultural Affairs, Recreation and Social Welfare 1981.

———*Migration, Minorities and Policy in the Netherlands (Report for OECD SOPEMI 1982)*, Rijswijk: Ministry of Cultural Affairs, Recreation and Social Welfare 1982.

Phizacklea, Annie and Robert Miles, *Labour and Racism,* London: Routledge & Kegan Paul 1980.

Phizacklea, Annie, (ed.), *One Way Ticket? Migration and Female Labour*, London: Routledge & Kegan Paul 1983.

Piore, Michael J., *Birds of Passage – Migrant Labour and Industrial Societies*, Cambridge University Press 1979.

Race and Class, a quarterly journal of black and Third World liberation, published by the Institute of Race Relations, London.

Rose, E.J.B. and others, *Colour and Citizenship*, London: Oxford University Press 1969.

Runnymede Trust and Radical Statistics Race Group, *Britain's Black Population*, London: Heinemann Educational Books 1980.

Reister, Hugo, *Ausländerbeschäftigung und Ausländerpolitik in der Bundesrepublik Deutschland*, Berlin: Fachhochschule für Verwaltung und Rechtspflege 1983.

Schlaffke, Wilfried and Rüdiger von Voss (eds), *Vom Gastarbeiter zum Mitarbeiter*, Cologne: Infomedia 1982.

Searchlight, a monthly journal published by the Campaign Against Racism and Fascism, London.

Sivanandan, A., *A Different Hunger*, London: Pluto Press 1982.

Smith, J. David, *The Facts of Racial Disadvantage: A National Survey*, London: PEP 1976.

Spaich, Herbert, *Fremde in Deutschland*, Weinheim and Basel: Beltz 1981.

Staeck, Klaus and Inge Karst (eds), *Macht Ali deutsches Volk kaputt?* Göttingen: Steidl Verlag 1982.

Studienkommission, *Das Problem der ausländischen Arbeitskräfte*, Bern: Bundesamt für Industrie, Gewerbe und Arbeit, 1964.

Tageszeitung, West Berlin daily newspaper.

Terre des Hommes (ed.), *Zur Situation der Ausländer in der Bundesrepublik Deutschland*, Darmstadt: Terre des Hommes 1982.

Tischler, Lothar C., *Ausländerreport Hessen '82*, Wiesbaden: HLT Gesellschaft für Forschung, Planung, Entwicklung 1982.

Turkei-Info-Redaktion, *Thesen zum Kampf gegen die Ausländerfeindlichkeit*, mimeo, 1982.

United Nations Economic Commission for Europe, *Labour Supply and Migration in Europe: Demographic Dimensions 1950–1975 and Prospects*, New York: United Nations 1979.

Die Volkswirtschaft/La Vie Economique, a Swiss government monthly, giving statistics on foreign workers and residents, Bern.

Ward, Robin and Richard Jenkens (eds), *Ethnic Communities in Business: Strategies For Ethnic Survival*, Cambridge University Press 1984.

Widgren, Jonas, *Report to OECD (SOPEMI) on Immigration to Sweden in 1978 and the First Half of 1979*, Stockholm: Swedish Commission on Immigration Research 1979.

Wirtschaft und Statistik, monthly journal published by the German Federal Statistical Office, giving statistics on foreign residents, Wiesbaden.

World Council of Churches Migration Secretariat (ed.), *Migrant Workers and Racism in Europe*, Geneva: World Council of Churches 1980.

Index

Note: To avoid undue repetition terms used very frequently, such as 'migration', 'migrant workers', 'settlement', do not appear in this index, as they would refer to nearly every page.